THE AGE OF REVOLUTIONS

Wellington crossing the Pyrenees at the close of the Peninsular War

A SURVEY OF BRITISH AND IRISH HISTORY

Book Two 1660-1815

THE AGE

OF

REVOLUTIONS

John Magee, M.A.

FALLONS

©

Fallons

Published by Fallons Educational Supply Company, C. J. Fallon (London) Limited, 33 King Street, Belfast and 1 Furnival Street, London E.C.4 and printed in the Republic of Ireland at Kingsbridge, Dublin, by Cahill and Company Limited.

Contents

Contents

SECTION THREE

THE AGE OF REVOLUTIONS (1763–1815)

List of Illustrations

List of Maps

Preface

This is the second book of a series that is intended primarily for students in the lower forms of Grammar Schools and in the Secondary Intermediate Schools of Northern Ireland, many of whom take the Junior Certificate Examination between fourteen and fifteen years of age. It should, however, meet the needs of other students of a similar standard elsewhere.

The preface to the first volume set out very fully the author's aims in preparing the series, and only a summary is required now. Topics are chosen which are likely to be of interest to children of the 13-15 age group, and, wherever possible, a biographical treatment has been preferred : thus the conquest of India has been told through the life of Robert Clive, with all the details about his boyhood and personality that the pupils find so attractive. The achievements of John Wesley, Captain Cook and Lord Nelson—to take three very different characters—are dealt with in a similar way. Some religious and political topics that the author knows, from a long experience, the children find neither interesting nor intelligible are treated here at some length, in the hope that the young student may be able to understand the issues involved and not just be satisfied to commit them to memory.

More space is given to Irish history than is usual in books of this kind. In addition to the usual political and constitutional topics, there are sections on the growth of Belfast in the eighteenth century, on Georgian Dublin, on the linen and cotton industries, etc. Irish history has been studied in schools almost exclusively from a political point of view ; the author believes it is time we broadened our approach to include economic and

social material as well. This is just as important, and the
pupils for whom the book is intended are likely to find it
more interesting.

Simple sketch-maps have been provided, each map containing only so much information as is required to illustrate the
text. As in the first volume, these maps have been specially
drawn by Mr. George Magee. There is also a number of
time-charts.

The author wishes to express his gratitude to V. Rev.
P. Rogers, M.A., D.Lit., Principal of St. Joseph's Training
College, Belfast, who read the proofs with great care and made
many valuable suggestions that are now incorporated in the text.

The Later Stuart Period
1660-1714

Time Chart : The Later Stuarts (1660-1714)

Reign	England	Ireland	Scotland	Abroad
Charles II (1660–1685)	1660: The Restoration 1661–1665: Clarendon Code 1665: The Plague 1666: Fire of London 1667: Fall of Clarendon 1670: Treaty of Dover 1672: Declaration of Indulgence 1673: Test Act 1678: Popish Plot 1679–1681: Exclusion Question 1683: Rye House Plot	1662: Act of Settlement 1665: Act of Explanation 1666: Cattle Acts 1672: Regium Donum 1681: Execution of Archbishop Plunkett	1679: Drumclog and Bothwell Bridge	1662: Bombay acquired 1663: Carolina 1665–1667: Dutch War 1667: Treaty of Breda 1670: Hudson's Bay Co. 1672: Royal African Co. 1681: Pennsylvania
James II (1685–1688)	1685: Monmouth's Rebellion 1687: First Declaration of Indulgence 1688: Second Declaration of Indulgence; Birth of Prince of Wales	1687: Tyrconnel Lord Lieutenant		1685: Revocation of Edict of Nantes

Reign	England	Ireland	Scotland	Abroad
William III (1689–1702)	1689: Bill of Rights 1694: Bank of England 1701: Act of Settlement	1689: Siege of Derry 1690: Battle of Boyne 1691: Treaty of Limerick	1689: Killiecrankie 1692: Massacre of Glencoe 1696–1698: Darien Scheme	1689–1697: League of Augsburg 1690: Beachy Head 1692: La Hogue 1697: Treaty of Ryswick
Anne (1702–1714)	1709: Coke used for smelting 1712: Newcomen's pump	1704: Test Act	1703: Act of Security 1707: Union of England and Scotland	1702–1713: War of Spanish Succession 1704: Blenheim 1706: Ramillies 1708: Oudenarde 1709: Malplaquet 1713: Treaty of Utrecht

Time Chart : The Later Stuarts (1660-1714)

CHAPTER ONE

The Restoration in England (1660-1685)

1. The Return of Charles II

The Landing at Dover : On the afternoon of Friday, May 25, 1660, Charles II stepped ashore at Dover after nine years of exile. With him were his brothers, the Dukes of York and Gloucester, along with a number of the friends who had been faithful to him in the days of his adversity, and who now were to share in his triumphant return. In the royal party, too, was the diarist, Samuel Pepys, who has left us an account of the landing. On the pier to greet the King were General Monk and the Mayor of the town, while an immense crowd of his excited and cheering subjects thronged the quays and the surrounding cliffs. "A canopy was provided for him to stand under, which he did, and talked a while with General Monk and others, and so into a stately coach there set for him, and so away through the town towards Canterbury, without making any stop at Dover. The shouting and joy expressed by all is past imagination." Four days later the King reached London. An eye-witness, John Evelyn, has vividly recorded the scenes which marked his arrival in the capital : "This day His Majesty, Charles the Second, came to London, after a sad and long exile, and calamitous suffering both of the King and Church . . . This also was his birthday, and with a triumph of above 20,000 horse and foot, brandishing their swords, and shouting with

1

inexpressible joy : the ways strewn with flowers, the bells ringing, the streets hung with tapestry, fountains running with
wine . . . the windows and balconies all set with ladies,
trumpets, and music, myriads of people flocking into the
streets . . . I stood in the Strand and beheld it, and blessed
God." At seven o'clock in the evening Charles reached Whitehall to be acclaimed by both Houses of Parliament, and his
long years of poverty and exile were now at an end.

The Declaration of Breda : Between the death of Oliver
Cromwell on September 3, 1658 and the return of Charles II
England had suffered nearly two years of anarchy. The Lord
Protector had nominated his son, Richard, to succeed him.
But Richard had none of his father's ambition or force of
character, and, after only eight months' rule, he abdicated
quietly and went abroad. A number of army officers then con-
tended with one another for control, while the country drifted
into disorder. Before government completely broke down a
strong man stepped forward and took over. He was General
Monk, a silent and morose soldier, who was in command of the
army in Scotland and had taken no part in the quarrels that
were going on. Monk marched on London, recalled the surviving members of the Long Parliament and persuaded them
to make arrangements for the holding of proper elections.

Meanwhile Charles II, at Breda in Holland, issued a declaration that was calculated to make his return popular with the
majority of his subjects. He promised four things :

(i) A general pardon for all who were prepared to " return to
the loyalty and obedience of good subjects ", but with any
exceptions that parliament might care to make.

(ii) " Liberty to tender consciences ", i.e. religious toleration.

(iii) Arrears of pay to the army.

(iv) That he would allow parliament to decide what was to be
done about the royalist estates which had been confiscated or
purchased during the previous eleven years.

The declaration of Breda made the restoration of the
monarchy certain. When the Parliament met, it declared that the

government of England " is and ought to be by the King, Lords
and Commons ", and invited Charles II to return. Thus the
restoration was greeted with joy, and celebrations marked
every stage of the King's journey from Dover to London.

Merrie England : After eleven years of strict Puritan rule
the nation rejoiced to see " the King enjoy his own again ".
Indeed the pendulum swung in the opposite direction, and
Charles earned the title of " the Merry Monarch " from the
enthusiasm with which he led the reaction against the drab
righteousness of the previous period. An early riser, the King
" was oft abroad between four and five in the morning ", and
his days were spent in strenuous exercise—hunting, shooting,
playing tennis, swimming, or sailing his yacht on the Thames.
Every spring and autumn he went to Newmarket, and under
his patronage horse-racing and gambling revived. He imported
a number of fleet-footed Arabian steeds to run there, and his
nick-name of " Old Rowley " was taken from one of his
favourite horses. His evenings were spent in dancing and card-
playing, and in visits to the theatre in Drury Lane or to the new
Opera House in Lincoln's Inn Fields. But his life abroad had
demoralized him, and his Court soon became notorious for its
frivolity and vice.

The nation at large followed the fashions set from above by
the King and his courtiers. In London the bear gardens and
the pits for cock-fighting were re-opened and drew great
crowds. Samuel Pepys describes a visit he paid to one of these
places, and his description gives us some idea of the brutality
of the spectacle. " I did go to Shoe Lane to see a cock fighting
at a new pit there . . . but, Lord, to see the strange variety of
people from Parliament men to the poorest prentices, bakers,
butchers, brewers, draymen and what not ; and all these fellows one with another in swearing, cursing and betting. I soon
had enough of it, and yet I would not but have seen it once,
it being strange to observe the nature of these poor creatures
(i.e. the fighting-cocks), how they will fight till they drop down
dead upon the table." In the country there was fox hunting,

beagling and a rough kind of football played on the village green, while the towns had their fairs with performing apes, tumblers, jugglers and fire-eaters. For a great many people— but not, as we shall see, for the Puritans and Catholics— this was indeed " Merrie England ".

2. What was Restored in 1660 ?

The Monarchy Was Restored : But it was not the sort of personal rule which James I and Charles I had tried to establish. Charles II had returned on the invitation of Parliament, and all the acts which had been passed in 1641 limiting the power of the King were retained. Never again could a monarch collect ship-money or forced loans on his own authority, or order the arrest of members of Parliament. In theory the King still had considerable powers : he appointed and dismissed his own ministers, and he controlled the foreign and domestic policies of the country. But in practice the financial arrangements which Parliament had made for the restored monarchy made it difficult for the King to follow a policy of which they disapproved. Charles II had given up a number of traditional feudal dues, and, in return, Parliament granted him taxes which were calculated to bring in £1,200,000 a year. In actual fact the taxes never brought in anything like this amount, and the King was consequently dependent on Parliament for further financial aid. But when Parliament made grants of this sort to the King they insisted on knowing for what the money was needed, and demanded a regular audit to ensure that the money was properly spent. Charles II resented the control that Parliament was thus trying to secure over his policy, but, as he was nearly always short of money, he had no alternative but to agree— except, of course, he could get money from another source, such as his cousin Louis XIV of France. When that happened he was sometimes able to defy Parliament and to follow a policy of his own. But he could never push a disagreement with Parliament too far lest he should provoke another Civil War ; for if there was one thing above all else that Charles II

Charles II is crowned in Westminster Abbey, 1660

was determined on, it was never to endure exile and poverty again. *Anything* was better than that.

Parliament Was Restored : Under the Commonwealth and Protectorate a real Parliament had ceased to exist. The House of Lords was abolished, and only those who were known to be supporters of Oliver Cromwell were allowed to sit in the Commons. In 1660 a Parliament of two chambers was restored, and Charles II had agreed to follow its advice in carrying out the promises he had made in the Declaration of Breda. As soon as the King returned, arrangements were made for the holding of a general election, but, in the meantime, the Convention Parliament (so called because it had not been summoned by a King) assisted Charles II in making a restoration settlement.

First they passed an Act of Indemnity and Oblivion granting a free pardon to all who had fought against the late King, except the surviving regicides, i.e. those who had actually signed the warrant for Charles I's execution. Thirteen of these were executed, while the bodies of Cromwell, Ireton and Bradshaw were taken from their tombs in Westminster Abbey and hanged in revenge on the gallows at Tyburn.

Next the army was paid off and dispersed. Only Monk's regiment of foot was retained in the royal service as the Coldstream Guards, and Monk himself was created Duke of Albemarle and left to command it.

The land settlement was a more difficult problem. During the Commonwealth many estates had changed hands. Lands belonging to the King, to the Church and to prominent Royalists had been confiscated. In addition, many other Royalists had been forced to sell their homes and property to pay the heavy fines that were imposed on them. In these circumstances it was not possible to suggest a solution that would satisfy everyone In the end it was decided that all lands which had been confiscated should be restored to their original owners, without any compensation being paid to their present occupiers ; but that those who had purchased lands which Royalists had sold should be allowed to retain them. Though it would be difficult to suggest a better arrangement than this, it is obvious that both the disappointed Royalists and the evicted purchasers of confiscated land felt bitterly wronged by the settlement that was made.

The Church Was Restored : During the Commonwealth the Anglican Church had suffered a great deal—its lands were confiscated, its great churches desecrated, its bishops and ministers driven into obscurity or exile. In 1660 it was restored as the national Church. The saintly old Bishop Juxon, who had walked with Charles I to his execution, was made Archbishop of Canterbury, and other surviving bishops returned to their sees. Charles II had promised " liberty to tender consciences ", and he hoped that it would be possible to arrange a religious settlement that would satisfy both Anglicans and Puritans. He called a conference at the Bishop of London's lodgings in the Savoy, London, hoping that the leaders of the two sides would work out an agreement about doctrine and worship. But neither side was prepared to compromise, and, in despair, the King left the question to be settled by the new Parliament, the elections for which had just taken place.

3. The Clarendon Code

The Cavalier Parliament : In May 1661 the elections were held for the first *real* Parliament to meet in England for nearly twenty years. There was a 'land-slide' in favour of the Royalists or Cavaliers, and the members (some only recently home from exile) came up to London determined to have revenge on the Puritans. They did so by means of a number of cruel penal laws that are known in history as the *Clarendon Code*.

The Earl of Clarendon : Edward Hyde was a barrister who in the early months of the Long Parliament had been an opponent to Charles I. Eventually, however, he had gone over to the side of the King and had fought in the Royalist army during the Civil War. After the defeat of Worcester (1651) he went into exile with Charles II and shared his hardship and

poverty. When the King was restored Hyde was made Earl of
Clarendon and Lord Chancellor. For the next seven years he
was Charles II's chief minister, and it is after him that the
cruel laws against the Puritans are called.

The Clarendon Code: The first of these laws was the Corporation Act of 1661 which compelled all mayors and members of town corporations to receive Holy Communion according to the rites of the Church of England, and to swear that it was unlawful in any circumstance to take up arms against the King. As most of the members of the House of Commons were representatives of boroughs and as borough representatives were usually chosen by the town corporations, this Act was designed to destroy the political power of Nonconformists or Dissenters, as the Puritans are called from now on.

In 1662 a revised Prayer Book was issued, and an Act of Uniformity insisted that all ministers use it in their services or resign their livings. Over two thousand resigned rather than violate their consciences, and were forced into poverty or menial occupations.

The King tried to call a halt to the persecutions at this stage for he disliked the manner in which the solemn promises he had made at Breda were being dishonoured. On December 26, 1662, he issued a Christmas message to his subjects saying that, if Parliament would agree, he would not enforce these laws against Nonconformists who lived peaceably. But Parliament was not prepared to allow this, and passed two further penal laws. By the *Conventicle Act* (1664) any meeting of more than four persons for the holding of a religious service other than that of the Church of England was declared an illegal assembly, and all present were liable to imprisonment for the first and second offences, and transportation for the third. Finally the *Five Mile Act* (1665) forbade any Nonconformist minister or schoolmaster to come within five miles of a city or corporate town. As the Puritans were mostly townsfolk this act was designed to deprive them not only of the comforts of their religion, but of education as well.

Effects of the Code : To what extent the law was enforced it is difficult to say, for a great deal depended upon the attitude of the local Justices of the Peace. Thus in Bristol, Norwich, Gloucester and Yarmouth, towns where there were large communities of Nonconformists, it seems that violations of the law were ignored. In other places the code was strictly enforced, and John Bunyan, the author of *The Pilgrim's Progress*, spent twelve years in Bedford goal, for illegal preaching. One effect the code did have, however. Before the Restoration there had been a considerable number of Puritans among the nobles and gentry : now many of the wealthier landowners, anxious to safeguard their social position and political power, conformed to the Established Church. Henceforth, more than ever before, Anglicanism was the religion of the upper classes, while the Nonconformists were strong in the towns and amongst the working and commercial classes. It was from the ranks of the latter that many of the leaders of industry were to come in the eighteenth century.

4. The Plague and the Great Fire

Two of the most sensational events of Charles II's reign were the Plague (1665) and the Great Fire of London (1666). The Plague was not confined to the capital, for other parts of the country suffered also, notably East Anglia. But in London, where people were crowded together in filthy and insanitary conditions, its effects were more obvious and tragic.

London : London had grown enormously in size during the seventeenth century, and, at the accession of Charles II, its population was estimated to be half a million, or about one-tenth of the total population of the country. It was situated mainly on the north bank of the Thames and was still officially bounded by its walls and ancient gates : Ludgate, Moorgate, Cripplegate, etc. Beyond the walls the poor were herded together in great slums in what were called the Liberties of St. Giles, Whitechapel, Stepney, etc.

In the city many houses were still built of wooden frames with lath and plaster walls. They overhung the narrow cobbled streets, shutting out both light and air, and their rooms were dark and dreary. Rivers of filth coursed down the middle of the streets, into which people poured their rubbish, and the passer-by often had to jump aside to escape the contents of a slop-pail.

Sanitation there was none. Great heaps of rotting filth were piled in corners, covered with flies and breeding germs of every description. In the slums of the Liberties the poor lived in hovels of indescribable squalor, infested with rats and fleas. Smallpox and fever haunted this part of London and frequently spread from there to the rest of the capital and to the kingdom as a whole.

The Plague : In the hot summer of 1665 the last of these great calamities struck London. It was first noticed in May, and with each succeeding month the number of victims increased, until in September there were more than 30,000 deaths. The unfortunate people who contracted it were stricken with a high temperature, swellings as large as eggs developed in their necks and under their armpits, and purple spots and sores appeared all over their bodies. Nowadays doctors call this Bubonic Plague and tell us that it is spread by fleas which carry the disease from infected rats. In the slums of some Asiatic cities where fleas and rats abound it is not unknown today.

The Court and the Government fled from London to the safety of the country, and most of the rich people followed their example. Those who remained tried bravely to deal with the Plague. Fires were lit in the streets to purify the air, tobacco was smoked and chewed to ward off infection, and, if a person showed sign of fever, he was locked in his house, which was then marked with a cross in order to warn others to keep away. But it was all in vain, for the poor people of the slums died

On the 2 of September in y.e Yeare 1666 (being the Lords day) in y.e begin.g of one M.
Farmer a Baker in pudding Lane which Continued till about 3 at night the Wednesday following, in which time it burnt eg Chur
ches, thirteene thousand & two hundred houses, 600 acres, & 97 Parishes within y.e walls, there was but 11 intire.
One Robert Hubert of Roane in Normandy, upon examination Confessed he was y.t that fired the first house (viz.) M.r Fam.
mers in Pudding lane, for which fact he was, after hanged at Tiburne.

Southwark

The Great Fire of London, 166

[British Museum]

in their thousands. Every night carts went round the streets to collect the dead, who were buried in enormous pits.

End of the Plague : After September the pestilence died down, and for the whole of the succeeding year there do not appear to have been more than 2,000 deaths. Indeed after 1665 there were no more serious outbreaks of the Plague in England. Several reasons are suggested for this, but the most interesting one is that about this time the country was invaded by a new large brown rat. He was shy of human beings, and avoided, if possible, the homes of the people ; but he did wage war on the small black plague-infected rat and caused his extinction. Another cause, in the case of London, was the Great Fire, which not only burned out the haunts of vermin but caused the building of new brick houses instead of the older wooden ones.

The Great Fire : London was just beginning to recover from the Plague when it was struck by another disaster. Early on the morning of Sunday, September 2, 1666 a bakery in Pudding Lane, near London Bridge, caught fire, and the flames spread rapidly from house to house along the narrow streets. Soon all of London inside the walls was ablaze, and the red glow in the sky could be seen by villagers fifty miles away. The people, terrified, seized what they could of their belongings and fled, leaving the fire, now driven by a strong easterly gale, to crackle and burn behind them. Only the King seems to have kept his head. He called out the train-bands (or militia) to act as fire-fighters and moved up and down amongst them, advising and encouraging them as the situation required, or sometimes, standing ankle-deep in water, he passed the buckets from hand to hand. Finally he ordered that a number of houses in the line of fire should be pulled down or blown up with gun-powder. In this way when a wide belt was cleared round the fire, it burned itself out.

Though there was little loss of life, nearly the whole of the city inside the walls and some of the Liberties beyond had been destroyed, and this included not only the homes of the people

Thackpu! Chackol

but many public buildings and churches as well. The Guildhall, the Royal Exchange, the old Cathedral of St. Paul and eighty-eight other churches had all disappeared. The capital would have to be rebuilt ; and almost before the fires were quenched Charles II was considering plans for the new city with Sir Christopher Wren.

Wren : Sir Christopher Wren (1632-1723) was Professor of Astronomy at Oxford and had some fame as an inventor and mathematician before he turned to architecture. After the fire Charles II asked him to draw up a plan for the rebuilding of London. Within a matter of weeks Wren produced his plan of the new city, with many wide streets running at right angles to one another, with St. Paul's Cathedral standing in a great open space, and broad thoroughfares radiating from it as centre. But like many a town-planner in our own day, Wren was to learn how difficult it is to put an ideal plan into practice. The merchants wanted to rebuild on their old sites, for they feared their businesses would suffer if they moved elsewhere. Yet in one respect the new London was better than the old ; the new houses were of brick and stone, and were fewer, better spaced and consequently healthier.

In the reconstruction of the churches and public buildings Wren had a free hand. In addition to St. Paul's he was engaged in rebuilding no fewer than fifty churches, but he regarded the cathedral as his great work. The cost of its building was met by a tax levied on all coal brought up the Thames to London. It was not completed until 1710, when Wren was seventy-eight years old. The last years of his life were spent in retirement at Hampton Court, but every year while he was able (he died in 1723 at the age of ninety-one) the old man made a pilgrimage to St. Paul's where he sat alone under the tall dome and contemplated his great achievement. There could be no better tribute to the best known of English architects than the Latin epitaph carved on the tablet above his grave in the cathedral : *Lector, si monumentum requiris, circumspice.* (Reader, if you want to see his monument, look around.)

5. Charles II and Religious Toleration

The King's Religion : Religious bitterness was totally alien
to Charles II's character, and he would have all his subjects
live together in peace and harmony whatever their views. As
for himself, he was young and gay and too much taken up with
the pursuit of pleasure to have much time for religion. Whenever a question of doctrine cropped up he was apt to brush it
aside with a smile and a witty remark. Whatever private inclina-
tions he had were towards Rome, and, in a vague sort of way,
he hoped, if possible, to ease the lot of his Catholic subjects.
His sister, Henrietta, Duchess of Orleans, was far more
enthusiastic about this than he was, and believed that, if
Charles II would ally himself with the King of France,
Louis XIV would provide him sufficient assistance to do so.
Charles II was cautious, for he knew the strength of anti-
Catholic feeling in England, but one aspect of his sister's plan
did appeal to him. He was hard up; Parliament was mean in
granting him supplies and critical of the ways he spent them;
if the French alliance provided him with sufficient money to
be independent of parliament, he was prepared to try it—
provided that the *real* aim of the alliance could be kept secret.

The Treaty of Dover (1670) : In 1670 the Duchess of Orleans
crossed over from France to Dover, ostensibly to stay with her
brother, but actually to carry out negotiations on behalf of
Louis XIV, and during her visit an agreement was made
between the two kings. By this treaty Charles II promised to
help Louis XIV in his war with Holland and to declare himself a Catholic at the opportune moment. In return Louis XIV
paid Charles the sum of £170,000 and undertook to provide
him with an army of 6,000 men if they were needed to force
Catholicism on England. Some historians are inclined to believe
that in this treaty Charles was simply using religion to get
some badly-needed money from the French King. He was far
too shrewd a man to think that Catholicism could be restored
in England as easily as that; and in actual fact the oppor-

tune moment to announce his own conversion proved to be on
his death-bed. Meantime he used the treaty to get as much
money as possible from Louis XIV.

The Declaration of Indulgence and the Test Act : A sham
treaty was shown to some of the King's ministers, but in a short
time rumours began to circulate about the clauses which
Charles wanted to conceal. These suspicions appeared to be
confirmed when, in 1672, the King issued a Declaration of
Indulgence, suspending the penal laws against both Catholics
and Nonconformists and permitting them to worship in public.
Parliament at once refused to vote any supplies unless the
Declaration was withdrawn, and the King's chief minister, the
Earl of Salisbury, supported the opposition.

Charles saw at once that he had gone too far and rather
shame-facedly agreed to withdraw the indulgence. Parliament
followed up their victory by introducing a Test Act whereby
all office-holders under the Crown had to take the Oath of
Supremacy, receive Holy Communion according to the rites of
the Church of England and repudiate the doctrine of transubstantiation. Charles was not prepared to risk a head-on
clash with Parliament on the subject, and thus, with all his
dreams of religious toleration shattered, he signed the Bill and
it became law (1673).

But the King's troubles were not ended. His brother, James,
Duke of York, who was heir to the throne, had recently become
a Catholic. Charles urged him to make at least an outward
show of conformity to the Anglican Church, but James refused
and resigned his office of Lord High Admiral. Then, to make
matters worse, he married Mary of Modena, a Catholic princess. This marriage opened up the prospect of a line of Catholic
kings, and the fears of Parliament were aroused once more.
The Earl of Shaftesbury resigned his post as Lord Chancellor,
and from now on he was an implacable enemy of Charles II,
determined to establish the authority of Parliament in the
government of the country and to use every means possible
to prevent James, Duke of York, from succeeding to the throne.

That explains why he gave so enthusiastic support to the ' Popish Plot '.

The Popish Plot (1678): In 1678 a clergyman named Titus Oates announced that he had discovered a Catholic plot to murder the King and to put his brother, James, Duke of York, on the throne in his place. The assassination, he said, would be followed by the landing of a French army, the massacre of prominent Protestants and the establishment of Catholicism by force. There was, of course, no such plot ; Oates was a thorough rascal who made up the story in the hope of being well rewarded. At first his story was not taken too seriously, and Charles, upon examining Oates, caught him out in some obvious lies. But then something occurred which convinced many that his story was true. Oates had sworn information about the plot before a London magistrate named Sir Edmund Berry Godfrey. A fortnight later Godfrey disappeared, and his body was found on Primrose Hill, near Marylebone, with a sword sticking in his back. Terror and hysteria were at once aroused, and a mob marched through the streets of London carrying the murdered man's body. A massacre of Protestants was said to be imminent, and all over the country Catholics were arrested and on the flimsiest of evidence condemned to death. These people were innocent and Charles II knew it. But to have intervened to save them would have endangered his throne, and he was not prepared to do that.

Shaftesbury and the Plot : The Earl of Shaftesbury used the plot unscrupulously for political purposes. In London his coach moved through the crowded streets every day, rousing the rabble who cheered and raised their ' Protestant flails ' as he passed by. In this way he hoped to stir up enough anti-Catholic feeling in the country to make the Duke of York's succession to the throne impossible. In Parliament, also, events played into his hands. There a letter was produced which the chief minister Danby had written, on the King's instructions, asking Louis XIV for money so that Charles II could be independent of Parliament. In the atmosphere of passion this aroused,

Shaftesbury demanded that the Duke of York be dismissed from the Royal Council and began to impeach Danby. Partly to save his minister, but more to prevent too many details of his agreements with the French King from being made public, Charles II dissolved Parliament in January, 1679

Thus after a life of eighteen years the 'Cavalier Parliament' came to an end. At its election it was described as being " more royalist than the King," and it had imposed a number of harsh penal laws upon the Puritans. At its end the whole atmosphere of the Parliament had changed. Charles II was no longer trusted, and there was a belief that he wished to set up a despotism in England similar to that of France and to force Catholicism on the country. Consequently there had grown up in the Parliament a strong opposition. This group, led by the Earl of Shaftesbury, wanted to secure control of the King's policy, to exclude James, Duke of York, from the throne and to gain freedom of worship for Nonconformists. In the beginning they called themselves the Country Party, but eventually they were known as *Whigs*. Those who supported the King and believed in the principles of hereditary succession and of the Anglican Church were called *Tories*.

6. The Exclusion Struggle

The First Exclusion Bill (1679) : The general election of February, 1679 was one of the most stirring in British history, and the first ever fought on party lines. Shaftesbury set up an elaborate organisation in London and sent out agents and agitators to every constituency in the country. They used the anti-Catholic feeling of the people without scruple, and where this was not sufficient (and it nearly always was) bribery was freely practised. Consequently the Whigs swept all before them, and, as soon as Parliament assembled, Shaftesbury introduced an Exclusion Bill, laying it down that if the King were to die without a legitimate heir he was not to be succeeded by the Duke of York. Charles II realised that Shaftesbury could carry the Bill through Parliament and that the feeling of the country was with him. Because of this he trod warily. First he got the Duke of York out of the way by sending him abroad ; then he announced that he was prepared to agree to an act limiting the Duke of York's powers when he became King, but that he could not accept any alteration in the succession to the throne. However Parliament was in no mood for compromise, and Charles dissolved it before the Bill could be passed.

The Oxford Parliament : In the following year (1680) when a new Parliament met, a second Exclusion Bill was actually passed through the Commons but rejected by the House of Lords. Charles II with his usual shrewdness saw that the anti-Catholic feeling was beginning to die down and that a certain amount of the old royalist spirit had begun to revive. Thus in January, 1681 he issued writs for the election of a new Parliament to meet in Oxford, where Shaftesbury would not have so many supporters. Once more the Whigs were victorious in the elections, and they went to Oxford armed to the teeth and threatening war if the Exclusion Bill were not passed. Charles went as far as he could go : he suggested that at his death James should inherit the throne, but that he should remain abroad and allow the country to be ruled in his name by his daughter Mary and her husband, the Prince of Orange. But the Whigs wanted the King's illegitimate son, the Duke of Monmouth, to succeed at Charles II's death. For some time the King seemed to hesitate; then one day he called both Houses together. They hurriedly assembled, expecting the King to give way, for they knew that he had been short of money for some time. But to their utter consternation he declared the Parliament to be at an end. The explanation, of course, was that in the nick of time Louis XIV had come to his aid and had left him independent of Parliament once more.

Rout of the Whigs : When the Whigs recovered from their shock, there was talk of another civil war. But it soon became obvious that the tide was running strongly in Charles' favour throughout the country and that there was a rising resentment against those who had attempted to humiliate their King. Charles took advantage of this new loyalty. Shaftesbury was driven into exile, and, after the Rye House Plot (1683) in which some desperate Whigs planned to murder the King as he drove home from the races at Newmarket, the opposition was completely routed and the Duke of Monmouth was banished from the country.

Charles' Last Years : Thus, after all his troubles, Charles in his last years ruled with an authority that his father or grandfather had never attained. He called no more Parliaments, being able with French subsidies and the revenue from the Customs to do without them. But, with his usual shrewdness, he seems to have realized that his victory was only a temporary one, and before his death in 1685 he said : " When I am dead and gone I know not what my brother will do. I am much afraid that when he comes to the Crown he will be obliged to travel again. And yet I will take care to leave my kingdoms to him in peace, wishing he may long keep them so. But this hath all of my fears, little of my hope, and less of my reason."

Questions and Exercises

1. Account for the Restoration of 1660. What else was restored as well as the King ?

2. Write a character-sketch of Charles II. Give examples of instances where he abandoned his principles to avoid going " on his travels again ".

3. Discuss the importance of each of the following in Charles II's reign : (a) The Declaration of Breda; (b) the Clarendon Code; (c) the Popish Plot.

4. Give a brief account of the Plague and the Great Fire of London. Add a note on the part played by Sir Christopher Wren in rebuilding the capital.

5. Write an account of the activities of the Earl of Shaftesbury during Charles II's reign. What new party did he form and what were its aims ?

CHAPTER TWO

The Restoration : Scotland, Ireland and the Colonies

1. Scotland under Charles II

Cromwell's Rule : The return of Charles II brought almost as much joy to Scotland as it did to England. In Edinburgh great crowds gathered in the streets : bells were rung, cannons were fired, and at the Market Cross there was a fountain of wine from which everyone could drink as he pleased. At night long tables laden with food were placed in the High Street, and bonfires blazed at every corner. There was no doubting the enthusiasm with which the Scottish people were welcoming the return of the Stuart King whom they had crowned at Scone nearly ten years before.

The intervening period had not been a happy one for Scotland. The country had lost its independence; the chair of state on which her Kings had sat and the royal robes had been brought to England. Cromwell had done what no English King had ever done : conquered Scotland, which from then on was represented in the Parliament of Westminster by thirty members. No doubt the merchants benefited from this arrangement through being able to participate in English trade, but it was a great blow to Scottish pride. The Highlands made one attempt, under the Earl of Glencairn, to regain their independence, but their rising was crushed at Dalnaspidal, at the head of Loch

Garry. It is thus easy to understand why the Scots celebrated the return of their King : they believed that it would bring an end to military rule, to interference in their daily lives, and to all the other evils they associated with Cromwell's rule. They were to be terribly disappointed.

Bishops Again : With the restoration of Charles II the union of England and Scotland was brought to an end, and on January 1, 1661 the Scottish Parliament met again in Edinburgh. Great pains had been taken to ensure that the members were all men of royalist views, and one of its first acts was to declare Charles Head of the Church as well as of the State. This was followed by the establishment of episcopacy and a declaration that from now on ministers were to be appointed by the bishops in whose dioceses they were. The Presbyterian ministers refused to accept these regulations (three hundred of them resigned their livings rather than do so) and demanded that Charles honour the promise he had made at his coronation in 1651 to accept the Solemn League and Covenant. Hence the ministers and their followers were known as *Covenanters.*

Persecution of the Covenanters : In an effort to force episcopacy on the Scottish people, a law was passed compelling them to worship in the parish churches and imposing heavy fines on those who refused. But in the south-west of the country, in the shires of Ayr, Lanark, Wigton, Dumfries and Kirkcudbright, the Covenanters refused, and flocked to services held by their own ministers in barns, in the fields and on the hillsides. By 1665 the services held by these " outed ministers " (as they were called) became so numerous that the government made the most strenuous efforts to suppress them. Ministers were forbidden to go within twenty miles of their former parishes, and soldiers were quartered on people who would not attend the parish churches. At length the treatment meted out to the Covenanters was so harsh that they rose in a hopeless little rebellion in 1666. The rising was crushed; fifteen of the leaders were hanged in Edinburgh, and many were imprisoned and cruelly tortured.

Drumclog and Bothwell Bridge (1679) : In 1668 the Earl of Lauderdale, who had himself once been a Covenanter, was entrusted by the King with the government of Scotland. First he tried to win some of the ministers to his side, but, failing in this, he then resorted to the most brutal methods. He sent nearly ten thousand soldiers into the south-west, where they looted, destroyed and murdered in every direction. The Covenanters, embittered now by persecution, struck back and in 1679 they murdered Archbishop Sharp of St. Andrews. From now on there was open war between the two sides. An army of Covenanters defeated a government force, led by Graham of Claverhouse, at Drumclog, a bleak moor on the borders of Ayr and Lanark, but were themselves defeated shortly afterwards by the Duke of Monmouth at Bothwell Bridge.

" The Killing Times " (1681-1687) : To the end of Charles II's reign the struggle between the Government and the Covenanters went on. Some of the more faint-hearted Scots eventually gave in and began to attend the parish churches, but there were many brave Covenanters whom neither imprisonment nor death would force to submit. In 1681 James, Duke of York, came to Scotland as Royal Commissioner. The fact that he was a Catholic incensed the Presbyterians even further, and the period from 1681 to 1687 is known as " the killing times " in Scottish history, when Covenanters were hunted down by government troops under Graham of Claverhouse. The result was that when the Revolution came in 1688 Scotland was seething with dis-content.

2. The Restoration in Ireland

The Land Settlement : Charles II was proclaimed King in Dublin on May 14, 1660. Naturally his return aroused great hopes among those who had lost their lands during the Crom-wellian Settlement. The Protestant Royalists, who had fought for his father in the Civil War and had suffered as a consequence, expected that their estates would be restored. The Catholics,

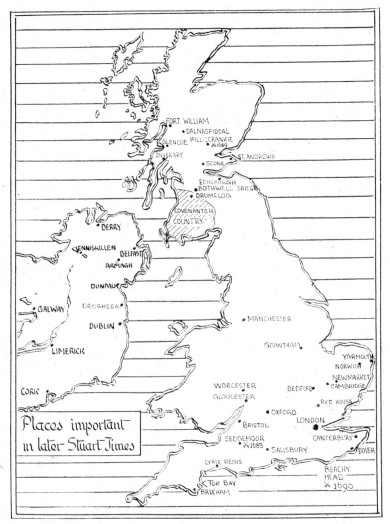

Places important in later Stuart Times

too, had high hopes, for many of their gentry had served Charles abroad in various capacities and now took it for granted that their loyalty would be rewarded. The King was anxious to help them, but certain facts could not be overlooked. The Cromwellian settlers were already in possession of much of the land, either as " adventurers " who had lent money to the government at the beginning of the rebellion or as soldiers who had been given estates instead of pay, and their claims could hardly be ignored. Apart from that, Sir Charles Coote and Lord Broghill, leaders of the Cromwellian forces in Ireland, had been in communication with Charles before he left Holland, and had got from him a promise that the " new settlers " would not be disturbed. One group or other was, therefore, bound to be disappointed; but so little knowledge had Charles of the real situation in Ireland that, in November 1660, he issued a proclamation promising to satisfy all genuine claims.

It soon became obvious that it would be impossible to do so. In 1662 the Irish Parliament passed an Act of Settlement, which confirmed the Cromwellian settlers in the possession of their lands, but also provided that Protestant Royalists and " innocent " Catholics (i.e. those who had not rebelled in 1641 or taken part in the Confederation of Kilkenny) should have their estates restored. If this entailed loss by the Cromwellian settlers, the latter were to be compensated elsewhere. A Court of Claims was set up to decide who were entitled to recover their estates under the act, but so many Catholics were able to prove their " innocence " that it soon became apparent that there would not be enough land for all. Thus the court was closed, with many cases still unheard, and a compromise was attempted by the Act of Explanation (1665), whereby the Cromwellians had to surrender one-third of their land to create a fund out of which Royalists and Catholics could be compensated. But even so, many who had formerly been land-owners never recovered their estates and were disappointed. Some of them sank into poverty as tenants-at-will or labourers; others, as after the Plantation of Ulster, took to the hills and became " Tories." This latter group did not regard the settlement as permanent but eagerly looked forward to the day when they could upset it.

The Church Settlement: The restoration of the monarchy was accompanied by a restoration of the Established Church. Dr. John Bramhall, a Yorkshire man, was made Archbishop of Armagh, and other bishops and ministers returned to their dioceses and parishes. As in England so also in Ireland, an Act of Uniformity was passed in 1662 imposing the Book of Common Prayer on the Church and providing that only ministers who had been ordained by bishops could hold benefices. The effects of this act were principally felt in Ulster, where, during the Cromwellian period, the Scottish settlers had organised their Church on the Presbyterian model and had in some cases occupied the parish churches and rectories. The bishops ejected them from these, especially in the counties of Antrim and Down where the Scottish settlers were numerous. But there was little actual persecution, and the Presbyterians in Ulster fared a great deal better than their brethren in Scotland. Indeed in 1672 they were given semi-official recognition when Charles began the payment of an annual grant, called the *Regium Donum*, to the Presbyterian ministers of the north.

The Catholics: The great majority of the Irish people were Catholics; as many as 800,000 out of an estimated population of 1,100,000. Most of them were not concerned at all with the problems of land ownership which we have discussed in an earlier section. They were labourers or tenants-at-will, occupying wretched cottages, sleeping on straw and living as a rule on milk and potatoes. During the middle part of Charles II's reign—from 1670 to 1678—when Lords Berkeley and Essex were Viceroys the Catholics did enjoy a fair amount of religious toleration. The harsh laws against their faith were still on the statute book, but except in isolated instances they were not enforced. Dr. Oliver Plunkett, descended from one of the old Anglo-Irish families of the Pale, was consecrated Archbishop of Armagh in 1669, and returned to Ireland as head of the

Church. His correspondence with Rome gives us some indication of the more favourable conditions prevailing. Writing in 1670 he said: "The Viceroy of this Kingdom shows himself favourable to the Catholics . . . . so that ecclesiastics may freely appear in public without suffering any annoyance, even when they are recognised as such." He also reported that Lord Berkeley had assured him that bishops and priests would not be molested if they did not interfere in political affairs. Dr. Plunkett was quick to take advantage of this toleration. He established a college at Drogheda for the education of priests and young Catholic laymen, and he summoned a number of national and provincial synods to reorganise the Church and to remove abuses into which both clergy and people had fallen.

In 1678 this policy of toleration was brought to an abrupt end. The Earl of Ormond, who was then Viceroy, was no more taken in by the Titus Oates' story than was Charles II, but so strong was the anti-Catholic feeling aroused among the English settlers that he feared to oppose the demand for persecution. In October 1678 the Council of Ireland issued a proclamation ordering all bishops and members of religious orders to leave the country and offering a reward for all who were captured after November 20th. Many prominent Catholics were imprisoned, and Dr. Talbot, the aged Archbishop of Dublin, died in prison. The bishops of course did not leave the country, but moved from place to place to attend the spiritual needs of their people. Oliver Plunkett evaded arrest for a time, but eventually he was taken in Dublin and accused of plotting to bring over the French to massacre the English. There was no real evidence to substantiate the charge, but after trials at Dundalk and London he was executed at Tyburn in 1681.

When the frenzy aroused by the story of Titus Oates subsided religious toleration was restored. But though Catholics were permitted to practise their faith quietly, they were still excluded from all official positions, from the town corporations and from the university.

Economic Affairs : During the Protectorate, when England,

Scotland and Ireland were under one parliament, there was free trade between the three countries; and, when the Navigation Act was passed in 1651, Irish merchants were allowed to trade freely with England and with any of her overseas settlements. At the Restoration this parliamentary union ended, and, when a new Navigation Act was passed in 1663, it contained no reference to Ireland, the intention being to exclude her from this traffic from now on. Irish merchants, however, continued to trade with the colonies, and so in 1670 another act was passed excluding Ireland by name from these markets as well. Because of these laws, raw materials and other commodities from the colonies could be imported into Ireland only through England, and because of the extra distance and the additional handling involved they cost a good deal more.

During this period the English Parliament tried to control the trade of Ireland in another way. Because of her equable climate and good pastures Ireland was particularly suited for pastoral farming, and large numbers of cattle and sheep were reared and exported to England and Scotland. But in 1666 a Cattle Act was passed prohibiting the import of Irish cattle into England. This embargo caused a good deal of immediate hardship, but the Irish merchants succeeded in finding a fresh outlet for their livestock. Large quantities of beef, mutton, pork and dairy produce were exported to Flanders, France, Spain and Portugal where they found a ready market. Indeed it is said that it was no uncommon sight to see twenty Irish provision ships lying alongside the docks of Dunkirk or Nantes or Ostend.

With regard to this commercial legislation there are two things we must remember. *First*, at that time England and other European countries regarded their colonies as means of enriching the mother country, either by supplying it with raw materials it could not produce itself, or by purchasing its manufactured goods. Thus the governments felt justified in passing any laws that were necessary to preserve a monopoly for themselves. This control was called the *Mercantile System*. *Second*, it was obvious that the English government was regarding Ireland as a " colony " in the matter of trade. This policy was continued in the reign of William III, and we shall see how bitterly the Protestant ruling class in Ireland came to attack it in the eighteenth century.

3. Colonies and Companies

During the reigns of James I and Charles I a number of English settlements had been made on the east coast of North America : Virginia, Maryland and the Puritan colonies of New England. At the same time the East India Company was very active in Asia and had established trading posts at Surat, Masulipatam, Madras and Hughli on the mainland of India. With the Restoration this work of expansion overseas continued, and by the end of Charles II's reign England controlled most of the east coast of North America, had acquired the island of Bombay, and had two more chartered companies.

(a) NORTH AMERICA

Carolina : In 1663 Charles II granted a large stretch of territory, lying to the south of Virginia, to a number of nobles in his court, including the Earl of Clarendon, the Duke of Albemarle (General Monk) and the future Earl of Shaftesbury. The purpose of this grant was to enable a settlement to be made there, and it was hoped that in time the territory would provide England with the silk, fruit and wine which had hitherto been imported from the Mediterranean lands. Two settlements were made : one at the Albemarle river in the north of the area, and the other at Charleston in the south. From these two settlements eventually developed the separate colonies of North Carolina and South Carolina. North Carolina did not prosper at first : it was difficult to get the right type of person to settle there, and many of its inhabitants turned to piracy or searched for gold instead of getting down to the hard work needed to make a colony a success. South Carolina was more fortunate and in the course of time attracted settlers from the West Indies and even from the other colonies. Huguenots exiled from France were introduced in the hope that they would establish the wine and silk industries of their native land. That did not happen, however, and South Carolina became a colony of large estates, worked by negro slaves and producing tobacco, sugar and rice.

Pennsylvania : William Penn was a son of that Admiral Penn who had captured Jamaica from the Spaniards in 1655. As a young man, when on a visit to Cork, William had gone to hear a preacher named Loe, and from then on he was a very devout Quaker. The Society of Friends (or Quakers as they were usually called) was a religious sect founded by George Fox about 1650. It had no ministers, dogma or formal services. Quakers were guided in matters of religion by "the inner light" or direct revelation from God, and they believed that in order to preach no special training was necessary. The Quakers were attacked by both Anglicans and Nonconformists and none suffered more than they did under the Clarendon Code. Because of this persecution Penn decided to found a colony in North America as a refuge where Quakers might live in peace.

In 1681 he obtained from Charles II a grant of land to the north of Maryland, and there he established Pennsylvania. About three thousand Quakers from England and Ireland immediately settled there, but Penn did not wish to confine his new colony to Quakers alone, and guaranteed religious liberty for all Christians. Neither did he wish to exclude other races, but advertised for settlers in Europe and attracted a considerable number of Germans and Swiss. He called the capital of his settlement Philadelphia, which means "the city of brotherly love," and that was the spirit in which he hoped the colony would develop. The Indians were treated fairly, and though eventually slavery was introduced the slaves were better treated than anywhere else.

The Middle Colonies : There was one part of the coastline between the Hudson and Delaware rivers that had not been settled by the English but by the Dutch. In 1623 a number of Dutchmen made a settlement at the mouth of the Hudson. Three years later they bought Manhattan Island from the Indians, and from these two settlements grew the colony of New Netherlands. Farther north a Swedish settlement, Delaware, was founded, but by 1655 it also was in Dutch hands. The English naturally resented these intrusions into an area which they regarded as their own, especially as the settlements placed a barrier between the New England colonies and those of the south.

This was only one cause for the enmity that existed between England and Holland. There was also rivalry between the merchants of the two countries in the Far East, and frequent disputes nearer home about fishing rights in the North Sea. Then in 1651, during the Commonwealth, a Navigation Act had confined trade between England and her colonies to British and colonial ships and had provided that goods from other countries could only be imported into England in either British ships or in those of the country which provided the goods. This act was aimed at Holland, which at that time was trying to secure a monopoly of the carrying trade of the world, and it led to the first Dutch War.

At the Restoration the Navigation Act was renewed, and by 1665 England and Holland were at war once more. The two sides were fairly evenly matched : Van Tromp and De Ruyter were in charge of the Dutch fleet and General Monk (now Albemarle) in charge of the British. Even before the two countries were actually at war Charles II had granted New Amsterdam to his brother the Duke of York. James sent out a fleet to occupy the area, and the Dutch, being unable to offer any effective resistance, were forced to surrender. By the Treaty of Breda (1667) at the end of the war Holland recognised British ownership of the territory, and from it were formed the colonies of New York, New Jersey and Delaware. These middle colonies were of great importance because they joined the Puritan settlements of the north to the plantation colonies of the south; and by the end of Charles II's reign twelve of the thirteen American colonies were already in existence. The thirteenth, Georgia, was founded very much later in 1732.

(b) INDIA

Bombay : When Charles II married Catherine of Braganza, sister of the King of Portugal in 1662, the island of Bombay was given to him as part of the marriage dowry. The King at first decided to hold it as a Crown Colony, but he found its administration so troublesome and expensive that in 1668 he handed it over to the East India Company. At first its progress was slow, but before the end of the century it had become the chief port of Western India, and had taken Surat's place as headquarters of the Company.

(c) COMPANIES

Two important companies were formed during Charles II's reign : the Royal African Company and Hudson's Bay Company.

The Royal African Company : The African trade in the seventeenth century consisted principally of slaves. Ever since the first voyage of John Hawkins to West Africa in 1562 several companies had been formed to carry on the trade, but they had all failed. In 1672 the Royal African Company was formed with the Duke of York at its first Governor. It carried slaves from the Gold Coast to the sugar plantations of the West Indies and to the southern colonies of North America, and the merchants of Liverpool and Bristol who participated in the trade made large fortunes. But the Company suffered from the competition of interlopers (individual merchants who were not members of the Company) and in 1750 a new company was formed to take over its liabilities and trade. Eventually in the early nineteenth century public opinion forced the government to put an end to the slave trade, and the companies carrying it on were abolished.

The Hudson's Bay Company : This company, founded in 1670, traded with the Indians round Hudson's Bay in North America. Certain English commodities were supplied to the natives in exchange for skins, hides and furs. One of the founders of the company was Prince Rupert, who had been Charles I's cavalry commander in the Civil War, and the area around Hudson's Bay was called Rupertsland in his honour. For some time the French competed with the English for this trade, but by the Treaty of Utrecht (1713) the territory was finally declared to be British. This is the only one of the seventeenth century chartered companies still in existence and carrying on the same trade.

4. The Royal Navy: Samuel Pepys

The Duke of York : The later Stuart period has been described by one historian as " the golden age of the British Navy ". This was largely due to the enthusiasm of James, Duke of York, who became Lord High Admiral at the Restoration. During the Commonwealth and Protectorate a considerable naval force had been built up under the command of Robert Blake, who as a soldier had distinguished himself in the Civil War. James now set about completing the work which Blake had begun, and in the opening years of Charles II's reign he devoted practically all his time to the task : examining plans for new ships, visiting docks and creating a service of full-time naval officers and men. His great difficulty was shortage of money. Parliament treated the King's request with suspicion, and, during the Second Dutch War, Charles was forced, through lack of money, to lay up the fleet at Chatham. Taking advantage of this, the Dutch Admiral de Ruyter sailed up the Thames, burnt some of the ships as they lay at anchor, and towed home in triumph the English flagship, the *Royal Charles.*

The Men : As well as attending to the building of better ships—and in this he had the assistance of the skilled shipbuilder Sir Anthony Deane—James also concentrated on improving the quality of the sailors who manned them. Boys were chosen and sent to sea as midshipmen "to learn the ropes". After two years they were examined, and, if considered proficient, they were commissioned as lieutenants. From their ranks in time the superior officers were chosen. The getting of good ordinary seamen was a more difficult problem, for pay was poor and conditions of service were very bad. James could do little about this, as he was unable to get the money it would have required. Thus crews continued to be press-ganged into service against their wills; but he did attempt to impose stricter discipline by a code which later developed into "the Queen's Regulations".

The Administration : James also created a new administration to supervise the navy. As Lord High Admiral he presided over the Navy Board consisting of the Treasurer, the Surveyor, the Comptroller and the Clerk, each of whom was responsible for a department—finance, stores, ships, etc. Thus the Royal Navy was in a very special way the creation of the Duke of York. But in this work he was fortunate to have the assistance of a devoted official named Samuel Pepys.

Samuel Pepys (1633-1703) : Pepys, the son of a London tailor, was educated at St. Paul's School in his native city and at Magdalene College, Cambridge. He was secretary to Admiral Montagu and accompanied him to Holland in 1660 in order to bring home the exiled Charles II. After the Restoration, when the Duke of York set up the administration described above, Pepys was appointed Clerk of the Navy Board. He was responsible for the provision of ships, material and pay during the Second Dutch War and did his work so efficiently that, when James was forced by the Test Act to give up his office of Lord High Admiral, Pepys took over as Secretary and carried out a great shipbuilding programme in the 1670's. At the time of the Popish Plot he was imprisoned for a time because of his friendship with James, but he was later reappointed to his

Samuel Pepys, 1633–1703

old post and remained at the Admiralty until the Revolution of 1688 when he finally retired.

The Diarist : Samuel Pepys is more famous for his diary, however, than for his part in creating the modern navy. He began to keep the diary in 1660, and under May 2 of that year he had a very vivid description of the King's return to London. He continued the diary for the next nine years, and in it he recorded, in cipher, even the most trivial happenings of his everyday life, without reserve and with great frankness. After his death in 1703 Pepys' diary went with his other papers to Magdalene College, Cambridge, and there it lay undiscovered until it was deciphered and published in 1825. It is of great value to the modern historian because of the lively and colourful account it gives of London life generally in the opening years of Charles II's reign.

Questions and Exercises

1. Give an account of the persecution of the Covenanters in Scotland during Charles II's reign.

2. Why did the Irish Royalists and Catholics hope for relief at the Restoration ? To what extent were their hopes realised by the land settlement ?

3. Describe the treatment of (a) the Catholics, and (b) the Presbyterians in Ireland during Charles II's reign.

4. Give an account of the colonies established or acquired by the English in North America in the period 1660-1685.

5. Describe the part played by James, Duke of York, in the development of the Royal Navy.

6. Write informative notes on each of the following :—
   (a) Samuel Pepys and his Diary;
   (b) The effects of English legislation on Irish trade and industry in the seventeenth century;
   (c) Hudson's Bay Company;
   (d) The acquisition of Bombay

CHAPTER THREE

The Glorious Revolution

1. The Reign of James II (1685-1688)

The Accession of James: The reign of the new king began well. So completely had Charles II triumphed over the Whigs that there was not even a murmur of opposition when James II ascended the throne. He was crowned in Westminster Abbey by the Archbishop of Canterbury, and he assured his Privy Council that, although he was a Catholic, he would do his utmost to uphold the Constitution and the Church of England. Because of this the Anglican ministers were fulsome in their loyalty and exhorted their congregations to give their allegiance to James as " the Lord's anointed sovereign ", An election held in May, 1685 returned an overwhelming majority of Royalists to the House of Commons, who granted him for life a revenue that was sufficient to meet all the ordinary expenses of government. Not one of his Stuart predecessors had enjoyed such a strong position at his accession as did James II; but we shall see how in the course of three years he antagonised the Church of England, lost the support of the members of Parliament and finally was driven from the throne.

Monmouth's Rebellion (1685): Within a few months of his accession two rebellions occurred which showed how strong the new King's position really was. You will remember that after Charles II had dissolved the Oxford Parliament (1681) many

James II
[*National Maritime Museum, Greenwich Hospital Collection*]

of the leading Whigs had gone into exile. When James came to the throne a number of these came together in the Netherlands and planned two invasions to take place simultaneously: one of Scotland led by the Duke of Argyle, the other of England led by the Duke of Monmouth. The Whig conspirators expected that there would be a general uprising of Scottish Covenanters and English Protestants in support of their invasions. Argyle's expedition came first; in May, 1685 he landed on the west coast of Scotland, but he failed even to raise his own clan, the Campbells, and he was executed at Edinburgh.

A few weeks later the Duke of Monmouth landed at Lyme Regis in Dorset with a hundred and fifty men and called upon the people of the south-west to help him overthrow " the Popish tyrant ". Most of the gentry held aloof, but the farm labourers, wool weavers and miners flocked to his standard, and he soon had an " army " of five thousand men. The general Protestant uprising that Monmouth had expected did not take place, however; instead Parliament voted an additional £400,000 to the king to enable him to send an army, led by Lord Feversham and John Churchill (later Duke of Marlborough), to crush the rebellion. The two forces met at *Sedgemoor,* near Bridgwater, on the night of July 5, 1685, and Monmouth's undisciplined horde was mown down by the King's troops. After the battle, the Duke, disguised as a peasant, tried to escape, but he was found hiding in a ditch in a bean-field near the New Forest and executed.

" The Bloody Assize " : Those who had joined in the rebellion were without doubt guilty of treason, for they had taken up arms against their King. A wise ruler, however, seeing how loyally the country as a whole had supported him, would have granted a general pardon to all but the leaders. But James showed no mercy, and the punishment of the rebels was very harsh. After the battle of Sedgemoor many of the peasants had been rounded up by Colonel Kirke and his soldiers (nicknamed " the Lambs ") and hanged without trial. Later, James sent Lord Chief Justice Jeffreys on a circuit of the counties of Dorset, Somerset, Wiltshire and Hampshire where he imposed such savage sentences on those brought before him that the episode has come to be known as " the Bloody Assize." Juries were bullied into giving the verdicts he wanted, prisoners were badgered, attacked and harshly handled. In the course of four weeks Jeffreys sentenced three hundred rebels to death by hanging, and over eight hundred were sold into slavery in the West Indies. This was cruel punishment, even for those days, and by tolerating it James shocked his most loyal supporters.

The King's Policy : The successes of the first few months of his reign had a disastrous effect upon James. Parliament was very loyal and had granted him generous financial aid; during the rebellion he had increased the strength of his army and had now nearly 30,000 men; his enemies were dead or disheartened. But what James overlooked was the fact that the loyalty of the Church, of the Parliament and of the people was conditional, and that it would quickly disappear if he violated the promises he had made at his coronation. This he now proceeded to do, and, by one reckless blunder after another, he turned friends into enemies and made it certain that he would lose his throne.

The Dispensing Power : When the army had been augmented during Monmouth's Rebellion, James had appointed a number of Catholic officers, although they were debarred from such service by the Test Act. Then when Parliament re-assembled in November, 1685 he asked it to repeal the Act so that these Catholics could continue in the army. But Parliament, for all its Tory loyalty, rejected the King's request : instead it asked James to reduce the size of his army and to dismiss his Catholic officers. His reply was to adjourn Parliament, which never met again during his reign.

If Parliament would not repeal the Test Act, James was determined to get around it in another way. It had always been accepted that the King had the right to free from punishment a person who had broken the law : this was called his *dispensing power*. But this power was only exercised in very special circumstances; as we see it occasionally used nowadays when

a murderer is " reprieved." James began to use it frequently to
secure the appointment of Catholics to positions from which the
Test Act excluded them. Catholics were appointed to the Privy
Council, a Catholic was put in command of the fleet and
another was made Lord Lieutenant of Ireland. To proceed in
this way was sheer madness, and even the Pope warned James
that he was going too fast. His most foolish act of all was to
antagonise his own supporters—the Church and the Universities.
He established the Court of Ecclesiastical Commission, with
Judge Jeffreys as its President, in order to enforce his religious
policy, and he appointed Catholics to important positions in the
Universities of Oxford and Cambridge which hitherto had been
reserved to ministers of the Anglican Church. James was now
openly violating his promise to protect the Church of England,
and many a parson, who had hitherto preached the duty of
obedience to the "Lord's anointed," began to wonder how
much longer he could himself give allegiance to the King.

The Declaration of Indulgence : In 1687 James began to use
even wider powers : he suspended laws altogether. Charles II
had tried to do this in 1672, when he issued his Declaration of
Indulgence suspending the penal laws against Catholics and
Nonconformists. Parliament had objected on that occasion, and
Charles had withdrawn the Declaration. James had learned nothing from that incident, however, and in 1687 he issued a fresh
Declaration of Indulgence, hoping to win the Nonconformists
to his side. But the latter were as bewildered as everyone else
by the policy which the King was pursuing and refused to co-
operate with him. In the next year (1688) James went even
further : he issued the Declaration once more and ordered that
it should be read from every pulpit in the kingdom. But
though bishops, in general, had been conspicuous for their
loyalty to the King, they were not prepared to help him under-
mine the privileged position of their Church. A few days before
the date arranged for the reading of the Declaration (Sunday,
May 20, 1688) Archbishop Sancroft and six other bishops petitioned James asking him to withdraw the order—*because they*

considered that his attempt to dispense with the laws was illegal.
James was furious; he arrested the bishops and put them on
trial for seditious libel. This turned the bishops into popular
heroes, and when, on June 30, 1688, the jury found them not
guilty there were celebrations throughout the country and
people lit bonfires to show their joy. By his actions during the
past three years James had driven Whigs and Tories together
and forfeited the allegiance he had been given in 1685.

The Birth of a Son : While the bishops were in the Tower
awaiting trial an event occurred which brought matters to a
head : a son was born to the King's wife, Mary of Modena.
Hitherto the heir to the throne had been James's daughter Mary,
who was a Protestant and married to the great Protestant
prince, William of Orange. Because of that the Tories were
prepared to wait for the King's death (he was fifty-five years
of age) when a Protestant ruler would succeed him. But a
Prince of Wales would ascend the throne before his sister, and
thus the country was faced with the prospect of a line of
Catholic kings. This proved too much even for Tory loyalty,
and on the very night that the bishops were acquitted seven of
the leading Whigs and Tories sent a letter to William of
Orange inviting him to come to England to save the
Constitution and the Protestant Church.

As soon as James discovered what was afoot he hurriedly
reversed his policy. He issued a proclamation promising to
uphold the law in both Church and State and to summon a
Parliament. He abolished the Court of Ecclesiastical Commission, replaced the Fellows he had expelled from Magdalen
College, Oxford and restored their charters to the boroughs
which had lost them. These concessions, had they been made
six months earlier, might have saved his throne; now they were
regarded as a sign of the King's weakness.

William of Orange : William, Prince of Orange, was the
ruler of Holland and the Stadholder or President of the seven
small provinces of the Netherlands, which were engaged in a
life and death struggle with Louis XIV of France. William's

William III on horseback

[National Maritime Museum, Greenwich]

mother was a sister of Charles II and he himself had married his cousin, the Princess Mary, daughter of James II, in 1677. But although he was married to the heir presumptive to the English throne, William was not particularly interested in English affairs. His whole life was dedicated to one task—to prevent the Netherlands being over-run by France. In 1688 another great war with Louis XIV was about to break out. William realised that in this contest England would be a useful ally and her help might make all the difference between victory and defeat. That was the spirit in which he accepted the invitation to come to England.

The Landing of William : On November 5, 1688 William landed at Brixham on Tor Bay with an army of 15,000 men.

From there he moved slowly towards London gathering support as he went. The King's only hope was in an immediate attack while his army was still intact, but James vacillated and delayed until his officers began to desert him in large numbers. Eventually when he did make up his mind and advanced as far as Salisbury, his best general, John Churchill (later Duke of Marlborough) went over to the side of William. Bewildered by the course events had taken James returned to London to find that his favourite daughter, Anne, had also forsaken him. In great distress he exclaimed, " Heaven help me, even my own children desert me."

Flight of the King : James now made his greatest blunder of all : he left the country. William had not claimed the throne; his banners proclaimed his object—" A Free Parliament and the Protestant Religion." Many of the Tories, sincerely attached to the principle of hereditary succession, were troubled in their conscience by what was being done. Had James remained in England could a compromise have been arranged that would satisfy both King and people? There is no means of knowing; but one thing is certain—by fleeing with his Queen and son to France in December, 1688, James made it inevitable that he would lose the throne. On his arrival in Paris he was presented by Louis XIV with the palace of St. Germain, was granted a pension of £40,000 a year for life, and was treated by everybody as if he were still King of England.

King William and Queen Mary : The flight of James left England without a government, and there was the danger of civil war if some action were not taken promptly. Thus before Christmas those members of the House of Lords and of the last Parliament called by Charles II, who could be assembled at once in London, requested William to take over the administration of the kingdom and to summon a Convention Parliament. When this body met on January 22, 1689 its first business was to decide who was to be King and on what terms. This revealed at once the dilemma of the Tories; though they had co-operated with the Whigs in overthrowing James they did not want to violate the principle of Divine Right (i.e. that monarchs were appointed by God to rule the country and that succession to the throne was hereditary). Thus they proposed that James, while remaining in France, would retain the title of King, and that William and Mary should govern the country as Regents. But the Whigs would have none of this : they said the throne of England was vacant and should now be filled. The argument between the two sides went on for weeks, until at last, his patience exhausted, William announced that if he were not at once made King he would return to Holland. That settled the issue; on February 6, 1689 Whigs and Tories joined in a declaration that James II had abdicated by running away, and invited William and Mary to be joint King and Queen.

2. The Revolution Settlement

The Bill of Rights : The Crown of England had not been offered to William and Mary unconditionally. Attached to the document which invited them to the throne was a *Declaration of Rights,* setting out conditions under which they were to rule. This was later expanded as the *Bill of Rights* which declared :

(a) That William and Mary were to hold the Crown jointly for their lives; at their death, if they had no heirs, Mary's sister, Anne, was to become Queen, to be followed by her children. But " all persons who shall hold communion with the Church of Rome, or who shall marry a Papist, shall be excluded from the Crown."

(b) That " the pretended power of suspending laws by royal authority as it hath been assumed and exercised of late " and the collection of taxes without the consent of Parliament were illegal.

(c) That the King must summon Parliaments " frequently," allow them to be elected " freely," and permit the members to speak their minds in debate.

(d) That " the raising and keeping of a standing army within the kingdom in time of peace " was illegal.

Other Limitations on Royal Power : Subsequent measures made it impossible for the King to do without Parliament from now on. The first of these measures was the new financial arrangement whereby the royal revenue was divided into two parts : one part (called the Civil List) was to meet the King's personal expenses and was granted for life; the other part was to meet the cost of government and was granted annually. Each year the King's ministers were expected to put before the House of Commons an estimate of government expenditure for the coming year and to obtain the approval of the House for the taxes that were imposed to meet it. This was the origin of the *Budget,* which is introduced by the Chancellor of the Exchequer each year, though the modern term did not come into use until about 1760.

The **Mutiny Act** of 1689 had precisely the same result. The Bill of Rights had made the keeping of an army within the kingdom in time of peace illegal; yet William III needed an army to help him in his war with France. The Mutiny Act allowed him to keep one, but for one year only. Thus if William (and succeeding Kings) wished to keep an army he had to summon Parliament each year to get its approval.

A finishing touch was put to the Revolution Settlement by the Triennial Act (1694) which provided for the holding of a general election every three years. This made more precise the declaration concerning " free " Parliaments " frequently " elected that had been included in the Bill of Rights.

The Toleration Act (1689) : An important decision was also taken about religion. The Nonconformists had rejected the overtures of James II when he issued his Declaration of Indulgence, and now William insisted that they should be allowed freedom of worship. This was done by the *Toleration Act* (1689) which gave the Nonconformists permission to have their own meeting-houses and their own clergy. But the Anglicans insisted upon retaining the Test and Corporation Acts, and Nonconformists were still excluded from public life. These laws remained on the statute book until 1828, but gradually in the eighteenth century the custom grew up of Nonconformists holding municipal and public offices from which the acts excluded them, and being forgiven for breaking the law by an annual Indemnity Act.

The Catholics did not fare so well. Many of them, naturally enough, had supported James II, and, after the Revolution, they were in consequence viewed with suspicion. In times of scare, when a Jacobite plot was detected or a French invasion was expected, they were still liable to persecution, but in general they were not molested as long as they went about their devotions quietly. The Catholics were a tiny minority now, and nearly everywhere consisted of aristocratic families with their dependents and servants. But as time went on, and one noble family after another conformed to the Established Church, the chief problem of Catholics was how to keep their religion alive in the midst of such a strongly Protestant community. It was only with Irish immigration in the nineteenth century that Catholicism in England began to revive.

Results of the Revolution : The Glorious Revolution is one of the most important events in English history and it had very far-reaching effects.

(a) A King who claimed to rule by Divine Right had been driven from the throne and replaced by William and Mary as joint sovereigns. William did not rule by Divine Right but by the favour of Parliament, and, while Mary was James II's daughter, she could not claim Divine Right while her father lived. Even when James died, his Divine Right would not pass to her but to the young Prince of Wales. Thus since 1688 no ruler of Britain has been able to claim that he or she has ruled by Divine Right.

(b) The great struggle between King and Parliament which had gone on all through the seventeenth century was finally settled : Parliament had established itself as an essential part of the machinery of government. Not only had it deposed one King and put another in his place, but also, by the Mutiny Act and the new financial arrangements, it had made it impossible for any future King to rule the country, even for one year, without the assistance of Parliament.

It would be a mistake to think, however, that the King of England lost all of his power in 1688. William III ruled very much as Kings had ruled before him : he chose his own ministers ; kept foreign affairs completely in his own hands and made treaties without consulting his ministers; he refused his consent to a number of Bills which had passed through Parliament. But Parliament, by its control of the purse and by its right of frequent meeting, was now in a better position to influence policy, and in time it became the ruler of the country.

(c) The Revolution led to a new policy—hostility to France. Except for a short time in the reign of Charles I, England under the Stuart Kings had been friendly with France; for the next hundred and twenty-five years the countries were enemies. During that period England and France fought six great wars. The wars fall into three groups. In the first group are two wars— the War of the League of Ausburg (1689-1697) and the War of the Austrian Succession (1702-1713)—which were fought against Louis XIV who was trying to dominate Europe. In the second group there are three wars—the War of the Austrian Succession (1740-1748), the War of American Independence (1775-1783), the Seven Years' War (1756-1763). In these wars the two countries were fighting for colonies, for trade and for supremacy at sea. Finally between 1793 and 1815 there were the Revolutionary and Napoleonic Wars. We shall learn something of these wars in subsequent chapters.

3. The Reign of William and Mary (1689-1702)

The New King : Once " the Protestant Revolution " was accomplished, William soon lost his popularity in England. A member of one of the oldest and proudest noble families of Europe, he lacked the common touch. Suffering from asthma and with a tubercular lung, he lived outside London at Hampton

Court, and, except for one tour he made of the Midlands in
1695, his subjects saw little of him. What little they did see
they disliked ; for William, pale, stooping and withdrawn, was
not an attractive figure. His only enthusiasm was for the defence
of Holland against the ambition of Louis XIV of France ;
everything else, even the kingship of England, was subordinate
to that. His wife, Mary, was very different : she had all the
charm and wit of the Stuarts, and her death from small-pox
in 1694 left William more isolated from his subjects than ever.
Yet he ruled his new kingdom well, and in defending Holland
he saved not only his own country but all Europe from French
domination. As well, by accepting the restrictions placed upon
his powers, he played an important part in the evolution of
constitutional monarchy.

Political Parties : The Whigs and Tories had joined in overthrowing James II and putting William and Mary on the throne;
but, apart from that, the two parties differed in nearly everything else. The Tories were opposed to any serious reduction
in the powers of the King ; the Whigs emphasised the rights of
Parliament. The Tories were determined to preserve the privileged position of the Established Church ; the Whigs wanted
greater toleration for Nonconformists. The Tories thought first
of the interests of landowners; the Whigs concentrated on the
needs of the business and commercial world. This division of
English politicians into two groups became a permanent feature
of English political life ; but it must be emphasised that Whigs
and Tories were not organised parties, similar to the Conservative and Labour parties of today. And, though the names
Whig and Tory were retained by political groups in the
eighteenth and nineteenth centuries, the political programmes
of the two parties naturally changed with time.

William regarded this division as a weakness at a time when
he wanted a united country behind him in his war with France.
He tried to choose his ministers indiscriminately from both
parties, but he found that they intrigued against one another
instead of concentrating on the serious business of government.

Thus towards the end of his reign he decided that the affairs of state would be conducted more efficiently if all his ministers were of the same political party—if possible the party which had a majority in the House of Commons.

The War of the League of Augsburg (1689-1697): The reign of William III was filled with wars. In his early twenties he began a struggle with Louis XIV which only terminated with his death in 1702. He had already begun to build up a Grand Alliance before he set out for England in 1688, and he then joined his new kingdom to Holland, Spain and the Holy Roman Empire in the War of the League of Augsburg. This war is also known as the War of the English Succession, because, if Louis XIV had won, he would undoubtedly have restored James II to the English throne.

The war was fought in three centres—in Ireland, on the sea and in the Spanish Netherlands. We shall deal with events in Ireland in our next chapter, and here shall confine ourselves to the other two centres. At sea things went badly for William at first. On June 30, 1690—the eve of the battle of the Boyne—a combined English and Dutch fleet was defeated by the French off Beachy Head. The French thus gained control of the Channel, and an army was gathered in Normandy for the invasion of England. But Louis XIV delayed too long, and, when the French eventually sailed in 1692, they were overwhelmed (off La Hogue) by a great Anglo-Dutch fleet under Admiral Russell. This victory was decisive, and for the rest of the war England had control of the sea.

By 1692 Ireland was also conquered, and William felt strong enough to cross to the Netherlands with the largest army that ever left England. For the next five years the war was dragged out by a series of sieges and dogged campaigns. William was defeated twice—at Steinkirk and Neerwinden—but he kept stubbornly on, and in 1695 his patience was rewarded by the capture of Namur. But neither side could hope to win a clear-cut victory in a war of this sort, and peace was made between them by the Treaty of Ryswick (1697). By its terms Louis XIV surrendered all his conquests except Strasbourg, recognised William III as King of England and promised to give no further help to James II. The Dutch were to be allowed to garrison a number of towns in the Spanish Netherlands as a precaution against any further French aggression. Clearly this treaty marked a great triumph for England, since Louis XIV was compelled to accept the revolution of 1688 ; for Holland, too, it had advantages since the occupation of " the barrier towns " gave her a greater sense of security. Yet neither side regarded it as a peace—only as a breathing space. Charles II of Spain was dying without direct heirs ; both Louis XIV and the Emperor of the Holy Roman Empire had claims to the throne. Thus it was almost certain that, as soon the the King of Spain died, war would break out again and on a larger scale.

The Bank of England (1694) : The English Government (i.e. the King's ministers and Parliament) was glad to be relieved of a war which cost the country £40,000,000. Such a large sum had never been spent on a war before and could not possibly be paid for out of ordinary taxation. Various expedients were tried such as a window tax and a new land tax, but it soon became apparent that the money would have to be borrowed. In his borrowing, Charles Montagu, who was in charge of the country's finances, introduced a new principle. In times past, Kings, like Charles II, had borrowed money for purposes of government or to fight wars, but the debt had been a personal one and had not always been repaid. Montagu borrowed in the name of the nation and with the approval of Parliament, and thus the money borrowed became the *National Debt*.

Montagu had difficulty in borrowing all the money he required, and so in 1694 a group of Whig business men, led by a Scot, William Paterson, undertook to raise £1,200,000 from the public and lend it to the Government at 8 per cent interest. The money had not to be repaid and the interest was guaranteed by Parliament. If a subscriber, for any reason, required his money back, he could sell his share in the loan to someone else who thus became entitled to his interest.

In return for their help, the subscribers were allowed to form a joint-stock company to carry on a banking business with the name of the *Bank of England,* and to issue bank-notes. These were " promises to pay " (i.e. receipts given to those who had deposited gold in the Bank), and, as people gained confidence in their worth, they were accepted as money in ordinary transactions. The Government allowed the Bank of England to issue more notes or " promises to pay " than it had gold to meet. This led to a crisis in 1696 when the London goldsmiths, who were traditional money-lenders, jealous of their new rival, collected all the notes they could lay their hands on and presented them for payment at the same time, hoping to bring the Bank down. But the Bank of England survived this and many other crises to become one of the most important institutions in the country.

The foundation of the Bank of England had important political consequences. Men who had lent their money to the Government were desperately anxious that James II should not recover his throne in case he would repudiate the National Debt. Thus the foundation of the Bank fostered loyalty to William III and helped to make the Revolution permanent.

The Act of Settlement (1701): William III, however, remained unpopular and his last years were very unhappy. Now that the war with France was over, the Tory majority in the House of Commons insisted on the King drastically reducing the army and sending home his favourite Dutch Guards. Taking this last action as a deliberate insult, William made up his mind to return to Holland, actually went so far as to compose a speech of abdication, and was only dissuaded from doing so by Lord Chancellor Somers. But relations between the King and Parliament did not improve, and, when the question of the succession to the English throne came up again for decision in 1701, it was settled in terms that were an indictment of William's rule.

Descent of the Stuarts

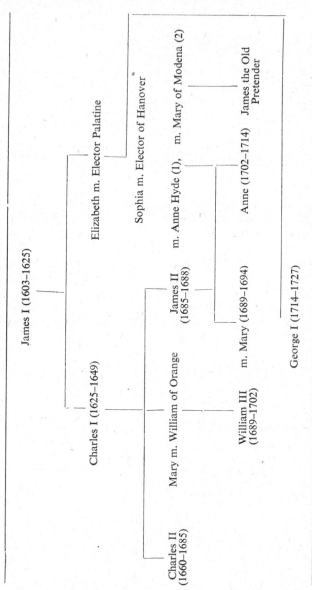

This table shows the succession of Stuart monarchs from Charles II to Queen Anne, and explains why George, the Elector of Hanover, succeeded to the English throne in 1714.

The Bill of Rights had arranged that, if William and Mary died without children, the throne should go to Mary's sister, Anne. Anne was married to Prince George of Denmark, and though she had fifteen children they had all died in infancy except one, the Duke of Gloucester. He died in 1700, and, as it was unlikely that Anne would have any more children now, it was necessary for Parliament to decide who should succeed her. The Act of Settlement (1701) laid it down that after Anne's death the Crown should pass to the Electress Sophia of Hanover (a grand-daughter of James I) and her heirs, provided, of course, that they were not Catholic. From now on it was not sufficient that the King be a Protestant: he must be a member of the Church of England. Sophia died before Queen Anne, and so in 1714 the Elector of Hanover, Sophia's son, became King of England as George I.

The Act of Settlement contained a number of other provisions which were inspired by the unpopularity of William III. The King could not go abroad or engage in a war in defence of his continental possessions without the consent of Parliament. No foreigners could be ministers or members of either House of Parliament or receive grants of land from the Crown. Most of these provisions were temporary or never went into effect. One provision, however, was permanent and it has become a very important feature of the British Constitution. Judges were to hold office *quamdiu se bene gesserint*—that is as long as they behaved well—and could not be dismissed except on an address from both Houses of Parliament. This made it less likely that a decision of the courts would be influenced by the King or his ministers, and the nation came to expect justice and impartiality from its judges as a matter of course.

The Death of William (1702): William's last years were taken up with the succession to the Spanish throne. For the last time he was in conflict with Louis XIV, and once again he had the support of the English Parliament and the English people. James II had died in 1701, and Louis had proclaimed James II's son to be King of England as James III. Both

William III and his subjects were angry and eager for war, and war was declared in 1702.

But William did not live to see the outcome of the War of the Spanish Succession. When he was riding in the grounds of Hampton Court his horse stumbled on a mole-hill and he was thrown. The shock was too much for the frail King and he died in March, 1702. But his unconquerable spirit survived to the end. His last words were "There have been times when I wished to die, but now I could wish to live a little longer."

Questions and Exercises

1. Explain briefly how James II united all classes against him and lost his throne.

2. Why did William, Prince of Orange, accept the invitation to England in 1688 ? Give an account of the War of the League of Augsburg.

3. Set out clearly the important features of the Revolution Settlement (1689-1694).

4. Give an account of the position of (a) Nonconformists and (b) Catholics in England after 1688.

5. What is meant by a Constitutional Monarchy ? Give an account of the Acts passed after 1689 which limited the power of the King.

6. Write informative notes on : the Bank of England ; Political Parties in William III's reign ; the Act of Settlement (1701).

CHAPTER FOUR

The Revolution in Ireland and Scotland

1. James II and the Williamite War

James II's Irish Policy : The accession of a Catholic King to the throne naturally aroused a good deal of anxiety among the Protestant settlers in Ireland. They feared that the recent confiscations and land settlements on which their wealth was based might be upset, and consequently were inclined to view every action of James II with suspicion. In these circumstances the King would need to exercise the utmost tact and discretion in his dealings with the settlers if their fears and anxieties were to be set at rest. But, as we have already seen, these were just the qualities that James lacked ; and thus, instead of exercising restraint as a wise King would have done, he followed in Ireland the same rash policy that lost him the English throne.

Shortly after his accession James appointed his brother-in-law, the Earl of Clarendon, as Lord Lieutenant of Ireland. But Clarendon was merely a figurehead, and the real ruler of the country was a swashbuckling soldier named Colonel Richard Talbot. In 1685 James made Talbot Earl of Tyrconnel and sent him to Ireland to carry out his policy. Tyrconnel began with the army : he dismissed the Protestant officers and men and replaced them by Catholics, so that it seemed he was building up a strong military force with which to crush any opposition. At the same time extensive changes were made in the administration and in the law-courts : Catholics were admitted to the Privy Council ; Protestant judges were removed from the Bench and replaced by Catholics ; the charters of corporations were revised so as to give Catholics control of the towns.

The Catholics, who formed the majority of the nation, were entitled to a greater share in the government and administration than they had hitherto enjoyed; but a fair balance would take time and patience to achieve. The rash behaviour of Tyrconnel made such an adjustment impossible. The settlers watched with growing alarm, not knowing where he was going to turn next. Clarendon warned the King of the consequences of this policy and emphasised the need for caution. " Landed proprietors feel so little security in the tenure of their estates," he reported to the King, " that they are trying to sell their land and leave the country. Many have actually gone ; quantities of money have also been sent away." But this advice went unheeded, and early in 1687, he was recalled and Tyrconnel became Lord Lieutenant in his place.

Tyrconnel as Lord Lieutenant : Under Tyrconnel all discretion was thrown aside : Catholic sheriffs were appointed to every county except Donegal ; only one Protestant judge remained on the Bench ; and eventually it was hoped to call an Irish Parliament which would reverse the land settlement and restore the old proprietors to their estates. The anxiety of the Protestants now turned to alarm, especially in Ulster where a large and vigorous Protestant colony had grown up in the 17th century. Hitherto relations had not always been friendly there between Anglicans and Presbyterians, but now past differences were forgotten, and they were ready to combine in self defence. The atmosphere was tense ; there were rumours of plots to murder Protestants, as had happened in 1641; the slightest incident anywhere might set the whole province ablaze. That incident came with the closing of the gates of Derry against the King's troops on December 7th, 1688.

The Siege of Derry: Tyrconnel had withdrawn the city garrison for service in England and sent a Catholic regiment, under the command of the Earl of Antrim, to replace it. Like most important towns in those days, Derry was surrounded by thick stone walls surmounted by towers, which could be entered only through a number of gates. When Antrim's regiment approached, the town council met to decide what they should do ; but before a decision could be taken thirteen young apprentice boys closed the Ferryquay Gate against them. Within a few minutes the other gates were closed ; crowds gathered in the streets, armed themselves and decided to defend the city with their lives. This defiance of the royal army is usually taken as the beginning of the Williamite War, and its anniversary is still celebrated by Orangemen.

Enniskillen, on the Erne, followed Derry's example, and thus it became vitally important for the *Jacobites* (as the supporters of James II were called) to subdue Ulster, for otherwise the province would provide William and his forces with an easy gateway into Ireland. This was the position when James himself landed at Kinsale on March 12th, 1689, bringing with him French officers and a considerable quantity of arms and ammunition. The Irish rallied to his support, and soon a large, if untrained, army was at his disposal. Tyrconnel sent part of this northwards, under Richard Hamilton, to surround Derry, and on April 19th 1689, the famous siege began. Shortly afterwards James arrived outside the walls, in the belief that his presence would be sufficient to secure the surrender of the town. But he was met by a cry of " No Surrender " and a burst of gunfire which killed several of those near him and narrowly missed himself. Thus began the siege of Derry which lasted 105 days.

The Jacobites placed a great boom of tree trunks and chains across the Foyle to ensure that no provisions should reach the city from the sea, and expected that hunger and hardship would soon force the people to surrender. But all through the spring and summer of 1689 the siege went on and the citizens endured the most terrible privations. When all the food was

The Siege of Derry, 1689

eaten, they were reduced to living on the animals—horses, dogs, even cats and rats—but still there was no thought of surrender. Every day watchmen on the cathedral tower looked anxiously out to sea hoping for relief, until at last, in the middle of June, a fleet of thirty ships was seen making for Derry and the people thought their long period of suffering was at an end. But the commander of the fleet hesitated about attacking the boom, and for six weeks his ships lay at anchor while the city continued to starve. Then at last on July 30th three food-ships, the *Mountjoy,* the *Jerusalem,* and the *Phoenix,* made their way up the Foyle, under heavy fire from the Jacobite guns which lined the banks. The *Mountjoy* crashed through the boom, and at ten o'clock that night the three ships sailed into Derry harbour bringing food to the starving people. There was now no point in the Jacobite army continuing outside the walls and next morning they marched away. The long siege was over.

Just as Derry was being relieved, the men of Enniskillen, on hearing that a Jacobite army was approaching from Dublin, went out to intercept it, and defeated it at Newtownbutler, on the borders of Fermanagh and Monaghan.

By their victories at Derry and Newtownbutler the Protestants had secured the north of Ireland for King William, and it was through Ulster ports that his army came into the country.

The Parliament of 1689 : Meantime James II had summoned the Irish Parliament to meet in Dublin on May 7th, 1689. Not surprisingly, in view of the changes which Tyrconnel had made in the charters of corporations and because of the conditions prevailing in Ulster, the Parliament was composed almost entirely of Catholics, though there was a sprinkling of Protestants in both the Upper and Lower Houses. James had no special interest in Ireland and no very great sympathy for its people. His intention was to use Ireland as a jumping-off ground for the recovery of his English throne, and he had summoned the Parliament in the expectation that it would provide him with the means to do so. But the members of Parliament were more concerned with their own interests. ' Old English ' and 'native Irish', united now as never before, were determined to take advantage of James II's difficulties in order to reverse the land settlements and to secure freedom of worship for themselves.

Religious toleration presented no difficulty at all : freedom of worship was guaranteed, and tithes were to be paid by the members of the different Churches to their own clergy instead of, as hitherto, to ministers of the Church of Ireland. But the land problem was different. As King of England James regarded it as his duty to uphold the Act of Settlement and was determined to make as few concessions on the question as possible. But he needed Irish help, and the members of Parliament warned him, "If your Majesty will not fight for our rights, we will not fight for yours." Thus, rather reluctantly, James gave way to the two measures for which this Parliament is best remembered. The *first* repealed the Acts of Settlement and Explanation and restored to the representatives of the former owners all lands confiscated since 1641, without paying any compensation to those who now possessed them. The *second* was an Act of Attainder against over 2,000 Protestants, who had fled either to England or to the North, the practical effect of which was to confiscate their lands. James opposed this legislation because he knew that it would be fatal to his cause in England, while it would turn the war in Ulster (where Derry and Enniskillen were still under siege) into a struggle for the survival of the Protestant colony.

Preparations For War : A fortnight after the relief of Derry a Williamite army commanded by Marshal Schomberg landed at Groomsport, near Bangor, Co. Down (August 13th, 1689). Marching round Belfast Lough, Schomberg took Carrickfergus Castle, and in a short time controlled the country as far south as Dundalk. James marched northwards to Drogheda, but no fighting took place, and both armies went into winter quarters to prepare for the battle that seemed likely to decide the issue. Louis XIV was anxious to drag out the war in Ireland as long as possible, and in March, 1690 he sent over 7,000 seasoned troops under the command of the Duc de Lauzun. Strangely enough, however, he did not use his supremacy at sea to prevent further Williamite forces from reaching Ireland, and eventually on June 14th, 1690 William himself landed at Carrickfergus with an army of Dutch, German, Danish and Huguenot soldiers. Both sides were now ready for war.

The main Jacobite army was at Ardee, and before moving against them William concentrated his forces at Loughbrickland, near Banbridge (Co. Down). On June 24th he began to move slowly southwards. Six days later, when he reached the River Boyne, he found the Jacobite army drawn up along its southern bank in the vicinity of Oldbridge. Historians differ as to the size of the armies on each side, but it seems probable that William had about 30,000 troops and James 20,000. Apart from the French, however, the Jacobite army consisted of untrained and poorly equipped recruits, whereas William's soldiers were either veterans or Ulster Protestants flushed with their successes at Derry and Newtownbutler. If James had shown inspired leadership, his men might have made up in valour what they lacked in experience, but on this occasion he displayed neither courage nor skill and was less concerned with the fighting than with keeping open a way of escape.

The Battle of the Boyne (1690) : On July 1st, 1690 the two armies faced each other across the Boyne. The nearest bridge across the river was at Slane six miles away, but there was a ford at Rossnaree on the left of the Jacobite army. If William could force a crossing there, he might be able, because of a bend in the river, to cut off the retreat of James's army from Oldbridge. James and de Lauzun were very frightened of this possibility and sent Sir Neil O'Neill to guard the ford.

William's main attack was launched at Oldbridge, but simultaneously Schomberg's son, Meinhart, attempted a crossing at Rossnaree. Meinhart was successful, and immediately panic seized the Jacobite leaders. Fearing that their retreat was about to be cut off, they moved the whole of the French infantry and Patrick Sarsfield's cavalry to the left flank. This greatly

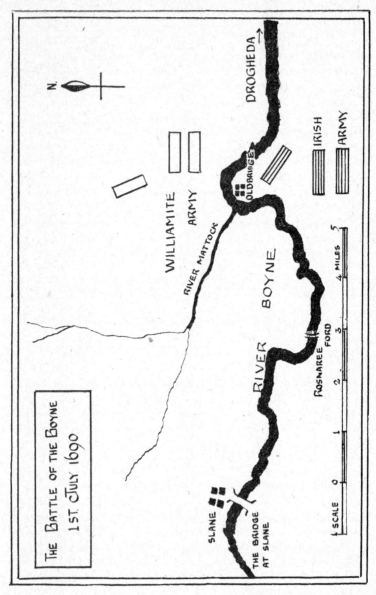

The Battle of the Boyne, 1st July, 1690

weakened the centre, and the Williamite forces had little difficulty in crossing the river at Oldbridge, though in doing so Marshal Schomberg was killed. The Jacobite army retreated in disorder, and might easily have been annihilated but for the courage with which the Irish cavalry and the French veterans covered their withdrawal. As for James, he did not even wait to see the end of the battle but fled to Dublin as fast as horses would carry him. The story is told that on his way into the city he met Lady Tyrconnel and said to her, " My cowardly troops have run away." " Then," said she, " Your Majesty has won the race." By July 20th James was back in France, bearing the news of his own defeat. From now on he had no real hope of ever recovering his English throne.

The Siege of Limerick (1690) : From the Boyne William marched rapidly to Dublin, and soon had the whole of Leinster under his control. Now that James had returned to France, William was anxious to finish off the war as quickly as possible in order to turn his attention to the main centre of operations on the continent. But the Irish army was determined not to yield without a struggle. They took the Shannon for their line of defence, and concentrated their forces at Limerick and Athlone. Limerick was defended by Patrick Sarsfield (whom James had created Earl of Lucan), the Irish hero of the Williamite War.

From Dublin William marched south through Naas, Carlow and Kilkenny to Carrick-on-Suir, and then west through Clonmel to Limerick. He reached the outskirts of the city on August 9th, 1690, but as in the case of Derry the gates were slammed against him by the defiant citizens.

William had a large army and could possibly have captured the city—de Lauzun said " it could be taken with roasted apples "—, but he decided to put off his attempt to storm the walls until the arrival of the artillery, ammunition and pontoon bridges that were on their way from Dublin. But, when Sarsfield learned that the siege-train was approaching, he decided on a daring adventure. In the middle of the night he stole out of

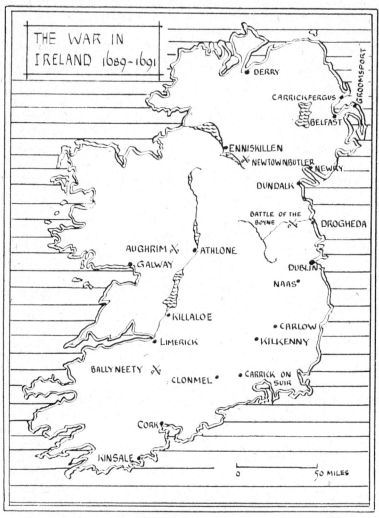

THE WAR IN
IRELAND 1689~1691

DERRY

CARRICKFERGUS

BELFAST

GROOMSPORT

ENNISKILLEN

NEWTOWNBUTLER

NEWRY

DUNDALK

BATTLE OF THE
BOYNE

DROGHEDA

AUGHRIM

ATHLONE

GALWAY

DUBLIN

NAAS

KILLALOE

CARLOW

LIMERICK

KILKENNY

BALLYNEETY

CLONMEL

CARRICK ON
SUIR

CORK

KINSALE

0   50 MILES

The War in Ireland, 1689–1691

Limerick with 500 horsemen, crossed the Shannon at Killaloe and lay in the hills to await the arrival of William's artillery. Eventually the siege-train reached Ballyneety and its commander decided to camp there for the night. Soon all were asleep except the sentry, and Sarsfield decided to take the camp by surprise. He was completely successful : the pontoon bridges were smashed, the ammunition destroyed and the cannons crammed with gunpowder and blown up. When William learned what had happened he sent a regiment to cut off Sarsfield's retreat, but the Jacobite leader eluded it and returned to Limerick.

Sarsfield's exploit postponed the attack on Limerick, but only for a time. William brought up more cannon, and, after a long bombardment, eventually made a breach in the walls. But the people of Limerick, with a courage equal to that of the men of Derry, repulsed the Williamite army and held the city. Eventually in September William ended the siege and returned to England, leaving a Dutch general, Ginkel, in command. This practically ended the fighting in 1690, except that in October John Churchill, later Duke of Marlborough, took Cork and Kinsale, thus cutting off easy communication with France.

Athlone and Aughrim : In the spring of 1691 the Jacobite forces were re-organised, and Louis XIV sent over General Saint-Ruth to command them. Their aim was still to hold the line of the Shannon, thereby protecting their only remaining ports of Limerick and Galway. Ginkel had also received reinforcements and had 5,000 men under arms at Mullingar. With these he advanced on Athlone, which Saint-Ruth was defending. The Jacobites destroyed the bridge over the Shannon at this point, but Ginkel crossed by a ford lower down the river and advanced into Connacht. Tyrconnel and Sarsfield then suggested that the Jacobites should fall back upon Limerick to await further help from France, but Saint-Ruth was eager for battle, and drew up his forces at the village of Aughrim, a few miles west of Ballinasloe (Co. Galway). There the greatest battle of the war was fought on Sunday July 12, 1691.

The two armies were of about equal size, and Saint-Ruth had chosen his position with great care. The Jacobite forces were drawn up along the brow of a hill that sloped away to a marsh. A frontal attack on their lines by cavalry was thus impossible, and St. Ruth took care to protect his flanks. Because of the position which the French general had chosen the Williamites were compelled to take the offensive. It was a spirited encounter and for a time it seemed as if the Jacobites were going to win. But as Saint-Ruth moved across the battlefield to repulse a threat to his left flank he was struck by a cannon-ball which carried away his head. Bewildered by the sudden loss of their leader, the Irish troops retreated in confusion and were defeated with great slaughter.

The battle of Aughrim decided the Williamite War. The defeated army withdrew towards Galway and Limerick with Ginkel in hot pursuit. After a short resistance Galway surrendered to the Williamite general and the Jacobites prepared to make a last stand at Limerick.

The Second Siege of Limerick : Tyrconnel sent an urgent appeal to Louis XIV and promised to defend the city until French help arrived. But the Irish had lost all heart for fighting, and had no intention of prolonging the struggle merely to serve the interests of Louis XIV. Some of them urged that negotiations be opened with Ginkel at once to obtain the best terms possible, for they knew that William III was as anxious as they were to end the war. Tyrconnel opposed this " peace party ", but his death at this time and a declaration made by Ginkel enabled them to have their way. On September 16th, the Williamite general offered pardon and a guarantee of their property to the Irish army and to the people of Limerick if they surrendered within eight days. Shortly afterwards Sarsfield and a Scottish Jacobite named Wauchope rode into the Williamite camp to begin negotiations and on October 3rd, 1691, the Treaty was signed.

The Treaty of Limerick (1691) : The treaty was in two parts

(a) the *military articles* which related to the treatment of the Jacobite army and its transport to France; and (b) the *civil articles* which were to apply to the country as a whole, and to those soldiers who were prepared to remain in Ireland as subjects of William and Mary.

The military articles were generous. All Irish soldiers who wished to go to France were permitted to do so, and Ginkel agreed to provide the ships to carry them abroad. Every effort was made, however, to encourage the Irish soldiers to remain at home (for England and France were at war), but several thousand of them, led by Sarsfield, joined the army of Louis XIV, and formed the first of the Irish brigades that were to fight so gallantly for France in her eighteenth-century wars. This going away of the Jacobite army is sometimes called " the flight of the Wild Geese."

The civil articles were also generous, and in keeping with William III's reputation for toleration. The Catholics were to enjoy such privileges in the practice of their religion as they had enjoyed in the reign of Charles II, and the King undertook to summon Parliament as soon as possible " to procure the said Roman Catholics such further security in that particular as may preserve them from any disturbance upon the account of their said religion." Those who were still in arms when Limerick surrendered were not to be deprived of their lands and were to be permitted to practise their " professions, trades and callings " as freely as they had done in the reign of Charles II, provided they took an oath of allegiance. They were not to be asked to take the oath of supremacy or any other oath distasteful to them.

The civil articles required Parliament's approval before they came into effect, but Article XII promised " that their Majesties will ratify these articles within the space of eight months or sooner, and use their utmost endeavours that the same shall be ratified or confirmed in Parliament." Historians are agreed that William III sincerely wished to honour the promises that Ginkel had made in his name; but the Irish Protestants were not as tolerant as the King. Archbishop Marsh of Dublin complained that the terms granted to the rebels were too lenient, while Bishop Dopping of Meath, preaching in Christ Church Cathedral, Dublin, argued that faith need not be kept with a people so treacherous as the Irish. Consequently when the Irish Parliament met in 1692, its members were required to take the oath of supremacy and to subscribe to a declaration against transubstantiation and other Catholic doctrines. This turned the Parliament into an exclusively Protestant body, and it refused to confirm the civil articles which William, in accordance with his promise, placed before them. Eventually in 1697 a Bill "For the confirmation of the articles made at the surrender of Limerick " was passed, but the promise that had been made to the Catholics in regard to the practice of their religion was not kept. In the same year an Act was passed ordering bishops and regular clergy out of the country, and this initiated a series of severe laws known as the *Penal Laws*— which Catholics believed had violated the Articles of Limerick. As time went on some of these laws were not enforced, but they did remain on the statute book until nearly the end of the eighteenth century.

The articles of the treaty which referred to property were more strictly observed, and there was no Act of Parliament that automatically confiscated the estates of those who fought for James. A modern historian has calculated that in 1688 Catholics owned between a quarter and a fifth of the land; the Williamite government confiscated about a third of this area leaving Catholics with about a seventh. Many of the leading Catholic peers—Antrim, Clanrickarde, Dillon, Dunsany, Gormanston, Iveagh etc.—were allowed to retain their estates; but so strictly were the Penal Laws regarding land enforced during the next fifty years that a number of these families conformed to the Established Church in order to save their property. Thus was created the Protestant Ascendancy that dominated the political, social and economic life of Ireland in the eighteenth century.

2. Scotland from Revolution to Union (1688-1707)

The Revolution in Scotland : The Scots had sent no invitation to William of Orange, and they might have continued to recognise James II as their King. But William was anxious to have Scottish support, and, shortly after his arrival, he said that if his expedition were successful he would restore to that " ancient kingdom " its laws and liberties, and have all its grievances attended to by Parliament. That settled the issue as far as the Presbyterians were concerned, and they immediately decided to support the Revolution. The Scottish Parliament met and drew up a document called *the Claim of Right,* in which it was claimed that James had broken the laws he had forfeited his right to the throne. It appointed a deputation to go to London and offer the Crown of Scotland to William and Mary. They accepted it (May 11th, 1689) and promised to rule according to the laws of the kingdom.

The Lowland Scots, who were mainly Presbyterian, accepted this decision without question, but some of the Highland clans were not prepared to see the House of Stuart overthrown without a struggle. Only a month after William had been crowned King, the Macleans, Macdonalds, Frasers, and Stuarts took up arms, under John Graham of Claverhouse, Viscount Dundee, to fight for James. General Mackay led a Williamite force against them, but he was ambushed in the steep-sloped Pass of Killiecrankie, near Pitlochry in Perthshire, and lost a great part of his men. Dundee was killed in the hour of victory by a stray bullet, and with him died James II's best hope of recovering the Scottish throne. Without a leader now, the Highlanders dispersed to their glens, and Scotland settled down under William's rule.

Presbyterianism Restored : After James II's flight the Presbyterians began to take back the churches from which they had been expelled. In Edinburgh a mob attacked and destroyed Holyrood Chapel, while, in the west, the Covenanters drove out " the King's Curates " often with great violence. But Presbyterianism was still not the Established Church, and, until it was so constituted, the country was not likely to settle down. For some time William did not know what to do, but eventually he was convinced that the Presbyterians were his staunchest friends, while the episcopalians could not be trusted. In 1690, therefore, Presbyterianism was restored as the Church of Scotland, and such it has remained to the present day.

The Massacre of Glencoe : Though the Highlanders had dispersed after Dundee's death, many of them were still in a restless state, and, if a French force should land in Scotland, they would almost certainly support it. To guard against this General Mackay was sent with an army into the Western Highlands, where he built a fort which he called Fort William in honour of the King, and a sum of money was distributed among the chiefs in an effort to win them over from Jacobitism. But some of the more spirited of the chiefs rejected what they considered as a " bribe ", and so the Government decided on a step that led to the terrible massacre of Glencoe.

In 1691 William announced that he would not punish any of the clans which had taken up arms under Claverhouse, provided that their chieftains took an oath of allegiance to him before the end of the year. By that date all the chieftains had made their submissions except MacIan, head of the Macdonalds of Glencoe. MacIan had every intention of taking the oath but had put off doing so until the last possible moment. On December 31st, 1691, he went to Fort William to take the oath, but the officer there told him that it must be taken before a magistrate, and that the nearest magistrate was at Inverary, three days journey away. MacIan was alarmed on learning this, and set out immediately through the snow ; but he was an old man, unable to hurry, and it was not until January 6th, 1696, that he took the oath.

This should not have mattered : all the chieftains had sworn their allegiance and Scotland might have settled down peacefully under William's rule. But the Secretary of State, Sir John

Monument of the Macdonalds murdered at Glencoe, 1692

[*J. B. White*]

Dalrymple, decided to make an example of the Macdonalds in order to pacify the Highlands forever. He reported to the King that MacIan had not taken the oath by the appointed day, and made it appear that the Macdonalds were still in rebellion. William therefore sent the following message to Dalrymple :

" *As for MacIan of Glencoe and that tribe, if they can be well distinguished from the rest of the Highlanders, it will be proper for public justice to extirpate that set of thieves. W.R.*"

Dalrymple entrusted the Campbells with this terrible task. Early in February, 1692, a troop of soldiers, commanded by Campbell of Glenlyon, visited the quiet valley of Glencoe in the north of Argyllshire, and were hospitably received by the Macdonalds. Then, when they had won their hosts' confidence, they made a surprise attack upon them in the early hours of the morning of February 13, 1692. The old chief was shot as he was getting out of bed, and an attempt was made to massacre the entire clan. But in the darkness many escaped into the surrounding hills, though thirty-eight in all were slain.

There may have been worse massacres than this in Scottish history, but the brutal and treacherous way in which the Campbells went about their task has made the massacre of Glencoe particularly odious. Instead of helping William, as Dalrymple had intended, he had only made his Highland enemies more bitter than ever.

The Darien Scheme : Another event which happened a few years later made William unpopular in the Lowlands as well.

As the Scots were not allowed to trade with the English colonies, they decided to establish a company of their own to carry on foreign trade. In 1695 " The Company of Scotland trading to Africa and the Indies " was formed, and it was hoped that English businessmen would invest their money in it. But the East India Company and the Royal African Company opposed the scheme, and English participation in it was stopped. The Scots then decided to go ahead by themselves, and to found a colony on the isthmus of Darien (or

Panama as it is now called), the narrow neck of land joining North and South America. A road was to be laid across the isthmus, and a port was to be built at each end of the road. It was believed that the settlement, situated between the Atlantic and Pacific oceans, would become the great centre of world trade and a distributor of the goods of East and West.

The project was supported by William Paterson, the Scottish businessman who had founded the Bank of England, and thus the company had no difficulty in raising money. Almost everyone who had money to spare took shares, hoping before long to make a large fortune.

But the scheme was not a good one. The isthmus belonged to Spain, which had no intention of allowing the Scots to make a settlement in her territory. The climate was hot and damp, and there were great malarial swamps which made it quite unsuitable for white settlement.

In July, 1698 the Company sent out its first expedition : three ships sailed from Leith carrying colonists who were to settle on the isthmus. But misfortune dogged the venture from the start ; fever broke out among the settlers, provisions ran short, they quarrelled among themselves, and worst of all they were under constant attack from the Spaniards. Two further expeditions were sent out without success, and it soon became apparent that the Company was involved in a hopeless business. Eventually, after 2,000 Scots had lost their lives and £200,000 had been squandered, the project was abandoned.

The Scots blamed the English for the failure of their scheme. They said that if the settlers in Jamaica and the other West Indian islands had come to their assistance the disaster might have been avoided. They were particularly angry when they learned that William had given orders to the English colonists that they were not to get involved in the business at all. Thus relations between the two countries were very bitter during the closing years of William's reign, and it sometimes seemed as if there would be a rebellion against him.

The Threat of Separation : Matters came to a head when,

in 1701, the English Parliament passed the *Act of Settlement* to arrange the succession to the English throne. By this Act Anne was to be succeeded by Sophia, the Electress of Hanover and grand-daughter of James I.* It was expected that the Scots would follow England's lead, as they had done in 1689—even though their Parliament had not been consulted before the Act of Settlement was passed; but this time Scotland decided to show its independence. In 1703 the *Act of Security* was passed which declared that Anne's successor on the Scottish throne would not be chosen until after the Queen's death, and was not to be the person chosen by the English, unless he or she would promise that Scotland would have complete freedom of religion, government and trade. This meant that on Queen Anne's death there was a very real danger of the union of the English and Scottish thrones, which had lasted for a hundred years, coming to an end. The English Parliament did not want this to happen, and it attempted to coerce the Scots by means of an Aliens Act. This declared that, if the Scottish Parliament had not adopted the English Act of Settlement by Christmas Day, 1705, Scots would be treated as foreigners and their exports debarred from England. But this only made matters worse, and both sides began to talk of war. In order to avoid war a number of prominent men of both countries came together at Whitehall, and after negotiations for nine weeks they signed an agreement. The Scottish Act of Security was to be dropped, and the Parliaments of England and Scotland were to unite on May 1st, 1707.

The Union of England and Scotland : The united kingdom was to be called Great Britain, and it was to have one sovereign, one Parliament, one army, one flag. There was to be free trade between England and Scotland, and between Scotland and the overseas settlements. Scotland was to keep her own religion and her own laws. Finally, England paid Scotland £400,000 which was to be used to reduce the National Debt, to encour-

---

* Sophia died before Anne, who was succeeded by Sophia's son, George I.

age industry and trade, and to compensate those who had lost money in the Darien Scheme.

There was little enthusiasm for the Union, and the leading men of both countries had recommended it because it seemed the only alternative to a war. There were demonstrations against it in the streets of Glasgow and Dumfries and copies of the agreement were burned. The £400,000 which the English had promised was a long time in coming. People began to jest about it, and say that the bridge at Berwick had broken down under its weight. Eventually when it did arrive in twelve wagons, the Edinburgh mob, enraged at the delay, stoned the dragoons who guarded it through the streets. The Jacobites were no doubt delighted to see how unpopular the Union was, and hoped that the Scots would come to wish for a return of the House of Stuart.

Questions and Exercises

1. Draw a large scale map of the British Isles. On it mark and name the following :
    (a) the ports at which William of Orange landed in England and Ireland respectively ;
    (b) the two Irish towns which successfully resisted siege during the Williamite War;
    (c) the scene of a Scottish massacre in 1692 ;
    (d) the battle which was followed by James II's flight;
    (e) the battles in which two Jacobite generals were killed almost in the hour of victory, one in Scotland, the other in Ireland;
    (f) the place where Sarsfield carried out a most daring adventure.

2. Make a time chart to illustrate Anglo-Scottish relations, 1660-1707.

3. Describe the policy followed by James II and the Earl of

Tyrconnel in Ireland (1685-1688) and discuss its political consequences.

4. Explain briefly.
   (a) the aims of (i) Louis XIV, (ii) James II, (iii) the Ulster Protestants and (iv) the Irish during the Williamite War ;
   (b) the importance of the Battle of the Boyne in (i) Irish history, (ii) European history.

5. Give a detailed account of Ginkel's campaign in Ireland after the departure of King William.

6. Describe fully the terms of the Treaty of Limerick, distinguishing between the military and the civil articles. Write a note on the manner in which the civil articles were carried out.

7. What events caused bad feeling between England and Scotland during William III's reign ?

8. When and under what circumstances were the Parliaments of England and Scotland united ? What were the terms of the Treaty ?

CHAPTER FIVE

The Wars with France (1689-1713)

1. The War of the League of Augsburg (1689-1697)

Le Grand Monarque : The period 1660-1715 has been called by historians the *Age of Louis XIV*.

During these years the great French King—le grand monarque—dominated the politics of Western Europe. He built for himself a magnificent palace at Versailles, on the outskirts of Paris, where he gathered round him the nobility of France in a court that was renowned for its splendour and ceremony. His word was law. " L'État, c'est moi " he is supposed to have said ; but whether he did so or not the phrase sums up accurately his position. The French Parliament, known as the States General, was not called once during his long reign, and he governed and taxed the people as he pleased. The arts and sciences flourished under his patronage, however, and during these years France set the fashion in manners, dress, literature and painting for the whole civilised world.

In the beginning it seemed as if the reign of the brilliant young King was to be peaceful and prosperous. With the assistance of his minister, Colbert, he adopted wise financial measures and gave great encouragement to industry and trade. But this happy period was short-lived, and, in 1667, he began a series of wars that filled most of the remaining years of his reign. Louis XIV's ambition was to extend the frontiers of France to the Rhine, and to make himself master of Europe. This policy was bound to bring him into conflict with the countries which barred his way: with Spain which owned the Netherlands, with the Holy Roman Empire and with Holland. As it turned out, only Holland was in any position to offer a formidable opposition to him. Spain had never recovered from the disaster of the Armada, and under Charles II was now a power in decline; while the Empire, for all its size, was weakened by the variety of the races within its borders and was already fully occupied in holding the Danube against the Turks. Thus the task of opposing Louis XIV fell mainly upon the Dutch, who were ably led by William, Prince of Orange. William formed an alliance called *the League of Augsburg,* consisting of Holland, the Empire, Spain and several of the smaller German states. But he was particularly anxious to get the assistance of England, for he believed that her navy might play a vital part in the struggle. That is why he welcomed the invitation to England in 1688 and readily accepted the English throne. Under him and his successor, Anne, England took part in two great wars against France. These are known as the War of the League of Augsburg (1689-1697) and the War of the Spanish Succession (1702-1713).

The War of the League of Augsburg : Louis XIV not only wanted to conquer Holland, he also wanted to put James II back on the English throne. In an effort to do so he sent money and men to help James in Ireland, and so the struggle there may be regarded as part of the War of the League of Augsburg. If William had been beaten there, Louis XIV could very likely have made himself master of Western Europe, and the Stuarts would have been restored to the English throne. That is why some historians have called this the *War of the English Succession.*

The war began well for Louis XIV. He had built up a great

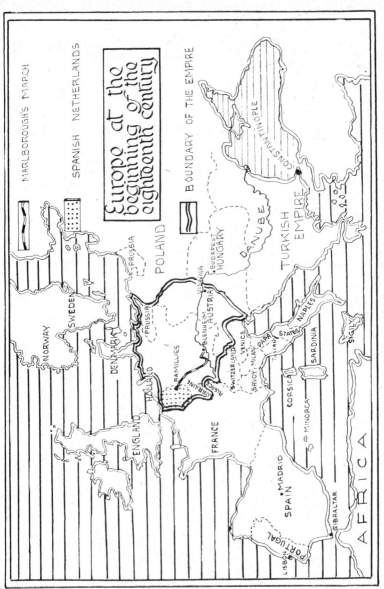

Europe at the beginning of the 18th Century

fleet and in a short time had control of the sea. Had he used his maritime supremacy he could have prevented the Williamite forces from landing in Ireland and might thus have made possible a Jacobite victory there. He failed to do so, but the great French victory off Beachy Head on June 30th, 1690—the day before the battle of the Boyne—emphasised how great his control of the sea was.

In 1692 Louis prepared an expedition for the invasion of England. He gathered a fleet and an army of 30,000 men at La Hogue in Normandy, and James II, who had high hopes that he would soon be back on his throne again, was there to see them off. Then suddenly, when preparations were almost completed, an Anglo-Dutch fleet swept down and scattered the French ships. Twelve of them ran aground in an effort to avoid capture, but Admiral Russell, who was in command of the Anglo-Dutch fleet, set them afire and burned them to the keels. The Battle of la Hogue gave England control of the seas for the rest of the war; and the maritime supremacy which she then established was the most important cause of England's victories over France in the many wars fought between them until 1815.

In Europe the chief centre of operations was the Netherlands, to which William himself had returned after his successful campaign in Ireland. But, on the land also, the opening stages of the war went in Louis XIV's favour, and William suffered a number of defeats—at Steinkirk in 1692 and Neerwinden in 1693. A less determined man than William might have lost hope, but for nine years he struggled on, until, in 1697, the French King was prepared to make peace.

The Treaty of Ryswick (1697) : By the terms of the treaty Louis XIV restored to their former owners all the towns he had captured during the previous twenty years, except Strasbourg in Alsace which he was allowed to retain. He also agreed that the Dutch should garrison a number of towns in the Spanish Netherlands as a guarantee against any future French aggression. Finally, Louis recognised William as King of England and promised to give no further help to James.

William and England had won the first round, and the ambition of *le grand monarque* had been checked.

2. Louis XIV and the Spanish Throne

Charles II of Spain : Louis XIV had agreed to the rather unfavourable terms of the Treaty of Ryswick principally because there was looming up a question of supreme importance that would require his full attention—and indeed that of all the other statesmen of Europe. The question concerned the succession to the Spanish throne. The King of Spain, Charles II, was seriously ill, and his death was expected at any time. He had no children or brothers, and the question was— who would succeed him ? The King of France and the Emperor Leopold I were both closely related to the Spanish royal family, and it was difficult to decide which of them had the better claim by descent. The problem was complicated, but it is not necessary for us to go into it, for it was not merely a question of deciding who had the better legal claim to the throne. What was involved was the whole Spanish Empire—Spain, the Netherlands, a large part of Italy and valuable colonies in Central and South America. If either Louis XIV or the Emperor got possession of this extensive territory, the balance of power in Europe would be seriously upset. France in particular was feared, for if this vast empire passed into Bourbon hands there was every likelihood of Louis XIV being able to make himself master of Europe.

Eventually, after prolonged negotiations in which England and Holland took a leading part, a settlement was arranged. By the *Partition Treaty of 1698* the greater part of the Spanish Empire (Spain, the Netherlands and the American colonies) would go to the Elector of Bavaria, a young prince who had also a claim and whose accession would not upset the balance of power. But hardly was the treaty signed than the young prince died and negotiations had to start all over again ! This

The Spanish Succession

Philip III of Spain

- Anne m. Louis XIII of France
- Philip IV
- Maria m. Emperor Ferdinand

Louis XIV m. Maria Theresa

- Charles II (died childless in 1700)
- Margaret Theresa (1) m. Leopold I m. Eleanor (2)

Dauphin

- Maria m. Elector Prince of Bavaria (died in 1699)
- Joseph I (died 1711)
- Archduke Charles

- Philip of Anjou (Philip V of Spain)
- Duke of Burgundy
- Louis XV

- Electoral Prince of Bavaria (died 1699)

time it was not so easy, for there was now no weak claimant who might be put on the Spanish throne. In the end a compromise was agreed upon: by the *Partition Treaty of 1699* the Archduke Charles, younger son of the Emperor, received Spain, the Netherlands and the American colonies, while the Spanish territories in Northern Italy went to Philip, Duke of Anjou, grandson of Louis XIV.

The Will of Charles II (1700): But the Spaniards were not prepared to see their empire carved up in this way. What right had these foreigners to decide who should reign over them? Charles II must have felt very much the same, for, shortly before his death in 1700, he made a will leaving the *whole* of his empire to Philip of Anjou—with the proviso that, if he did not accept it, the inheritance was to pass *intact* to the Archduke Charles of Austria.

What would Louis XIV do now—accept the will or stand by the Partition Treaty of 1699? After some hesitation he accepted the will in a dramatic fashion: assembling his courtiers at Versailles he presented to them his grandson Philip and said, " Messieurs, voici le Roi d'Espagne." By this act Louis was breaking the solemn promise he had made to the other powers. However, neither England nor Holland was at that stage prepared to go to war to uphold the treaty of 1699, and, if Louis had been tactful, a European war need not have taken place. But the French King went out of the way to provoke his old adversaries. In violation of the Treaty of Ryswick he re-occupied the barrier fortresses and expelled their Dutch garrisons; he excluded English and Dutch ships from the Spanish colonies in America; and finally, when James II died in 1701, he recognised his son as King of Great Britain. The English and Dutch consequently rallied behind William, and he was building up an alliance against France when he died in 1702. Naturally he was disappointed to leave his old enemy undefeated behind him, but he died confident that John Churchill, Earl of Marlborough, whom he appointed as Captain-General of the allied army, would finish the work which he had begun. He calculated correctly, for it was in the War of the Spanish Succession that Marlborough showed his great gifts as a soldier.

3. Marlborough and the War of the Spanish Succession (1702-1713)

The Duke of Marlborough (1650-1722): John Churchill was born at Ash House, near Axminster in 1650. His father was Sir Winston Churchill who had supported Charles I during the Civil War and, as a result, had suffered some poverty during the Commonwealth period. With the Restoration, however, the family fortunes improved and Sir Winston became a member of the royal household in London. The young John was made a page to the Duke of York, and the two men became fast friends. But John's great ambition was to be a soldier, and the Duke got him a commission in the Foot Guards in 1667. Five years later, when England and France were allies against the Dutch, he served in Flanders under Louis XIV's great general, Turenne. From him Churchill learned the art of war so brilliantly that many consider him to have been the most able soldier that Britain ever had.

In 1678 Churchill married Sarah Jennings and introduced her into the household of the Duke of York, where she became an intimate friend of the Princess Anne. These two friendships —that of Churchill with the Duke of York and that of his wife with the Princess Anne—ensured the rapid promotion of the young soldier, when James II succeeded to the throne. In 1685, when the first attempt was made to overthrow the King, Churchill fought valiantly for James and was largely responsible for the defeat of Monmouth at Sedgemoor. Three years later, however, when Whigs and Tories combined to invite William, Prince of Orange, to England, Churchill not only went over to the winning side himself, but, through his wife, was also instrumental in the desertion of her father by the Princess Anne. He took part in the Williamite Wars in Ireland, and in

The Duke of Marlborough

the autumn of 1690, after a brilliant campaign in Munster, he captured Cork and Kinsale, thus cutting off the Jacobite lines of communication with France.

Despite the very great assistance which Churchill was giving the King (and for which he was made Earl of Marlborough in 1689), William soon discovered that he was at the same time carrying on a correspondence with James II. In this Marlborough was no worse than the other leading politicians of his day, for, in a period of uncertainty, most men were anxious to be on the winning side. For a time William turned a blind eye to their duplicity, but eventually, fearing lest a Jacobite plot might succeed in dethroning him, he struck at Marlborough. The Earl was dismissed from all his high offices and imprisoned in the Tower of London, but his detention did not last long. He and his wife, however, continued their close association with Anne and hoped with her accession to recover their influence. But the occurrence of the Spanish succession question and the failing health of William III brought about Marlborough's return to office sooner than he had expected. William realised that he would now be unable to accomplish the task he had set himself (i.e. the defeat of Louis XIV), and so, before his death, he pardoned Marlborough for his past treacheries and entrusted him with the conduct of the War of the Spanish Succession.

The Opening Years of the War : The fact that William's successor, Anne, was an intimate friend of Marlborough's wife meant that in England the Earl was given a good deal of freedom in planning the opening moves of the war. But on the continent he was confronted by a host of difficulties. The Empire, Holland, Denmark and a number of small German states had joined with England to form the Grand Alliance against Louis XIV, but their rulers were jealous and distrustful of each other, and it needed all Marlborough's very great gifts as a diplomatist to keep them together. The Dutch, in particular, were awkward allies; they were more concerned with securing their own frontiers than with winning victories, and on several occasions prevented battles that might have won and ended the war. But Marlborough had unlimited patience and showed a skill in negotiation that was little inferior to his superlative talents as a commander.

His first task was to repel the French attack on Holland which had already begun, and then, if possible, to liberate the Spanish Netherlands as well. The first part of this task was accomplished without a great deal of difficulty, but in the Netherlands the French were so strong that it was impossible to expel them. Nevertheless, the first year's campaign had been successful, and Marlborough was made a Duke by the Queen.

In 1703 he planned to capture Ostend and Antwerp : Ostend because it would give him a new line of communication with England, and Antwerp because it would make easier his advance into the French fortress zone. But the Dutch would not support him in this, and " the great design ", as he called it, had to be abandoned.

The Battle of Blenheim (1704) : Meanwhile in Germany an event had occurred which threatened the alliance with disaster. The Elector of Bavaria, who had fought against Louis XIV in the War of the League of Augsburg, now went over to the French side. Louis sent an army to support him, and it soon became evident that a large force was being collected for an attack on Vienna. The Emperor was already fully occupied in putting down a revolt in Hungary and would be unable to defend his capital. This was a critical moment, for, if Vienna were captured, the greatest power in the alliance would probably be forced out of the war. Marlborough therefore decided that Vienna must be saved. But the Dutch were not prepared to support him in this; they feared that, if their troops were moved to the defence of the Austrian capital, Louis XIV hight over-run the Netherlands once more. The matter was urgent, and, as the Duke could not afford the time to persuade the Dutch, he decided to deceive them instead. He told them that he wanted to advance to the river Moselle in order to attack the French from the rear. The

Dutch gave their consent, and on May 19, 1704 he set off on his 600 mile march to the Danube at the head of 50,000 men.

It is necessary to emphasise the danger into which Marlborough was putting himself by this deception. If he failed to win a resounding victory over the French and save Vienna, he would be in disgrace once more and could possibly be put to death as a traitor. The Grand Alliance would break up and Louis XIV would at last achieve his life-long ambition. But on the other hand, if he succeeded, he might in one great battle win the war. Marlborough was gambling with his life, but he considered that the risk was justified.

He marched up the Rhine at the head of an army of English, Dutch and German soldiers until he reached the town of Heidelberg. There he turned south-east, and a startled Europe realised that he was not heading for France (as they had supposed) but for Bavaria and Austria. He captured Donauwörth on the Danube, joined forces with Prince Eugene of Savoy, the Emperor's best general, and finally confronted the French and Bavarian armies, under Marshal Tallard, at the village of Blenheim. There on August 13th, 1704 the famous battle took place, and Marlborough won a resounding victory. This was a turning point in the war. By his success the Duke had saved Vienna, conquered Bavaria and ended the war in Germany. A large part of the enemy forces was destroyed, and 13,000 men, including Marshal Tallard, were taken prisoner. Louis XIV was stunned by the defeat of his " invincible " army and from now on was mainly concerned with securing an honourable end to the war.

As for the Duke, he was given a hero's welcome when he returned to London, and he was granted, as a gift from the nation, the manor of Woodstock in Oxfordshire, on which the palace of Blenheim was built to the design of Sir John Vanbrugh.

The War in Spain : Meanwhile fighting had begun in Spain. In May, 1704 an Anglo-Dutch fleet, under Sir George Rooke and Sir Clowdesley Shovell, captured Gibraltar, and thus

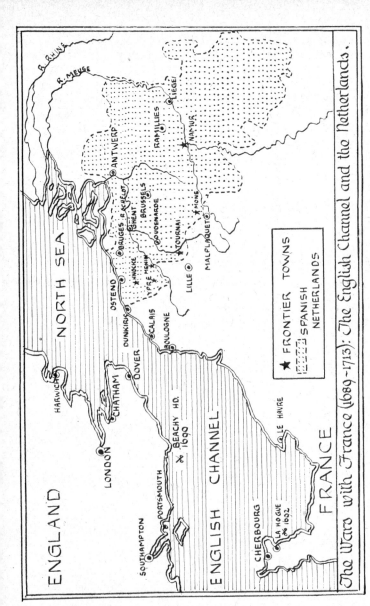

The Wars with France (1689-1713) : The English Channel and the Netherlands

gained control of the narrow entrance to the Mediterranean. Encouraged by this success the allies then tried to drive Philip from the Spanish throne. In 1705 the Earl of Peterborough, accompanied by the Archduke of Austria, captured Barcelona and proclaimed the Archduke as Charles III. A second English army moved eastwards from Lisbon and occupied Madrid. But the Spaniards were loyal to their King, Philip, and would not have the Austrian prince. In 1707 they defeated the allies at Almanza, and this settled the issue as far as the Spanish throne was concerned, though the war dragged on for another six years.

Louis XIV Offers to Make Peace : Elsewhere in Europe the war continued to run in the allies' favour. In 1706 they won two great victories. Prince Eugene won a victory at Turin and drove the French out of northern Italy, while Marlborough showed his military skill once more in the battles of *Ramillies* (1706) and *Oudenarde* (1708). The French had now been driven out of the Netherlands, and one of the principal aims of the war had been achieved. Peace might have been made then, for the French had grown weary of a war that brought them nothing but want and suffering. But the terms proposed by the allies were too severe. They demanded that Louis XIV should join with them in driving his grandson, Philip, from the Spanish throne. It is hardly surprising that the French King rejected these terms and decided to continue the war. He appealed to his weary subjects to support him, and they responded so magnificently that Marlborough's victory at *Malplaquet* (1709) was the hardest won of all and cost him 25,000 soldiers' lives.

Malplaquet was the Duke's last success. War-weariness was not confined to the French, and Englishmen began to complain about the cost of a struggle that did not appear to be bringing any advantage to them. It began to be said that Marlborough was dragging on the war for his own ends ; every year he was growing richer and more important. Finally, when he asked Anne to appoint him Captain-General of the Forces for life, the word went round that he was planning to overthrow the

Queen and make himself a military dictator. At the same time Anne was tiring of her Whig ministers and of the over-bearing Duchess of Marlborough. She dismissed the Duchess from her Court and replaced her by the less haughty Mrs. Masham. The war might have gone on for some years but for the fall of the Whig Government in 1710. The new Tory Government, led by Robert Harley and Henry St. John, favoured peace. Marlborough's days were clearly numbered.

Dismissal of Marlborough : In 1711 the Emperor died without children and was succeeded by his brother the Archduke Charles, the Austrian candidate for the Spanish throne. This made nonsense of the aim of the Grand Alliance, for to put the Emperor on the throne of Spain would have upset the balance of power more than by allowing Philip to remain there. Harley and St. John, therefore, pressed for peace and opened secret negotiations with Louis XIV. Since Marlborough was opposed to this policy he was removed from his command. But the Tories were not satisfied with his mere dismissal ; they accused him of taking bribes and of embezzling public funds. The charges could not be proved, because in the main they were not true. But popularity is a transient thing, and the crowds who cheered the victor of Blenheim now shouted " Stop, thief " when his carriage drove through the streets of London. In deep disgust Marlborough left England and remained abroad for the rest of Anne's reign. George I recalled him, but he was by then a physical and mental wreck, and died in 1722. With Marlborough out of the way the Tory ministers continued their negotiations with Louis XIV ; but Holland and the Empire were in no mood for peace and wanted to continue the war. Prince Eugene came to London in an effort to persuade the Government to change its mind. He failed to do so, and when he later laid siege to Quesnoy, the Duke of Ormond, who had taken Marlborough's place as commander, received orders from St. John that he was not to help him. Without England's help Eugene's position was hopeless and he was defeated at the battle of Denain (1712) in which many of his troops were driven into the Scheldt and drowned. Though Austria continued to fight for another year, the great war was over, and peace was made at Utrecht in 1713.

The Peace of Utrecht (1713): What is called the Peace of Utrecht was in fact a number of separate treaties made between the states which had taken part in the war. The terms agreed upon may be summarised as follows :—

1. Louis XIV's grandson, Philip V, was recognised as King of Spain and of Spanish America on condition that he gave up all claim to the French throne. The rest of the Spanish territories—the Netherlands, Milan, Naples and Sardinia— were given to the Emperor Charles, Sicily was given to the Duke of Savoy.

2. Louis XIV was allowed to retain all the conquests he had made before the outbreak of the War of the Spanish Succession, except for a few towns along the Netherlands border. In return he recognised Anne as Queen of Great Britain had promised to expel the Old Pretender from France. He also agreed to the Dutch having a line of fortresses to protect them from future French aggression.

3. Great Britain gained most from the war. In Europe she was allowed to retain Gibraltar and Minorca, which she had captured; in North America France recognised her claim to Newfoundland, Nova Scotia and the lands round Hudson Bay. She also made a treaty with Spain, called the *Asiento,* whereby she gained a monopoly of the slave trade with South America, and the right of sending one ship each year, laden with merchandise, to Porto Bello on the isthmus of Panama.

Results of the Treaty: When Queen Anne announced in Parliament on April 9th, 1713 that these terms had been agreed upon, church bells pealed and bonfires blazed in the streets to show the people's joy. The treaty marked the end of an epoch in the history of both Europe and of England. Louis XIV died shortly afterwards, his great dream unrealised, leaving France disappointed and utterly exhausted. No one mourned his death; as a cynic said at the time, " The people had shed too many tears during his life to have any left for his death." Holland, too, had over-reached herself in the long struggle, and after 1713 she never again became one of the great powers. But for Britain the treaty marks her emergence as a maritime, commercial and colonial power. The end of the war left her in control of the entrance to the Mediterranean Sea, solidly planted in North America, from which she was eventually to expel the French, and with important trading rights in South America. It is for this reason that a modern historian has described the treaty as " a milestone on the road that led to the first British Empire ".

Questions and Exercises.

1. Draw a large scale map of Europe to illustrate the War of the Spanish Succession (1702-1713). On it mark and name the following :—

    (a) The boundaries of France, Spain, the Spanish Netherlands, Holland, the Empire, Bavaria.

    (b) The rivers Lys, Scheldt, Meuse, Rhine and Danube.

    (c) The sites of Marlborough's victories at Ramillies (1706), Oudenarde (1708) and Malplaquet (1709).

    (d) By means of a coloured line Marlborough's march to Blenheim (1704), and the names of any large towns near which he passed.

    (e) An island and a fortress captured by Britain during the course of the war.

    (f) Britain's gains by the Treaty of Utrecht shaded in colour.

2. Why is the War of the League of Augsburg sometimes called the War of the English Succession ? Give a brief account of the war.

3. What exactly was the Spanish Succession Question? Describe the attempts made to arrange a peaceful solution and explain why they failed to prevent war.

4. Give an account of the career of John Churchill, Duke of Marlborough.

5. Set out clearly the most important terms of the Treaty of Utrecht. To what extent did the treaty secure the objectives for which England had fought from 1688 to 1713?

CHAPTER SIX

Life and Literature in The Later Stuart Period

1. Social Conditions in Rural England

Palaces and Halls : The later Stuart period has been called " a golden age ". Harvests were good and foodstuffs found a ready sale in the growing towns; industry and commerce were flourishing and bringing in new luxuries from many lands. All this was reflected in the life of the upper classes. At the top of the social scale were the great nobility, who built for themselves the places that still astound us by their magnificence and size: Blenheim Palace at Woodstock, presented by the nation to the Duke of Marlborough in gratitude for his services against France; Castle Howard in Yorkshire built by the Earl of Carlisle; Houghton in Norfolk, the home of Sir Robert Walpole. Even the " Halls " of the lesser nobility were impressive, while in the countryside the large farmers built for themselves stone, brick and half-timbered houses.

The internal arrangements were in keeping with the architecture. The rooms were high and well-lighted by large windows, and, for the first time, they opened out onto corridors instead of from one another. The floors were covered with carpets and rugs imported from Turkey and Persia ; the walls were panelled or hung with pictures by Italian and French masters. Mahogany was brought from the West Indies for the making of furniture, and elaborately carved tables and high-backed chairs were popular in the homes of the wealthy. There, also, great four-poster beds were to be found, with ornamented head-boards and heavy curtains. They may not have been as comfortable as our beds to sleep in, but they certainly looked more impressive.

Living in Style : The Dukes, Marquises and Earls were the most important people in the land. The Government was chosen almost exclusively from their ranks; they owned many " pocket " and " rotten " boroughs and usually decided who should represent their counties in Parliament : they very often controlled appointments in the Church of England. Their style of living was in keeping with their importance. In their great rural palaces they lived like princes, entertaining on a lavish scale and being waited on by troops of servants. Many of the nobles were men of culture who built up libraries of French, Italian and Latin authors or made collections of valuable works of art. Others spent their days out-of-doors, hunting the fox or shooting pheasant and partridge. Nearly all of them ate enormous dinners at night and drank far too much port and claret. Some built " town houses " in London, in the newly developed and fashionable areas of Covent Garden, Bloomsbury and Piccadilly, where they lived for part of the year. In June when " the season " was over they either returned to their country houses, or adjourned to Bath which the aristocracy were beginning to patronise because of its medicinal waters.

The Squires : Beneath the nobility were the squires, a large class whose estates varied in size, some of them bringing in as little as £300 a year. The wealthy amongst them tended to imitate their " betters ", taking their families to London for " the season " to engage in the fashionable round of entertainments and parties. But the majority of squires were content to remain at home, supervising their estates and visiting the markets of the near-by towns. They played an important role in the life of the community. As Justices of the Peace they tried people accused of small offences, administered the system of poor relief, supervised the repair of roads, and fixed the price of bread and ale in their areas.

The essayist, Joseph Addison, has left us a picture of a typical squire of Queen Anne's reign in a series of articles which he wrote for the *Spectator*. He called him Sir Roger de Coverley and this is how he described him :

" He is now in his fifty-sixth year, cheerful, gay and hearty; keeps a good house both in town and country . . . . His tenants grow rich, his servants look satisfied, all the young women profess to love him; when he comes into a house he calls the servants by their names, and talks all the way upstairs to a visit. I must not omit that Sir Roger is a Justice of the Quorum; that he fills the chair at a Quarter Sessions with great abilities, and three months ago gained universal applause by explaining a passage in the Game Act."

Addison's picture of Sir Roger at church brings out very clearly the deference paid to the squire by the village community: " As Sir Roger is a landlord to the whole congregation, he keeps them in very good order, and will suffer nobody to sleep in (the church) besides himself; for, if by any chance he has been surprised into a short nap at sermon, upon recovering out of it he stands up and looks about him, and if he sees anybody else nodding, either wakes them himself, or sends his servants to them. Several other of the old knight's peculiarities break out upon these occasions; sometimes he will be lengthening out a verse in the singing of psalms half a minute after the rest of the congregation have done with it; sometimes when he is pleased with the matter of his devotions, he pronounces Amen three or four times to the same prayer, and sometimes stands up, when everybody else is upon their knees, to count the congregation or see if any of his tenants are missing.

As soon as the sermon is finished, nobody presumes to stir till Sir Roger is gone out of the church. The knight walks down a double row of his tenants, that stand bowing to him on each side, and every then and now inquires how such a

one's wife or mother, or son, or father do, whom he does not
see at church; which is understood as a secret reprimand to the
person that is absent."

The Yeomen : Next in the social scale were the farmers: the
freeholders, copyholders and tenants. Of these the freeholder
was the most important. He was for all practical purposes an
independent owner, and, if his land was worth forty shillings
a year, he was entitled to a vote at parliamentary elections.
However, he sometimes held a piece of land as a tenant in
addition to the piece owned, and when this happened the squire
usually controlled his vote. The later Stuart period, as we have
seen, was a prosperous period for agriculture, and this was
reflected in the new stone and brick houses which the farmers
built, and in the better dress which they and their families wore.
They were frequently referred to as the " yeomen," and contemporary writers called them " the back-bone of England."

The Landless Labourers : At the bottom of the scale were
the landless labourers and poor tradesmen. They had benefited
little from the improved conditions but lived in squalid settlements on the outskirts of villages. An act of Elizabeth I's reign
had ordered that no cottage should be built without having
four acres of land attached to it, but the law was ignored and
many of the country poor erected crude one-roomed timber
huts and roofed them with straw. They had practically no
furniture and sometimes slept on the ground, with their goats
and fowl. Windows were rare for glass was expensive, and
there was seldom any outlet for the smoke except through the
door. Logs were used for heating and cooking, and such lighting
as there was came from rushlights or candles.

Work was irregular and badly paid. A typical wage for a
farm labourer was eightpence a day, and tradesmen, like masons
and carpenters, might earn a shilling. Wives helped when they
could in the fields, but they were lucky if they earned fourpence
a day. One cannot judge a labourer's conditions on the basis
of wages alone, however, for he sometimes brought home with
him butter, eggs and cheese from the farm As well most

families sent their children out to work at an early age or employed them at home in some branch of the textile industry. Their principal diet was bread, ale and cheese. But in the winter months when work was scarce and food dear, they were driven to the verge of starvation. Then they snared wildfowl, which were plentiful in forests or marshes. In really bad years the more desperate labourers might be driven to take animals or game from the squire's estate, but most people hesitated to do so, for the penalties for poaching were severe.

The Game Laws : At the beginning of the Stuart period game were so plentiful that there were no restrictions on hunting or trapping. The introduction of the shot-gun changed that, and the squires began to fear that partridge and pheasant would be killed off so rapidly that their traditional sport would die out. Thus in 1617 a law was passed which forbade freeholders of under a hundred pounds a year—i.e. the majority of farmers— to kill game even on their own lands. Nor was this all. Fox-hunting was becoming popular in the later Stuart period, and the richer squires kept their own packs of hounds. Frequently they invited their friends to join in a wild chase across the country at large, irrespective of the ownership of the land or the crops which the field contained. The farmers were annoyed by this but could do nothing, for the law was on the side of the squires.

Amusements : The ordinary people worked too hard to have much time for recreation, but the traditional sports of football and wrestling were still carried on, and cricket was becoming popular especially in the southern counties. Football was a violent and disorderly game, played without rules, boundaries or time limit, and sometimes whole villages participated. Cricket was more refined, but was marred by a good deal of gambling, as the following notice for a match to be played on Clapham Common shows : " These are to inform gentlemen, or others who delight in cricket playing, that a match of cricket of ten gentlemen of each side will be played for £10 a head each game (five being designed) and £20 the odd one." Later, in the eighteenth century, betting rose to fantastic heights, as much as £20,000 being wagered on a match. It was not until the M.C.C. became the controlling body, early in Queen Victoria's reign, that the evil was entirely eliminated.

Other pastimes were cudgel-play, boxing, bull-baiting and cock-fighting. Horse racing was becoming popular, under the patronage of the Royal Family, and meetings were frequently held in country places. These were gay and boisterous occasions: fiddlers and ballad-singers were present, and acrobats and jugglers performed before the incredulous gaze of the villagers. During the races, the spectators ran up the course behind the horses, cheering on their favourites. Afterwards all adjourned to the local inn for dancing and merry-making. The squire drank claret or port, the ordinary people ale, for tea or coffee were still unknown in country places. Everyone drank too much, for drunkenness was the great evil of the time.

Travel : The roads of the country were still in a shocking condition. Signposts were unknown and travellers were obliged to hire guides to help them from place to place. Thus Samuel Pepys, riding from Huntingdon to Biggleswade, employed two countrymen to lead him through the floods that covered the roads. Every few miles travellers had to ford a stream for bridges were few, and many of the larger rivers could only be crossed by ferry. Celia Fiennes, a courageous woman who travelled through England during William III's reign, describes how she went along a road in Gloucestershire " over one common of some miles length on a narrow causeway that a coach can scarce pass, all pitched with slatts and stones. Our coach was once wedged in the wheel in the stones that several men were forced to lift us out ".

The reason for this deplorable state of affairs was that no satisfactory scheme had yet been devised for maintaining the roads of the country. In Tudor times each parish was made responsible for its own highways, but the work was either neglected or only half done. After the Restoration it was decided that those who used the roads should pay for their upkeep, and in 1663 the Justices of the Peace in the counties of Hertford, Cambridge and Huntingdon were empowered to place gates across the main roads passing through their area and to collect tolls from those who used them. The money collected was to be used for the upkeep of the roads. Thirty years later this method was used again on the roads from London, and Daniel Defoe was very impressed by the improvement in conditions that took place: "These roads were formerly deep, in time of floods dangerous, and at other times, in winter, scarcely passable. They are now so firm, so safe, so easy to travellers and carriages, as well as cattle, that no road in England can equal them."

People usually travelled on horseback, the women sometimes riding pillion behind the men. Coaches had been introduced into England in Tudor times, but they were heavy uncomfortable vehicles and not much used. In the seventeenth century they were improved in a number of ways: the body was slung from leather straps attached to pillars set in the axles of the front and back wheels and windows were provided with glass. After the Restoration coaches became more popular and rich people took a great pride in their "turn-outs". Samuel Pepys was particularly proud of his, and in 1689 he describes in his diary how he drove "through the town with our new liveries of serge, and the horses' manes and tails tied up with red ribbons and new green reins."

For carrying goods pack-horses were used or great heavy wagons drawn by teams of horses. At various times during the seventeenth century attempts were made to limit the number of wagons used for carrying goods on the plea that they cut up the roads. A Highways Act, passed in 1662, restricted the number of horses that could be used, and required carts to have wheels not less than four inches wide. But such restrictions could not be tolerated when industry and trade began to expand, and eventually it was realised that the proper course was to build roads strong enough to stand up to the traffic. But it was not until the middle of the eighteenth century that England got a road system adequate to her needs.

2. London under the Later Stuarts

A Great City : After the Great Fire of 1666 London was re-built, and began to grow more rapidly in size and population than it had ever done before. Already it was the largest city in the world with a population of over half a million, and only Paris could rival it as a capital. The City proper extended from the Tower to London Bridge, and this was the most densely inhabited part of England, but London had already broken through its old boundries and was spreading over the surrounding fields. To the west, great new " Squares " were being laid out at Covent Garden, Bloomsbury and Piccadilly, and houses were being built there by the nobles and squires who came to London for " the season ". But, in the older parts of the city, streets were narrow and dirty, and open drains ran along many of them giving off a foul smell. They were crowded with coaches, wagons and barrows, which created a great noise as their wheels crunched over the cobble stones. To add to the din there were the cries of the street traders—the fishmongers, the fruit-sellers, the men with the sedan chairs shouting for customers. The river was almost as crowded as the streets, and far more boisterous. London Bridge was the only road over the Thames, and most of the traffic was carried across the river by barges. On the north bank, between London Bridge and the Parliament House, there were thirty flights of steps at which boats could be hired by people wishing to travel along the river or across it. The boatmen were tough and grizzly, and their coarse language was notorious. They added a great deal to the noise of the city, and nothing at all to its refinement.

At the end of the Stuart period, therefore, London was a busy, noisy and exciting place: it was, also, the seat of government, a leader of fashion, the centre of intellectual and cultural life and the chief commercial area of the country.

Commerce and Industry : The merchants and businessmen lived in the centre of the capital, in many cases over or beside their premises. Shops, as we know them, were then beginning to appear for the first time, with large glass windows showing a selection of the merchants' wares. Many had large swinging signs that creaked in the wind and added to the general din of the traffic. There were also large warehouses where goods imported from all parts of the world were stored, before being distributed in England or sent to the continent. The port was crowded with ships from many lands. There were no docks in our sense of the word, and so the boats discharged their cargoes into lighters which brought them to the wharves on either bank. London was also a manufacturing centre with a great variety of industries. Some supplied local needs—breweries, distilleries, sugar refineries, the making of furniture—but others served a wider market. London cutlery was said to be better than that of Sheffield, and her clocks were the best in the world.

The Poor : The poor, who supplied the labour for these industries and trades, lived in the utmost squalor. They were herded together in great slums, sometimes five or six families to a house, or occupied dark and filthy cellars that we would not put our animals in today. Sanitary arrangements were primitive and there were frequent outbreaks of plague. Over half the children born died before they reached five years of age.

Many of the unfortunates who lived in these slums drank themselves to death on the cheap beer and spirits that were sold in such quantities in London. Others turned to crime, as pickpockets, highwaymen and thieves. Streets were poorly lighted (after 11 p.m. not at all), and there were no police to patrol them. Thus it was easy for thugs to waylay pedestrians at night and to take their purses. Even members of parliament were liable to be attacked in this way; consequently it was customary for them to travel in groups for safety, and the cry " Who goes home ? ", with which each night's sitting of the House of Commons still ends, is a survival from those dangerous days.

High Life : The life of the well-to-do was a great contrast to that of the poor. The nobles and gentry came up to the capital for the " season " and occupied their lovely mansions in Bloomsbury and Piccadilly. Their " chairmen " carried them about the city streets, or else they were driven in their carriages to the parks, where they met their friends to discuss the latest scandal or the progress of Marlborough's campaign against France. The " Court " was no longer the centre of a gay life as in Charles II's reign, for neither William III nor Anne liked London and came there only when they had to. But the aristocracy made their own amusements: in the evenings there were balls and parties — or even more exciting a visit to the theatre or to the opera.

The theatre was in many ways different from that which the Puritans had closed and resembled more the theatre with which we are familiar today. The whole house was roofed over, and the stage, oblong in shape, was viewed by the audience through a frame to give the effect of looking into a room. Scenery was now used, and female roles were played by actresses and not by boys as formerly. There were two theatres in London —Drury Lane and Covent Garden—and it was to these that the upper classes went to see the comedies that were fashionable at the time. Most of these were concerned with courtiers and rakes, their vanities, love affairs and intrigues. Some of the dramatists —notably William Wycherley and George Etherege—were outspoken and coarse in the treatment of their themes, and made " Restoration Comedy " notorious; but the plays of William Congreve and George Farquhar, who wrote during the reigns of William III and Anne, had greater merit.

Coffee Houses : The first coffee-house in London was opened by a Greek in 1652. Tea followed shortly afterwards, and one of the earliest English newspapers, the *Mercurius Politicus,* announced in 1658 : " That excellent, and by physicians approved China drink, called by the Chineans Teha, by other nations Tay, Alias Tee, is sold at the Sultaness Head, a cophee-house in Sweeting's Rents, by the Royal Exchange." After the accession of Charles II, the number of houses selling coffee, chocolate and tea increased until, in Queen Anne's reign, there were nearly five hundred of them in London. They resembled the modern club, and men met there, in the morning and afternoon, to talk, arrange business deals or read one of the newspapers that were kept there for customers. Each group tended to have its own coffee-house : the Tories went to the Coffee Tree and the Whigs to St. James'. Writers and actors were usually to be found at Will's near Covent Garden, fashionable gentlemen and gamblers at White's. One of the best known coffee-houses was that kept by Edward Lloyd in Lombard Street. He was interested in shipping and trade, and the merchants came to him for advice and information. In order to help them he erected a pulpit from which he read out the latest shipping news, and eventually this practice turned Lloyd's into the greatest centre in the world for marine insurance.

3. The Royal Society: Boyle and Newton

The Royal Society : In 1645 a number of men interested in science and mathematics began to meet regularly in London to discuss scientific topics and to carry out experiments. In the beginning there were only seven members in the group—among them an Irishman, Robert Boyle—and their studies were interrupted by the Civil War and its aftermath. After the Restoration they began to meet again, and Charles II informed them that " the King did well approve of this design and would be ready to give encouragement to it." The members, thereupon, petitioned the King for a royal charter, and in 1662 this was granted. The official title of the group from now on was " The Royal Society of London for the Advancement of Natural Knowledge," but it was generally known as " The Royal Society." Today it is the most celebrated scientific society in the world, and a person who is entitled to put the letters F.R.S. (Fellow of the Royal Society) after his name is a scientist of distinction. One of its founders was Robert Boyle, and an early president was Sir Isaac Newton.

Robert Boyle (1627-1691) : Robert Boyle was born at Lismore Castle in 1627 and was the fourteenth child of the Earl of Cork. His father had come to Ireland as a penniless man in 1588, but had gradually acquired a great estate in Cork and Waterford, and had set up an iron smelting and a linen industry. Young Robert was educated at Eton and then studied abroad at Geneva, Florence and Paris. On his father's death he inherited estates in Ireland and Devonshire, but he was more interested in scientific studies than in land. In 1654 he settled in Oxford, built a laboratory there, and carried out a number of experiments on air and respiration by means of his improved air pump known as " machina Boyleana." He described these experiments in his first book, " New Experiments Physico-Mechanical " (1660), and in 1662 he announced his discovery that the volume of gas, confined in a vessel, becomes proportionately smaller in volume as the pressure upon it is increased. This is known as *Boyle's Law*.

Before Boyle's day very little was known about chemistry, and a great deal was accepted as true that had not been proved. Boyle questioned many of the traditional views, and in 1661 he published a book, " The Sceptical Chemist," in which he gave the death blow to alchemy (the idea that one metal might be made into another) and the belief that such things as earth, air, fire and water were basic elements. He defined as an " element " something which could not be changed by chemical means into anything simpler. In addition he discovered a method of preparing phosphorus, used colouring matters like litmus as acid-alkali indicators, and was the first in Britain to make a sealed-in mercury thermometer. He was one of the earliest of British scientists and is often called " The Father of Modern Chemistry."

Sir Isaac Newton (1642-1727) : Newton was born in the village of Woolsthorpe, near Grantham in Lincolnshire in 1642. His father died before Isaac was born, and his mother hoped that, when he grew up, he would work the family farm. But young Isaac was more interested in making mechanical toys or repair-

Sir Isaac Newton

ing clocks, and only with reluctance would he work on the land. At the age of eighteen he went up to Trinity College, Cambridge, to study mathematics and he took his degree in 1665. The following year the Great Plague spread to Cambridge, and Newton returned home for eighteen months. During this period he continued his studies and made some of his most important discoveries.

Since his boyhood Newton had been interested in astronomy, but he was dissatisfied with the telescopes he used, and in his attempts to improve on them he began to study the nature of light. He made a number of experiments. First he passed the sun's rays through a glass prism and broke it up into a band of seven colours: red, orange, yellow, green, blue, indigo and violet. Next he used two prisms, placing them so that the rays would pass first through one and then through the other which he turned upside down. He found that the second prism combined the seven colours again to give a ray of colourless light. Newton now realised that what was wrong with his old telescope was that the lenses broke up the light and caused patches of colour to be seen. So he built himself a new telescope with an opening in its side, through which the observer saw the image reflected in a mirror placed inside. This was known as a " reflecting telescope " and its invention earned Newton his F.R.S. in 1672.

This achievement would have been enough to satisfy most scientists, but Newton was already at work on a greater problem. Copernicus and Galileo had shown that the sun, not the earth, was the centre of the universe, that the earth rotated on its axis every day, and that every year it made a complete revolution round the sun. By Newton's time this teaching was generally accepted. But no one had yet explained *why* the earth and the other planets moved around in this way. It is sometimes said that the answer came to Newton one evening as he sat in his garden. He heard an apple drop from a tree and strike the ground. He knew that the apple's fall was due to gravity, i.e. to the force pulling everything on the earth to its centre. He knew, too, that, if a weight was attached to a cord and then sent whirling round, the pull on the cord kept the weight flying round and round. Might not the same thing, on a gigantic scale, explain the movement of the heavenly bodies, the moon moving round the earth, and the earth moving round the sun? He made a number of calculations that confirmed his theory, but he does not appear to have done anything about it, until his friend, the astronomer Halley, persuaded him to write a full treatise on the matter. The result was his great work, *Principia,* published in 1687, in which he enunciated his theory, explained why the earth had an elliptical orbit, and proved that tides were caused by the action of the moon.

Newton was now a scientist of distinction. In 1696 he was made Warden of the Mint and three years later its Master. In 1703 he was elected President of the Royal Society, and in 1705 he was knighted by Queen Anne. For the next twenty years he was the most famous man in England. He built a fine new mansion in Kensington and his friendship was sought by the greatest in the land. In 1727 he died and was buried in Westminster Abbey. Newton was perhaps the greatest of all English scientists, but he was a most humble man and well aware of the debt he owed his predecessors. " If I have seen farther than most men," he said, " it is by standing on the shoulders of giants."

Questions and Exercises

1. Give an account of the life of the ordinary people in rural England during the later Stuart period under the following headings (a) houses; (b) standard of living; (c) work; (d) amusements.

2. Write an essay on " Travel in England in the Seventeenth Century ".

3. Describe the growth of London, and give some indication of the extent and variety of its trade.

4. Write notes on (a) London Coffee-Houses; (b) The Restoration Theatre; (c) Robert Boyle.

5. Give an account of the life and work of Sir Isaac Newton (1642-1727).

The Struggle for Colonial Supremacy (1714-1763)

The Hanoverians and the Pretenders

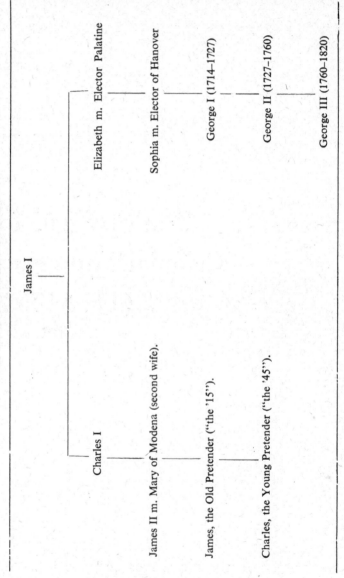

James I

Charles I — Elizabeth m. Elector Palatine

James II m. Mary of Modena (second wife). — Sophia m. Elector of Hanover

James, the Old Pretender ("the '15"). — George I (1714–1727)

Charles, the Young Pretender ("the '45"). — George II (1727–1760)

George III (1760–1820)

CHAPTER SEVEN

A Hanoverian or Stuart King? The '15 and the '45

1. The Stuarts in Exile

James II : His defeat at the Boyne did not end James II's hopes of recovering his throne, and as soon as he reached France he once more sought the help of Louis XIV. The French King was just then anxious to direct William III's attentions from the Low Countries, and a fleet was prepared for the invasion of England. Before it could sail, however, an Anglo-Dutch squadron attacked it in the harbour of La Hogue (1692), and after this James never made any other serious effort to regain his throne. The final blow to his hopes came in 1697 when, by the Treaty of Ryswick, Louis XIV was forced to acknowledge William as King of Great Britain. For the rest of his life James lived in the beautiful palace of St. Germain surrounded by the faithful followers who shared his exile. They were known as *Jacobites* or followers of James from the Latin word *Jacobus* meaning James. He died on September 16th, 1701.

The Pretender : The son of James II was only thirteen years old when his father died. The Jacobites proclaimed him as

James III of England and VIII of Scotland, and recognised his mother, Mary of Modena, as Regent. A year later William III died, but James who was commonly referred to in England as the Pretender was not invited to ascend to his father's throne. His Protestant half-sister Anne succeeded and for the next twelve years ruled England. During nearly the whole of her reign England was engaged in the War of the Spanish Succession, and, when James was old enough, he joined the French army and fought against his fellow-countrymen in the battles of Oudenarde and Malplaquet.

The Act of Settlement (1701): Anne was married to Prince George of Denmark, and though she had seventeen children none of them survived infancy except one, the Duke of Gloucester. He died in 1700 at the age of eleven, and thus it was necessary to decide who should succeed to the throne after the Queen's death. This was done by an Act of Settlement, whereby it was arranged that, if Anne died without issue, the Crown was to go to her cousin the Electress Sophia of Hanover and her heirs *being Protestants* and that from now on the Sovereign must be a member of the Church of England. James II's descendants were thus barred from the throne.

Jacobite Hopes: In 1707 the Union of England and Scotland took place. We have seen that in its early years the union was very unpopular in Scotland, and consequently many Jacobites urged James to take advantage of the situation to seize the Scottish throne. They believed that, once he were established in Scotland, he could come to terms with Anne, who was thought to be against the Hanoverian succession. Louis XIV also favoured the project, and a force was collected at Dunkirk in 1708. The expedition sailed on March 9th, but, due to bad French planning and to the energy of Admiral Byng who commanded the British fleet, the attempt failed, and the Pretender returned to France. Had he been allowed to land as he wanted to, there would undoubtedly have been a rebellion in his favour, and it is just possible that the Queen might have made an arrangement with him concerning the succession. As it was, the government had learned a lesson, and from now on Scotland was kept under strict control. The Habeas Corpus Act was suspended, and a watch was kept on all those noblemen and Highland chiefs who were suspect of being in touch with James. Though Scotland remained quiet for the rest of Anne's reign, attachment to the Stuarts did not end : given favourable circumstances and an inspiring leader the Scots would rally to their cause.

A Hanoverian or Stuart King? : The last years of Anne's reign were very unsettled. Sophia, the Electress of Hanover, was dead, and the heir to the throne was now her son, George. The Queen's Tory ministers, the Earl of Oxford and Lord Bolingbroke (formerly St. John) did not favour George because he was friendly with the Whigs and distrustful of the Tories. They decided that, if an acceptable arrangement could be made with James, they would put him on the throne, instead of George, when Anne died. The main difficulty was the Pretender's religion: unless James became a Protestant it was unlikely that the nation could be persuaded to accept him. Oxford sounded James on the subject, but the Pretender was not prepared to change his religion, and thereby gave up his best chance of recovering the throne. Anne was nearing her end now, and the Tories were growing desperate. Oxford, bewildered and without a plan, was drinking heavily, so Bolingbroke decided to act on his own. He would proclaim the Pretender as James III as soon as the Queen died. But events moved too fast for him, and he could not make the necessary arrangements in time. On August 1, 1714 Anne died, and the Elector of Hanover was proclaimed as George I. If James wanted the throne, he would have to fight for it.

George I : The new King was not a very attractive figure. A dull middle-aged German, who spoke no English and whose private life was scandalous (for more than thirty years he shut his wife up in a fortress), he had been accepted by the English people only because he was a Protestant and all the nearer heirs were Catholic. But he could never be popular. " Wha' the de'il hae we gotten for a king," sang the Jacobites, "but a wee, wee German lairdie!" In these circumstances it is not surprising that support for the Stuarts should grow in England and Scotland. On April 3, 1715, there were riots in London; in the following month the celebration of the King's birthday was marked by grave disorder in Oxford. In June sympathy for the Jacobite cause began to spread, and there were demonstrations in the North, the Midlands and the West Country. In Somerset the church bells were rung at Norton St. Philip and Woolverton, and the health of James III was publicly drunk. In Gloucester the Jacobites came together in the *Swan* and drank toasts to James whom many expected soon to return. The movement spread, and plans were made for a rising in the West Country. Bristol and Plymouth were to be seized, and through the latter port the Pretender was to come. The conspiracy came to nothing, however. The government acted quickly, arrested the plotters and moved strong detachments of troops into the disaffected areas. Fearing for their lives the Jacobite leaders, Bolingbroke and Ormonde, fled from the country.

All this time James was at St. Malo on the north coast of France, waiting patiently for the signal that never came. When eventually he learned what had happened, he changed his plans and decided to join those who were already in revolt for his cause in Lancashire and Scotland.

2. The Rebellion of 1715

The Rising in Scotland : In the Highlands a Jacobite rebellion was planned by the Earl of Mar, a vain and ambitious man whose conduct over the years had been so inconsistent that he was known to his countrymen as " Bobbing John." He had first offered his services to George I, but the new King had refused them, whereupon Mar fled to Scotland, determined to raise the Highlanders on behalf of the Pretender. On September 6, 1715, he invited a number of Highland chiefs to meet him at Braemar on the Dee in order to take part in hunting the

PETERHEAD

ABERDEEN

BRAEMAR

MONTROSE

PERTH · DUNDEE

SHERIFF MUIR
STIRLING · 1715

EDINBURGH

KELSO

NEWCASTLE

CARLISLE

PRESTON

THE JACOBITE
RISING OF 1715

0   100
          MILES

The Jacobite Rising of 1715

deer. But the hunting party was only a pretext, and when the chiefs and their followers had gathered, Mar raised the Stuart standard and called upon his countrymen to restore, " not only our rightful and native king, but also our country to its ancient, free and independent constitution, under him whose ancestors had reigned over us for so many generations." There was a tremendous response in the Highlands to this appeal : before long Mar was at the head of 5,000 men with whom he advanced towards Perth, while in the south-west of Scotland, in Dumfries and Galloway, Lord Kenmure and the Earl of Nithsdale were able to collect a following. In the whole country there were only 3,000 government troops, and they were dispersed in small groups. Thus the rebellion had a very good chance of success had Mar taken advantage of the situation and captured Edinburgh. Instead he remained in Perth while the Duke of Argyll, whom the government had appointed to command the royal forces, occupied Stirling and thus blocked his way to the south.

The Rising in Lancashire : Meanwhile in the north of England the Jacobites had risen under Thomas Forster, a squire of Northumberland, and the Earl of Derwentwater. They first attempted to capture Newcastle, but Forster was, if possible, a worse leader than Mar, and the attack failed. Bewildered as to what to do next, Forster finally decided to cross the border into Scotland with the intention of joining the forces of Kenmure and Nithsdale. Before he could do so, however, the Lowland Jacobites who had no clear plan either, moved south and joined him. The combined force then crossed back into Scotland and camped at Kelso.

It was now obvious to Mar that a military success was necessary if the rebel forces were to be held together. The obvious course was for him to advance against the Duke of Argyll, and, using his superior numbers, to destroy the only considerable government army in Scotland. But with remarkable stupidity he decided instead to send 2,000 men, under Brigadier MacIntosh, into the Lowlands to reinforce the army of Lord Kenmure. On

October 22, MacIntosh reached Kelso. Even then success might have been achieved if Mar had advanced against Argyll, while Forster, Kenmure, and MacIntosh had launched an attack from the rear. Instead it was decided that the army at Kelso should invade England once more, for Forster declared that Lancashire would welcome the Jacobite soldiers and rise to support them. The whole force consequently marched through Cumberland and Westmorland and Lancashire, but at Preston they were surrounded by government troops and forced to surrender (November 13th, 1715).

The Battle of Sheriffmuir : On the same day as Forster surrendered at Preston the fate of the Jacobite rebellion was decided in Scotland. Mar had at last left Perth with the intention of forcing his way past Argyll and following Forster into Lancashire. But as soon as he began to move, Argyll advanced from Stirling to Dunblane, where he chose as his battlefield an undulating upland called Sheriffmuir. Mar had three times as many men as his opponent and should have won the battle without difficulty, but the Jacobite leader was no soldier, and, after a day of charging and counter-charging, neither side could claim a victory. After the battle Mar retreated to Perth and his army began to disperse. This was the turning point in the rebellion and ensured victory for George I.

The Pretender in Scotland : Nearly two months afterwards James landed in Scotland, but by then it was too late. Mar's great army had melted away, and the Pretender was not the kind of man likely to bring them into the field again. Cold and reserved he lacked the resolution required to turn defeat into victory. He joined the remnants of the Jacobite army at Perth, but when Argyll advanced against them Mar and he fled to Montrose and took ship to France. The rising of 1715 was over.

Fate of the Rebels : Those who had taken up arms had now to pay the penalty of failure. The Earl of Derwentwater and Lord Kenmure were executed together on Tower Hill, London. It was intended that the Earl of Nithsdale should die along with them, but, while awaiting execution, he escaped and made his way to France. Thomas Forster was committed to Newgate but also made his escape by using false keys. Relays of horses had been arranged, and he rode without stop to the Essex coast where a ship waited to bring him to France. Of the less distinguished rebels twenty-two were hanged in Lancashire and four in London, while several hundred of those captured at Preston were shipped to the American plantations.

Causes of Failure : At the beginning the rebellion seemed to have every chance of success. In Scotland there was great discontent with the way the country was being ruled, and in the Highlands there was genuine affection for the Stuarts. In England the new King was far from popular, for he scarcely concealed the fact that his heart was in Hanover and he spent as little time as possible in his kingdom. The " fifteen " might have succeeded if James had been prepared to change his religion, but he was not. He was prepared to guarantee liberty of conscience to his subjects, but he also claimed it for himself. Lack of co-ordination between the English and the Scottish uprisings, and the incompetent leadership of Mar and Forster were contributory causes. Finally the Pretender himself failed to inspire those whom he claimed as his subjects. When he heard of the retreat from Sheriffmuir he said sadly: " It is no new thing for me to fail." Princes of this stamp are not likely to lead successful revolts.

3. From the '15 to the '45 : Sir Robert Walpole

The Triumph of the Whigs : The failure of the rebellion meant final success for the Whigs. George I was convinced that the Tories could not be trusted: when Anne died they had tried to keep him off the throne, next they had tried to overthrow him. As far as he was concerned Jacobite and Tory were synonymous terms. During the whole of his reign and of that of his son George II (1727-1760), only Whigs held office. These Whig ministers were the real rulers of the country. They had a majority in the House of Lords, and they were able to gain control of the House of Commons. In those days the right to vote was confined in the counties to landowners and in the towns to the well-to-do tradesmen and merchants, so that the number of voters was small. There was no secret ballot such as we have to-day, and it was customary for candidates to buy the support of those who had votes. In the Commons members were kept loyal to the government by the distribution of positions and pensions either to themselves or to their friends. There was a solid block of over a hundred " placemen " in the House of Commons who consistently supported the government, while in the country every important position in the Church, in the Services and in Local Government was filled by their friends. This system of ' patronage,' as it was called, was used by Sir Robert Walpole to keep himself in power for over twenty years and to gain support for a policy of peace which he believed was in the best interests of the country. To that extent the system could be justified, but it did lead to an absence of ideals among the ruling classes, and often meant that politicians were ready to change their views for money.

Sir Robert Walpole : One of the greatest of the Whig politicians was Sir Robert Walpole, the third son of a rich Norfolk landowner. He was born on the family estate at Houghton in 1676, and as a young man was intended for the Church. But both of his elder brothers died, and so he was trained for the life of a country gentleman. He learned about farming and the management of estates, and he devoted a great deal of time to hunting and shooting. Had his brothers lived he might have been a bishop in the Church of England; instead he became a stout and jovial squire, who loved a good dinner and jolly company, and who drank a lot of claret and port. Behind this bluff exterior Walpole hid a great ambition and love of power and a shrewd grasp of political affairs. He entered Parliament in 1702 and soon proved to be one of the ablest men in the Whig party. After 1715 his policy was clear: to end all sympathy for the House of Stuart and to unite the whole nation happily under the Hanoverian Kings. His methods were : *firstly* to avoid war at all costs, for he believed that an enemy abroad was likely to join forces with the Jacobites ; *secondly* to make the country prosperous and happy by reducing taxation, increasing trade and dealing more tolerantly with Nonconformists. He had difficulty in persuading his colleagues to support such a policy, and, when in 1717 Lords Stanhope and Sunderland proposed to take part in a war which had broken out in Europe, he resigned. For the next four years he was out of office, but in 1721 he was recalled to deal with the great financial crisis known as the South Sea Bubble.

The South Sea Bubble : In 1711 the South Sea Company had been formed for trading with the Spanish colonies in America. Two years later Britain was given permission, by the Treaty of Utrecht, to send one ship a year to Porto Bello in South America, and also to supply the Spanish colonies with negro slaves. The Government handed over these rights to the South Sea Company, which expected to make a large profit from the trade. In return for this, the company proposed to take responsibility for the National Debt (that is the money which the Government owed to individuals from whom it had borrowed) and in addition to pay over to the Government a sum of £7,500,000. This transaction convinced many people that the South Sea Company must be making enormous profits if it were able to finance such a deal. The result was that everyone with money to invest rushed to buy shares in the company, and £100 shares were soon being bought for £1,050.

As soon as it became obvious that the public was eager to invest money in the hope of making fortunes, all sorts of companies were formed, some sensible enough, but many for the most absurd purposes : for importing jackasses from Spain, for obtaining gold from sea-water, and, most foolish of all, " for carrying on an undertaking nobody to know what it is ". It is hard for us to understand how people could be deceived in this way, but in a frenzy " to get rich quick " an excited public threw discretion to the winds. Of course many of these " bubble " companies went bankrupt, or the men who formed them disappeared with the money that foolish people had entrusted to their care. The result was a panic, and, where previously people had been anxious to buy, now they were anxious to sell. Even the South Sea Company was affected, and the price of its £100 shares fell, until they were being sold for as little as £150. The Company did not fail, but its shares returned to something like their real value. Many people were ruined, and a great outcry arose against the Government for allowing so much foolish speculation to take place. Then it was discovered that several ministers had taken bribes from the South Sea Company. The Postmaster-General committed suicide, the chief minister Stanhope died of shame and disgrace, and the Chancellor of the Exchequer was put in the Tower. For a time it seemed as if the country might drift into disorder, a circumstance that would raise once more the hopes of the Jacobites. But at the critical moment Walpole was brought into office to save the situation. He took back the National Debt, restored the £7,500,000 which the Company had given the Government, and forced the directors to surrender some of their own wealth, thus creating a fund which he used to compensate investors. But in spite of his efforts many people were ruined.

The Rule of Walpole (1721-1742) : For the next twenty years Walpole controlled the government of the country, and it was during this time that the Hanoverian dynasty was firmly established on the throne. He set out deliberately to win the support of the whole nation—the squires, the merchants, the Nonconformists. To please the squires he lowered the land tax. This had been started in the reign of William III in order to pay for the war with France, and was levied on income from land. When Walpole came into office it was four shillings in the pound; he reduced it by stages until it was only a shilling.

To gain the support of the merchants he examined seriously their grievances, particularly the numerous duties which they said were hindering their trade. Many of these duties had been imposed haphazardly over the years and brought in little revenue. Walpole abolished some of them, reduced others and in this way stimulated trade. He also began a system of bonded warehouses. These were locked and sealed sheds in which cargoes of tea and coffee were stored, and merchants only paid import duties on the goods as they were taken out for sale. In 1733 he tried to extend this system to wines and tobacco, but his proposals were misunderstood. People protested because they believed that their houses would be searched and that their tobacco and wines would cost more. Walpole thereupon abandoned the scheme, for what he wanted above all things was peace and order. " Let sleeping dogs lie " was his motto.

It was the same with the Nonconformists. He knew that if he proposed to repeal the Test and Corporation Acts, which prohibited them from holding office, he would stir up the opposition of the Church of England. What he did therefore was to allow them to hold office, and each year he passed an Indemnity Act cancelling any punishments that Nonconformists had incurred by breaking the law. This curious compromise lasted until the repeal of the Test Act in 1828.

The War of Jenkins' Ear (1739) : Walpole believed in " letting sleeping dogs lie " in foreign affairs as well as at home. Wars cost money and interfered with trade, besides providing the Stuarts with potential allies; therefore at all costs he tried to avoid them. After George I's death in 1727 this was not easy. The new King, George II, was a fiery little man, anxious to display his prowess in battle. Walpole used his influence with the Queen, Caroline, to keep peace, and when war broke out between France and Austria in 1733, he boasted to her, " Madam, there were 50,000 men slain this year in Europe, and not one an Englishman ".

As time went on Walpole became less popular. He was dictatorial in manner, and a minister who disagreed with him was forced to resign. Thus he created a number of enemies who criticised the methods he adopted to keep himself in power.

Others said he was so anxious for peace that he was prepared to see British interests suffer abroad rather than run the risk of a war. They seized on an incident that occurred in Central America to prove their point. Ever since the Treaty of Utrecht the British had the right to send one ship each year to Porto Bello laden with merchandise. This privilege was abused, and a great deal of smuggling went on. The Spanish coastguards were consequently very strict and dealt harshly with those whom they suspected of breaking the law. In 1738 Captain Jenkins of the *Rebecca* claimed that his ship had been stopped by the Spaniards on his way home from Jamaica, and that in a scuffle one of his ears had been cut off. The opposition used this incident to create a scene in the House of Commons. They brought Jenkins to the bar of the House, where he showed his ear preserved in a bottle to the horrified members. There was a loud cry for war with Spain, and, against his will, Walpole gave way. But his heart was not in it. " They are ringing their bells now," he said, when the chimes of London rang out the news; " they will soon be wringing their hands." He ought to have resigned; instead he remained in office, conducting the war in a half-hearted manner. Opposition to him continued to grow, and eventually in 1742 he was forced to resign.

After Walpole's fall the War of Jenkins' Ear became merged in a general European struggle known as the War of the Austrian Succession. He saw in this the end of all his hopes, and, before his death in 1745, he warned the Government to prepare themselves for another Jacobite rebellion.

4. The Jacobite Rebellion of 1745

Bonnie Prince Charlie : After the failure of the first Jacobite rebellion the Pretender became ' Jamie the Rover ' once more. In 1719 he married a Polish princess, and in the following year they had a son, Charles Edward, who was given the title of Prince of Wales. This was the ' Young Pretender ' or ' Bonnie Prince Charlie ', who was to play such an important part in the

'45. During the years of his youth there was a marked decline in the strength of Jacobitism in England ; but in Scotland loyalty to the Stuarts remained strong, and there was little doubt that, given a chance, the Scots would rise again. Their opportunity came when, after Walpole's resignation, England went to war with France. Louis XV offered Charles 15,000 men if he would lead an insurrection in Scotland. A fleet was gathered at Gravelines and the Young Pretender joined them there in February, 1744. Before they could put to sea, however, a violent gale shattered the ships in the harbour, and after this disaster the French showed little further interest in the Jacobite cause.

Charles was a very different man from his father: gay, charming and daring, he could persuade his followers to face hopeless odds for his sake. He decided to act without French aid and was convinced that, if he reached Scotland, the Highlanders would immediately rally to his standard. " I will go," he said, " if I have only a single footman." He almost kept his word, for when he sailed for Scotland in July, 1745 he had only seven companions—an Englishman, two Scots and four Irishmen. They landed on Eriskay, a small island on the west coast between South Uist and Barra. A local laird named Macdonald advised Charles to go home. " I am come home," he replied. From Eriskay he crossed to the mainland and landed at Moidart. Would the Highlanders join him ? For a time the chieftains held back, for they knew the risks they would run by joining a rebellion. But the Pretender's confidence and enthusiasm proved infectious, and before long Macdonalds, Camerons and other Jacobite clans were gathering by the hundred round his standard.

The Battle of Prestonpans : Most of the Government troops were abroad fighting in the war, but a small army was sent north under Sir John Cope to deal with the rebels. The two forces met at Corryarrack and a battle seemed imminent. At the last moment, however, Cope changed his mind, retreated towards Inverness and left open the road to the south. Charles

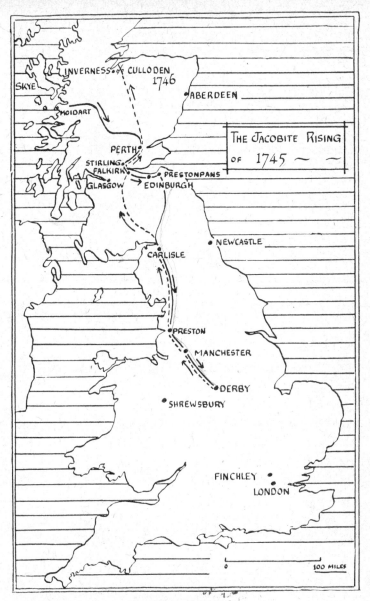

THE JACOBITE RISING
OF 1745 ~ ~

SKYE
INVERNESS • CULLODEN
1746
• ABERDEEN
MOIDART
PERTH
STIRLING
FALKIRK
GLASGOW
EDINBURGH
PRESTONPANS
NEWCASTLE
CARLISLE
PRESTON
MANCHESTER
DERBY
• SHREWSBURY
FINCHLEY •
LONDON

0   100 MILES

The Jacobite Rising of 1745

took advantage of his good fortune, captured Perth, and only
a few weeks after landing occupied Edinburgh. There his
father was proclaimed as James III of England and VIII of
Scotland, and Charles was declared to be his Regent.

Meanwhile Cope had brought his troops by sea from
Aberdeen to Dunbar, and now advanced on the capital.
Charles went out to meet him, and the two armies came face to
face at the village of Prestonpans, nine miles east of Edinburgh.
The battle was over in less than ten minutes. The Government
forces could not withstand the wild Highland charges and fled
towards Berwick and the Scottish border.

Prince Charles in England : The news of the loss of Edinburgh and of the defeat of Prestonpans caused consternation in
England where the Government had no troops ready. Orders
were given that the British armies were to be brought back
from the Low Countries, but if Charles had invaded England
at once he might have taken London by surprise. Instead he
delayed in Edinburgh for over a month, and, when his march
south eventually began, the Duke of Cumberland was back
from the continent with an army of veterans. Nevertheless,
Charles captured Carlisle, passed through Preston and Manchester and reached Derby on December 4, 1745. It was on
this march that he met his first disappointment. No Englishman of note had joined him, and only in Manchester did
he find any support for his cause. The Highlanders were
depressed and homesick; the Jacobite chiefs had lost their confidence and enthusiasm. They advised Charles to retreat, though
he was now only 130 miles from London. "Rather than go
back I would go ten feet underground," he protested, but his
advisers had their way, and on December 6 the retreat began.
Charles was never the same again; all his old gaiety and charm
of manner disappeared, and he now rode at the rear of his
army, gloomy and irritable.

The Battle of Culloden : Charles returned to Scotland to
find that Edinburgh had fallen and that most of the Lowlands had been subdued by the Government troops. He won

a victory over General Hawley at Falkirk, but the retreat to the Highlands continued, and he reached Inverness in February, 1746. The Duke of Cumberland pursued him, and it was obvious that the decisive battle of the rebellion was about to be fought.

The odds were against a Jacobite victory : many of the Highlanders had returned to their homes; Charles was not on friendly terms with several of the chiefs, and they were on bad terms with one another. Cumberland, on the other hand, had a highly trained and experienced army, and was well supplied with artillery. Charles sought to minimise Cumberland's advantage by launching a surprise attack. On the night of April 15, 1746, he led his forces on Nairn, where Cumberland was now encamped, with the intention of attacking his soldiers as they slept in their tents. But, when he came within two miles of Nairn, day broke and the sound of a drum in the English camp showed that the army could not now be taken by surprise. Accordingly Charles ordered a retreat, and the Jacobites returned, weary and disappointed, to Culloden Moor. Hardly had they reached there than Cumberland launched an attack against them. It was a fierce and bloody battle. Recklessly the Highlanders threw themselves against the better armed Government forces, and it seemed for a time as if they might carry the day. But Cumberland had trained his men to thrust their bayonets not against the soldiers in front of them but against the soldiers to their right. The tactic succeeded, and the wild rush of the Highlanders was stemmed. " Their bodies," said a Scottish writer, " were afterwards found in layers three and four feet deep, so many, it would appear, having in succession mounted over a prostrate friend to share in the same certain fate." Soon the remnants of the Jacobite army were in flight. In their pursuit no mercy was shown by the Government troops, while on the battlefield itself the wounded were massacred where they lay. " Our men," wrote an English officer, " what with killing the enemy, dabbling their feet in the blood and splashing it about one another, looked like so many butchers." Cumberland may have been determined to teach the Highlanders such a lesson that they would never rise again. He certainly did that, but he also earned for himself an unenviable reputation for cruelty.

End of the Rebellion : Charles remained with his followers as long as there was any hope, but, when the retreat began, he knew that all was now lost, and made his escape with a few friends. Great efforts were made to capture him, and a reward of £30,000 was offered for his arrest, but no Highlander could be persuaded to betray him. His intention was to remain in hiding until he could escape to France, but so thoroughly did the Government pursue him that he had to be constantly on the move. Eventually he reached the west coast, and then, disguised as Betty Burke, an Irish maid in the service of Flora Macdonald, he escaped to France.

This was not the end of the Jacobite movement. For some years the Tory squires in England continued to hold their glasses over the finger bowl, and thus drank a toast to " the King over the water ", while in Scotland the Jacobites sang to Charles " Will ye no' come back again ", but the chance of his ever doing so became more and more remote. He found little support for his plans in France, and finally settled in Rome. When his father died in 1766, he assumed the title of Charles III, but by then the gay and charming prince had become a morose and slovenly drunkard. Such was the inglorious end of the proud House of Stuart.

Questions and Exercises

1. Draw a map of England and Scotland. On it mark and name the following :

    (a) The place in the Scottish Highlands where Mar raised the Stuart standard in 1715.

    (b) The site of an indecisive battle between Mar and the Duke of Argyll.

    (c) The Lancashire town in which Forster surrendered.

(d) The port from which the Old Pretender sailed away in 1716.

(e) The place in the Western Highlands where Prince Charles landed in 1745.

(f) The village near Edinburgh where he defeated Sir John Cope.

(g) The route followed by Prince Charles in his invasion of England, and the town at which he turned back.

(h) The site of the last battle of the '45.

2. Why were the Whigs able to monopolise political power under the first two Hanoverian Kings?

3. Sir Robert Walpole's policy was "let sleeping dogs lie". Explain what this means, and show how Walpole carried it out.

4. Give an account of the rising of 1715. Why did it fail?

5. Who were the Jacobites? Give an account of the career of "Bonnie Prince Charlie".

Do part two of Q. 5.
Into. good book.

CHAPTER EIGHT

Ireland 1691-1760 :
The Penal Laws

1. The Laws against Catholics and Presbyterians

After Limerick : When the first Irish Parliament of William III's reign was summoned in 1692, a number of Catholics were elected, and attended the opening of the House of Commons. They were asked to take an oath of supremacy, and, when they refused to do so, they were not allowed to take their seats. This had the effect of turning the Irish Parliament into an exclusively Protestant body and deprived the Catholics, who formed four-fifths of the population, of any representation at all. The Treaty of Limerick had promised them the same freedom as they had enjoyed in Charles II's reign, but, against King William's wishes, the treaty was ignored, and a series of cruel laws were passed against the Irish Catholics. These are known as the **Penal Laws.**

Religious persecution was common enough in the seventeenth century, for men had not yet learned to respect each other's points of view or to live together in peace and harmony. In England, after the Restoration, Parliament had passed the Clarendon Code in an attempt to force the Nonconformists into the Established Church. In France, Louis XIV was persecuting the Huguenots almost at the same time as the Irish Parliament was persecuting the Catholics. But historians have pointed out a number of differences between conditions in Ireland and those prevailing elsewhere. *Firstly,* the Catholics formed a majority of the nation and not a tiny minority: *Secondly,* what prompted the members to act as they did was fear rather than religious zeal. The Catholics had taken the side of James II in the late war, and, in the Parliament which he had summoned at Dublin in 1689, they had attempted to overthrow the land settlements of the seventeenth century. The Protestants were determined that a situation like this would never occur again. The aim of the penal laws, therefore, was to impoverish and degrade the Catholics, and to deprive them of leaders and of social influence. In this they succeeded. The native aristocracy either conformed to save their estates or were reduced to the level of an impoverished peasantry; while the ordinary people, deprived of leaders, property, education and self-respect, sank gradually into a state of apathy and despair. They were not likely to take up arms again to restore the Catholic Stuarts to the throne, and the Jacobite rebellions of " the '15 " and " the '45 " produced no disturbance in Ireland.

The Penal Laws: The penal laws were passed at different times during the reigns of William III, Anne and George I, but it is more convenient to deal with them in groups than to take them in chronological order.

(a) **Religion:** In 1697 a law was passed ordering all archbishops, bishops and members of religious orders to leave the country under pain of transportation. Parish priests were allowed to remain, but only one priest was allowed in each parish. This was followed by an act of 1704, ordering every priest to register his name and address with the authorities and to provide two securities for his good behaviour. Under this act over one thousand priests registered; they were allowed to say Mass and to minister to their flocks. But it was expected that Catholicism would eventually die out for want of priests. Bishops were banished, and consequently there could be no ordinations. Priests were not allowed to enter the country. Thus within a generation there would be few of the registered clergy still alive. It did not turn out that way: a number of bishops succeeded in evading capture and moved about their dioceses administering the sacraments, while young men were smuggled abroad to study for the priesthood in Rome, Paris, Salamanca and Louvain. As the years passed and the fear of Jacobitism died away, a more tolerant spirit showed itself among the ruling classes, and bishops as well as priests carried out their duties in comparative freedom. But the religious laws still remained on the statute book and could be revived at any time. It was not until 1778 that the first of them was repealed.

(b) **Land :** The laws against property were more strictly enforced than those against religion. A Catholic landowner could not leave his estate to his eldest son : he must divide it in equal shares among all his sons. If his eldest son became a Protestant, he inherited the whole estate. No Catholic could purchase or inherit land or take land on lease for more than thirty-one years. Thus the amount of land in Catholic hands could not increase and was almost certain to diminish.

(c) **Education :** Catholic schools were forbidden, and children were not to be sent abroad to be educated. The theory was that parents must send their children to Protestant schools or allow them to remain ignorant; but illegal schools, called " hedge schools ", sprang up all over the country, and some children were smuggled out to France and Spain.

(d) **Political and Social Disabilities :** A Catholic was not allowed to sit in Parliament or even to vote at parliamentary elections. He was debarred from all government posts and might not serve on the corporation of his town. No Catholic could be a judge, a barrister or a solicitor, and the army and navy were closed to him. He was forbidden to possess arms or to own a horse worth more than £5. A Protestant might obtain a horse from its Catholic owner by offering him £5 for it.

Evil Effects of the Laws: The penal laws could not be rigidly enforced. It was impossible to keep track of bishops or unregistered priests, who moved about the country in disguise, keeping alive the Catholic faith. One of the most famous of the fugitive bishops was Dr. Donnelly of Dromore. He registered as a priest in accordance with the act of 1704 and lived in a hut on the slopes of Slieve Gullion, near Newry. But masquerading as a wandering harper—" Bold Phelim Brady, the Bard of Armagh "—he moved around his diocese attending to his episcopal duties. Eventually he was betrayed and arrested, but there was no real evidence against him, and he was released. Even the land laws were evaded, and some Catholic gentry, like the Earl of Kenmare and Lord Trimleston, managed to retain their estates intact, usually with the co-operation of Protestant neighbours. But, in general, the penal laws succeeded in their purpose, and the Catholic population was rendered poor, ignorant and degraded. Some of the more enterprising and ambitious Irishmen, rather than remain in a country that provided no scope for their talents, went abroad to serve in foreign armies. In later years their families sometimes rose to fame and fortune in France, Spain and Austria. Those who remained at home had no encouragement to work, for it was impossible for them to advance themselves in the world. They gradually lost their self-respect and grew lazy and improvident. Worse still, they could have no respect for the law which oppressed them, and they avoided obeying it when they could.

Even the Protestant ruling classes were affected. Arrogant and over-bearing in manner, they treated the poor with great harshness. Arthur Young, who toured Ireland between 1776 and 1778, was horrified by some of the things he saw. He wrote :

" The landlord of an Irish estate, inhabited by Roman Catholics, is a sort of despot who yields obedience in whatever concerns the poor to no law but that of his will . . . A landlord in Ireland can scarcely invent an order which a servant, labourer or cottier dares to refuse to execute. Nothing satisfies him but an unlimited submission. Disrespect or anything tending towards sauciness he may punish with his cane or his horsewhip with the most perfect security, a poor man would have his bones broke, if he offered to lift his hand in his own defence."

The Laws Against Presbyterians : Though the Presbyterians of Ulster had not been shown much kindness by members of the Church of Ireland during the seventeenth century, they had made common cause with them in the war against James II, and had played a conspicuous part in the siege of Derry. William III received an enthusiastic welcome to Belfast, when he halted there for a few days on his way south to the Boyne. After the war, the King showed his gratitude for this Presbyterian support by renewing the *Regium Donum,* a royal grant first paid to the Nonconformist clergy in the reign of Charles II. William increased the amount available for distribution to £1,200 a year, thus providing a payment of £15 for every Presbyterian minister in Ulster. The Presbyterians would have liked some form of legal recognition by the Irish Parliament, and made several efforts to have bills passed " for the ease of Protestant Dissenters ". But the Church of Ireland did not require Presbyterian help after 1691, and Parliament was more inclined to restrict the liberties of Dissenters than to extend them. By the Test Act of 1704 all office-holders and members of town corporations had to take the sacrament of Holy Communion according to the rites of the Church of Ireland. Presbyterians could not in conscience obey this law, and, where it was enforced, they were excluded from office. In this way they lost control of the government of a number of northern towns, including Belfast. However, in 1715, at the time of the first Jacobite rebellion, when there was a fear of a Catholic uprising in favour of the Pretender, some Presbyterians accepted commissions in the militia, and thus made themselves liable for the penalties provided in the Test Act. No action was taken against them, and, four years later, an indemnity act was passed forgiving those Presbyterians who had broken the law by accepting office. Thus from 1719 onwards they enjoyed a legal toleration, though the Test Act remained on the statute book until 1780.

Another serious grievance of the Presbyterians was that the marriages performed by their ministers were not recognised in law. All good Presbyterians, naturally, wanted to be married by their own clergymen, but, in the eyes of the state, the children of such marriages were illegitimate, and their claims to property were frequently contested in the courts. In the early years of the eighteenth century some Church of Ireland bishops were very active in prosecuting Presbyterian ministers who officiated at weddings of members of their congregations, but the passage of time brought greater toleration, and the number of such prosecutions decreased. It was not until 1782, however, that marriages performed by Presbyterian clergymen were recognised as valid.

Many strong-willed Presbyterians were not satisfied with this grudging toleration, and began to look across the Atlantic to a land where they might practise their faith with absolute freedom. In 1717 emigration to America began as a trickle and grew steadily throughout the century, until, at the outbreak of the American Revolution, there were said to be half a million people of Ulster descent in the colonies.

2. The Government and Parliament of Ireland

The Government : The first thing that strikes one about the Irish system of government is its superficial resemblance to that of Britain. At its head were the Lord Lieutenant who represented the King but was nominated by the British Government, and a Chief Secretary who sat in the Parliament of Westminster and was a member of the cabinet there. These two, with a number of other officials, formed the *executive,* which carried on the actual business of ruling the country and of seeing

that the laws were obeyed. But, as they were usually Englishmen and owed their responsibility to the British Government
rather than to the Irish Parliament, it was mainly the interests
of Britain which they served.

The Irish Parliament : The Parliament consisted of a House
of Lords and a House of Commons. The House of Lords was
smaller than that of Britain, and many of the Irish peers were
absentees and seldom visited the country. The bishops of the
Established Church also had seats in the House and, as they
were more regular in their attendance than the other members
and frequently formed a majority of the House, the Government
took great care in making episcopal appointments. The bishops
were usually Englishmen, and were chosen—not because they
were likely to be zealous in the care of their flocks, but because
they were prepared to obey the commands of the Lord
Lieutenant and his Government.

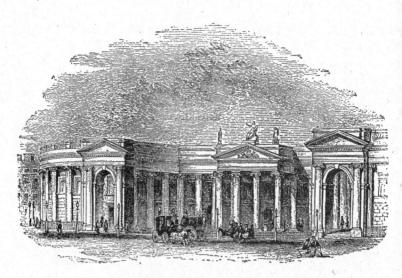

The Irish Parliament House

The Irish House of Commons consisted of three hundred members elected as follows : sixty-four elected by the counties, and two hundred and thirty-four elected by one hundred and seventeen boroughs, and two elected by Trinity College, Dublin. All members had to belong to the Established Church. No Catholic sat in Parliament after 1692 or voted at elections after 1727. Presbyterians had the franchise but were excluded from Parliament by the Test Act of 1704. Even when they were admitted, under the indemnity acts from 1719 onwards, few of them managed to secure election. The country was thus ruled by the representatives of a tiny minority.

The County Members : Each county returned two members, and these were elected by the forty-shilling freeholders who cast their votes in the County Courts. This meant that in a large county voters had to travel long distances to the polls, and this involved a great deal of organisation for the candidates and their agents. Polling went on for several weeks, and, as voting was done publicly with a crowd looking on, there was tremendous excitement whenever an election was closely contested. Few Irish counties had more than a thousand voters.

County elections were notoriously expensive. The County Armagh election of 1753 is said to have cost William Brownlow (who was successful) £14,000, and Francis Caulfeild (who was not) £10,000. The lavish entertainment provided for all and sundry was responsible for much of this expense, but there was, in addition, much bribery and open purchase of votes. A number of accounts survive for the County Louth election of 1768, and these give us some indication of the ways in which a candidate's money was spent : 3,628 dinners, 2,511 breakfasts and 246 suppers were served at Dundalk ; and 523 dozen bottles of claret and port, 276 gallons of spirits etc., etc. were distributed. Small wonder that brawling marked many an election.

Parliament usually lasted for the life-time of a King, and there was no general election during the long reign of George II

(1727-1760). However in 1768 an Octennial Act was passed, and from then on elections were held every eight years.

The Borough Members : These comprised 80% of the House of Commons and were elected on a medley of franchises. There were boroughs as " rotten " as any in England : Bannow in Wexford and Harristown in Kildare had no inhabitants, yet each was represented by two members in the Irish Parliament. Many were " pocket " boroughs, and obediently returned the candidates chosen by the local landlord. There were four main classes of boroughs.

1. 53 ' Corporation' boroughs, where the two members were chosen by the town corporation. This consisted of twelve men called ' burgesses ', who very often did not even live in the town and who invariably chose the candidates recommended by the local landlord. Some of these boroughs were big towns like Belfast, others were small places like Killyleagh in County Down.

2. 46 ' Freeman' boroughs, where, in theory, every male Protestant was given the vote when he reached the age of twenty-one. Carrickfergus was the best example of this kind of borough, but even there large numbers of non-resident ' freemen ' were created in order to swamp the local inhabitants at election time. In fact the local landlord usually decided the election.

3. 11 ' Pot-walloper ' boroughs, where every Protestant householder who had a hearth on which he could boil a pot qualified for the vote. Five of these boroughs were in Antrim and Down—Antrim, Lisburn, Randalstown, Newry and Downpatrick. At election time there was lavish entertainment of voters, and public houses were thrown open to the electors at the candidates' expense.

4. 7 ' Manor ' boroughs, where the landlord decided who the members of Parliament should be. The electorate was small—often only a dozen voters—and the election was purely a matter of form.

An Unrepresentative Assembly: It is apparent that the House of Commons did not even represent the Protestant section of the population and that political influence was concentrated in the hands of the great lords who controlled the boroughs of one sort or another. It has been calculated that, in 1783, only seventy-two of the three hundred members of the House of Commons were freely elected, and that, of the rest, one hundred and twenty were chosen by fifty-three lords, and ninety-one by fifty-two commoners. Lord Shannon returned sixteen members of Parliament; Lord Hillsborough, nine; the Duke of Leinster, seven. This system put tremendous political power into the hands of a small number of men, and it was with these that the Lord Lieutenant negotiated when he wanted to be sure of Parliament's support. Their support could only be obtained by promises of titles, places and provisions for themselves or their relatives, and thus there was a good deal of corruption and sordid bargaining during every session of the Irish Parliament.

Powers of the Irish Parliaments: Besides all this, the Irish Parliament was almost powerless. A law passed in 1494, known as Poynings' Law, stated that the Irish Parliament could not meet until permission had been given by the King and his Council in London, not only for the calling of Parliament but also for the laws that it was proposed to pass. This act had been amended from time to time, but in the period we are considering the essential point was retained: the Irish Parliament could not pass a law until it had been approved by the British Government. In 1698 William Molyneaux had protested against this subservience of the Irish Parliament in his book *The Case of Ireland's being bound by Acts of Parliament in England, stated*, but his views were condemned by the authorities as " bold and pernicious ", and the book was burned by the common hangman. Then in 1719 the Declaratory Act (sometimes known as the " Sixth of George I ") put the matter beyond question, by asserting that the British Parliament had " full power and authority to make laws and statutes of sufficient force and validity to bind the kingdom and people of Ireland ". The Irish Parliament had thus very limited powers, and this, as we shall see, was to become a matter of controversy in the future.

Restrictions on Trade : There was one sphere in which the British Parliament actually legislated for Ireland, and that was in matters of trade. In Charles II's reign the export of Irish cattle to England was forbidden, with the result that the Irish had developed an overseas trade in provisions and had built up a promising woollen industry. The English manufacturers were alarmed by the latter development and appealed to William III to " restrain " the export of Irish woollen cloth. The King was prepared to help them and persuaded a subservient Irish Parliament in 1698 to put such a heavy duty on fine material shipped out of the country that the industry gradually died out. At first rough woollen cloth was exempt from the duty, but in 1699 an act passed by the Parliament at Westminster forbade the export of any kind of Irish woollen cloth to a country other than England, and even there high duties were imposed on it.

Other industries suffered in the same way, and during the first half of the eighteenth century silk, cotton and glass were all placed under restrictions of one kind or another. The most obvious exception was the provision trade, and for most of the eighteenth century there were large exports of beef, pork, butter and hides, especially to the British colonies across the Atlantic.

Results of Restrictions : An immediate result of these restrictions was that smuggling was carried on extensively in the eighteenth century. Wool was smuggled out to France, and brandy, wine and silk carried back in return. Irishmen of all classes were involved in this illegal trade—landlords, clergy and peasants, Protestants and Catholics. The Government was powerless to stop it, and for generations it flourished all round the coasts.

Another result of the commercial restrictions was the growth of a more independent spirit among the Protestant settlers in

Ireland. In 1699 they had agreed to William III's request to crush the Irish woollen industry " in grateful acknowledgement of his majesty's royal care, favour and protection ". A quarter of a century later they felt differently. The Catholics had been depressed by the penal laws and were no longer regarded as dangerous : thus some Protestants were bold enough to question England's right to control Ireland's trade or even to interfere in her internal affairs. The episode known as " Wood's Halfpence " gave this group an opportunity to bring their views out into the open.

Wood's Halfpence : In the early part of the eighteenth century there was a scarcity of small money in Ireland, and that was the cause of much hardship, especially for the poor. Because of this, one of the King's favourites, the Duchess of Kendal, was given permission to issue halfpence and farthings to the value of £108,000. She sold her right to a Wolverhampton iron-merchant named William Wood, and it was calculated that he would make a profit of £40,000 on the transaction. The Irish Parliament had not been consulted on the matter at all, and, roused to action by this slight, both Houses petitioned George I, asking that the new copper coinage be withdrawn. But Wood had influential supporters, and, though the Irish Parliament stirred up strong feelings on the matter, the British Government would probably have had its way, were it not for the intervention of Jonathan Swift.

Jonathan Swift : Swift was born in Dublin in 1667 and educated at Trinity College. After his ordination he lived in England, where he was on terms of close friendship with Oxford and Bolingbroke, the Tory ministers of Queen Anne, and he became the centre of a brilliant literary circle which included Pope and Congreve, Addison and Steele. Returning to Ireland, he was made Dean of Saint Patrick's, Dublin in 1713, and for the next thirty years he wrote a succession of brilliant pamphlets, attacking and satirising the abuses and evils that surrounded him. In bitter words he assailed the Irish Parliament

with its crowd of pensioners and place-seekers ; he attacked
the commercial laws restricting Ireland's trade; he condemned
the custom of appointing only Englishmen to the high offices
of Church and State. But his great chance came with the
" Wood's Halfpence " affair. In the assumed character of a
shopkeeper, he attacked the proposal in the famous *Drapier's
Letters*, pouring ridicule upon Wood and his coinage and
urging the Irish people to reject them. The pamphlets were
eagerly read in the capital and whipped up a storm of indigna-
tion. In his fourth *Letter*, published in 1724, Swift attacked
the whole system of English rule in Ireland, and rejected the
claim of the British Government to legislate for the country as
a usurpation.

The Lord Lieutenant offered a reward of £300 for the discovery of the author, but no one would come forward to
identify him. Then the printer of the pamphlets was arrested,
but no jury would convict him. Eventually the British Government admitted defeat, and Wood's contract was withdrawn.

' The Patriot Party ' : This episode is of some importance as
it indicates a change in the attitude of the ruling class towards
Britain. Just after the Revolution, when they still feared a
Catholic uprising, they were inclined to be servile, to regard
themselves as " an English colony " in a foreign country. Thus
they had accepted without question the commercial restrictions,
and had not seriously protested when the British Parliament
claimed the right to legislate for Ireland. But by the middle of
the eighteenth century a number of members of Parliament
adopted a more independent attitude. They formed a small
group called " The Patriot Party ", led by Henry Flood, Charles
Lucas and Lord Charlemont. In the beginning their demands
were simple; they wished to limit the life of Parliament to five
or seven years; to have a Habeas Corpus Act so that a man
could not be imprisoned without trial ; to reduce the number
of place-men and pensioners in the House of Commons—in
other words, they claimed for themselves the constitutional
rights that Englishmen had gained from the Revolution of

1688. The Catholics did not come into their calculations at all. Some of the " Patriots " were prepared to allow them to practise their religion or even to acquire property, but that was as far as they were prepared to go. " In a country unfortunately circumstanced like Ireland," said Lord Charlemont, " where the many are to be governed by a few—there are two points which never can with safety be ceded by the governing few, namely the free and uncontrolled use of arms, and a share in the legislature ". He was prepared to extend to Catholics full religious liberty and every economic benefit that did not entitle them to political power. The Protestant ascendancy must be maintained.

3. The Irish Land System in the Eighteenth Century

Confiscation of Irish Land : From Tudor times onwards the greater part of Irish land had gradually passed into the hands of English settlers. In Queen Elizabeth's reign, after the Desmond Rebellion, more than half a million acres were confiscated in Munster; while the defeat of O'Neill and O'Donnell at Kinsale was eventually followed by the Plantation of Ulster, when six of the northern counties were handed over to English and Scottish colonists. Nearly fifty years later there occurred the Cromwellian Settlement, by which the supporters of the Parliamentary side in the struggle with Charles I were given large estates in Leinster, Munster and the unplanted parts of Ulster. Finally there were the confiscations that followed the Irish defeat at the Boyne and the treaty of Limerick, when over a million acres belonging to Jacobite supporters were forfeited to the Crown. Thus at the opening of the eighteenth century, the land owned by Catholics probably did not exceed one-twentieth of the area of the country.

The Landlord : Many of those who acquired Irish land did not live on their estates but spent practically all their time in

London and Dublin or on other estates they might happen to have in England. Their only interest in their Irish lands was in the rents they collected from them : these they wanted punctually paid and without too much trouble on their part. Thus came into existence the " middleman system ". The landlord would let his estate, or part of it, perhaps ten thousand acres, to a head-tenant on a long lease and for a low rent. The head-tenant in his turn would divide the land into a number of smaller estates and let them again at a higher rent. Further subdivision and sub-letting took place, and there were sometimes four or five persons between the landlord and the cultivator of the soil. In such circumstances rack-renting was almost inevitable. Where the landlord did not let his land in this way, he often handed over its management to a local agent who squeezed the last penny out of tenants for rent, and expected to be bribed with poultry, eggs and butter into leaving the peasant in possession of his farm.

The Tenants: Whenever a tenant's lease expired, his farm was put up for auction, and a new lease was granted to the highest bidder. Thus a peasant had no security and might find that his farm had been granted to someone else. A number of serious consequences followed from this state of affairs. The farmer had no inducement to maintain the quality of his land as the end of his lease drew near. On the contrary, he knew that the better the cultivation had been the more likely the landlord's agent would be to demand a higher rent.

Very often the tenant had no lease at all but could be evicted at any time, even though his rent was paid. If he had built a good house, drained his fields and built ditches, all these became the property of his landlord, who let them to his successor at a higher rent. All initiative and ambition were killed, and every encouragement was given to sloth and to bad farming. The more impoverished his land, the more miserable his hovel, the more ragged and dirty his family, the less likely was a peasant to be disturbed.

Living Conditions : From the writings of contemporary

travellers we can get some idea of the terrible conditions under which these peasants lived. Arthur Young has left us this picture :

" The cottages of the Irish, which are called cabins, are the most miserable looking hovels that can well be conceived : they generally consist of only one room : mud kneaded with straw is the common material of the walls ; these are rarely above seven feet high and not always above five or six ; they are about two feet thick and have only a door which lets in light instead of a window, and should let out smoke instead of a chimney . . .

The roofs of the cabins are rafters, raised from the tops of the mud walls, and the covering varies ; some are thatched with straw, potato-stalks or with heath, others only covered with

An Irish Cabin

sods of turf cut from a grass field ; and I have seen several that were partly composed of all three. The bad repair these roofs are kept in, a hole in the thatch being often mended with turf, and weeds sprouting from every part, gives them the appearance of a weedy dunghill . . .

The furniture of the cabins is as bad as the architecture ; in very many consisting only of a pot for boiling their potatoes, a bit of a table and one or two broken stools ; beds are not found universally, the family lying on straw."

The peasant and his family usually went barefoot and were scarcely covered with their tattered clothing. Their food consisted almost entirely of potatoes.

Tenant Right : Conditions in Ulster were better than in the rest of the country. Relations were happier there between landlord and tenant : over large areas they were of the same religion, spoke the same language and inherited the same traditions. Most important of all, there had grown up a custom in the northern counties, known as *tenant right,* which practically guaranteed a farmer security as long as his rent was paid. If he wished to give up his land he was compensated by his successor for the improvements which he had made. Farming methods were consequently better, and standards of living were higher in Ulster than in the rest of the country. A contributory factor was the manufacture of linen, which was scattered widely throughout the area and gave the farmer a second income. But the north had its grievances, also, as the revolts of the " Oakboys " and of the " Hearts of Steel " show.

The Whiteboys : Considering the conditions under which many of the peasantry held their lands, it is not surprising that they should have banded together in a number of agrarian societies to try to improve their lot. One of the most famous of these was the " Whiteboys " and they were active in Munster in the opening years of George III's reign. The Whiteboys are said to have got their name from the practice of moving about the country at night, wearing white shirts over their clothes, pulling down enclosures, ploughing up grassland, maiming cattle and sheep, and stirring up resistance to the payment of tithes. But a more unsuitable garb for men who wished to escape detection than a white shirt would be difficult to imagine, and it is possible that the name had some other origin. The movement began in Tipperary and spread from there to other counties. For a time the authorities believed that the disturbance was being organised by French spies or that it was a " popish plot " directed against Protestants, but there is little evidence to support these views. Lord Charlemont was nearer the truth when he said the causes of the revolt were " exorbitant rents, low wages, want of employment, misery, want and oppression." The government acted promptly: strict laws were passed against secret societies and volunteers were enrolled to assist the magistrates in restoring law and order. By these means the Whiteboy movement was crushed, though agrarian crime in one form or another continued in Ireland until near the end of the nineteenth century.

The Oakboys : During these years also, disturbances began to occur in Armagh and Tyrone, and gradually spread from there to the other Ulster counties. For the most part the insurgents were Presbyterians who rose in protest against the attempts of the ministers of the Established Church to increase their tithes, and against a Road Act which forced them to contribute six days unpaid labour to the repair of highways each year. Large crowds of men, wearing oak leaves in their hats, gathered in many parishes and forced clergymen to promise not to demand excessive tithes. An unpopular minister, Dr. Clarke of Clonfeacle, came in for special attention. He was driven around the countryside tied to the top of his own carriage and greeted everywhere by the shouts of the crowds. As in Munster, the authorities acted promptly, and the movement was suppressed. But the Road Act was repealed and a new one put in its place.

The Hearts of Steel : This was the most exciting revolt of the period and was largely confined to Antrim and Down. In 1769 many of the leases on the estate of Lord Donegall to the north and west of Belfast came to an end. Instead of following the usual custom of granting new leases to the tenants at a moderate increase of rent, the landlord's agent demanded in addition a lump sum or fine from each tenant, the amount depending on the size of the farm. The tenants refused to pay, and immediately the agent offered their farms to the highest bidders. A number of wealthy Belfast merchants, hoping to benefit from the high price of provisions, took the land and made large grazing farms. The angry tenants struck back. They formed an association called the " Hearts of Steel," and began to maim the cattle of those who had taken their lands. Matters came to a head on December 1, 1770, when a leading Belfast merchant, Waddell Cunningham, arrested David Douglas of Templepatrick and charged him with slaughtering cattle. The Hearts of Steel decided to rescue Douglas, and over a thousand of them, armed with guns, swords and pitchforks, marched on Belfast. They surrounded the barracks and demanded the release of Douglas. When this was refused, they proceeded to the house of Waddell Cunningham in Hercules Lane (present Royal Avenue) and began to loot it. Fearing that they would eventually burn the town, if their wishes were not granted, the authorities released Douglas, and he was brought back in triumph to Templepatrick.

After this the movement spread, and attacks on farmhouses and cattle increased. Large numbers of soldiers were sent into the disturbed areas, and several " Steelboys " were tried at Carrickfergus but acquitted. In 1772, however, twelve were hanged and from then on the insurrection gradually subsided. But the peasantry were far from satisfied, and the more peaceful conditions which followed were the result of the wholesale emigration of the malcontents to America.

Questions and Exercises

1.   Describe the chief penal laws against (a) Catholics and (b) Presbyterians in the first half of the eighteenth century. Were these laws always strictly enforced?

2. How were the powers of the Irish Parliament restricted by
    (a) Poynings' Law, 1494, (b) the Sixth of George 1, 1719?

3. Describe how members of the Irish Parliament were elected
    in the eighteenth century, and compare it with the method
    used today.

4. Give a full account of the " Wood's Halfpence " affair.

5. Who were the leaders of the " Patriot Party " in the period
    before 1760? What was their policy?

6. What were the principal defects of the Irish land system
    in the eighteenth century? How did Ulster differ from the
    rest of the country?

CHAPTER NINE

The Struggle for India:
Robert Clive

1. British and French Rivalry in India

European Trades : The Far East has always held a fascination for the peoples of Europe. In the Middle Ages Venice had developed a valuable trade with it through the Red Sea and the Persian Gulf, and the market places of the city were thronged with merchants who bought and sold spices, silks and other oriental luxuries. Then in the sixteenth century, following the voyage of Vasco da Gama round the Cape of Good Hope, Portugal took the place of Venice as the chief distributor of eastern goods, and Portuguese merchants made settlements at Goa, Bombay and other places on the West Coast of India. No other European nation was permitted to trade in these areas, and merchants wanting silks and spices had to purchase them in Lisbon. But when Philip II of Spain conquered Portugal in 1580 this trade was upset. Philip was not on friendly terms with England and Holland, and he refused to allow their merchants to visit his ports. From then on, if English or Dutch merchants wanted eastern products, they were compelled to make the long journey to India for them. The Dutch went first and were soon bringing home cargoes of pepper, nutmegs and other spices from the islands which lay to the east of India. They charged very high prices for their goods and forced up the price of pepper from three shillings to eight shillings a pound. In protest against what they described as "the unchristian price of pepper" a number of London merchants met in the Lord Mayor's parlour in September, 1599 and decided to form a company of their own to trade with the East. Queen Elizabeth was appealed to, and on December 31, 1600, the merchants received a royal charter by which they were given a monopoly of the trade between England and the lands which lay to the east of the Cape of Good Hope. This was the origin of the East India Company, which not only brought great wealth to England, but also, in time, established a vast empire in India.

The East India Company : The Company's first venture was a fleet of five small ships which left London on February 13, 1601 under Captain James Lancaster, an Englishman who had been in the service of Portugal and had already sailed round the Cape of Good Hope. The expedition was a success, and, when the ships returned in two years, they carried valuable cargoes that made a handsome profit for the members of the Company. At the beginning the English merchants were inclined to concentrate on Java, Sumatra and the other islands which lay to the east of India and which were the chief source of the spices that Europe demanded. But the Dutch were determined to keep this area to themselves and did everything possible to hinder their rival's trade. The Company, therefore, appealed to James I for protection, and he entered into negotiations with the Dutch, as a result of which a treaty was signed in 1619, whereby the two countries agreed to share the trade. But the Dutch merchants in the East were not prepared to honour the agreement made by their government at home, and four years later they seized a number of English traders and, after terrible torture, put them to death.

From then on the East India Company confined its attention to the mainland of India. This was a vast country, inhabited by many different races, speaking different languages and having different social customs and religions. The largest of these groups were the Hindus, but at the beginning of the sixteenth century a Moslem chieftain named Baber had gained control of the Indo-Gangetic plain and had established an empire there. His successors, who were known as the Mogul Emperors, extended the area of their rule until they dominated nearly the whole of India. It was with one of these Mogul Emperors, Jehangir, that the East India Company had to deal when they sought permission to trade with the mainland of India. Sir Thomas Roe was sent as ambassador by James I to the Mogul Emperor in 1615 and was ordered to obtain trading rights for the East India Company. He was successful, and merchants of the Company were given permission to settle and to trade at Surat, in the north-west of the peninsula. This was the first English settlement in India, but during the seventeenth century several similar trading posts were established: at Masulipatam on the east coast in 1622, at Madras in 1639, and at the mouth of the Ganges in 1642. When Charles II married Catherine of Braganza, a Portuguese princess, in 1662, the island of Bombay was given to him as a marriage dowry, and he rented it to the East India Company. Thus at the end of the seventeenth century the most important trading posts of the Company were at Calcutta, Bombay and Madras, and in their warehouses great quantities of spices, silks, cottons and calicoes were stored to await the arrival of ships (the " East Indiamen " they were called) to bring them to England. After the Restoration two new commodities were added to the cargoes as tea and coffee became more and more popular as drinks with the well-to-do.

The East India Company called its trading posts *factories,* because they were in charge of factors or agents. Each factory was built round a central quadrangle or courtyard. The buildings were two storeys high, with offices and warehouses on the ground floor, and dormitories and living rooms upstairs. Because of the valuable goods which they contained the factories were surrounded by high walls and the merchants were armed to defend their property in case of an attack. Each factory was controlled by a president and council chosen by the merchants. There were also writers or clerks and young men called apprentices who had come out to India to learn the business. All were badly paid, but they were permitted to engage in private trade, and the more enterprising or less scrupulous could exercise their wits against the natives in the bazaars.

The French in India : In 1664 a French East India Company was formed and set up factories at Pondicherri, south of Madras, at Mahé on the west coast and at Chandernagar on the Ganges delta. The English now had trading rivals, but for a time the two companies got on very well as there was plenty of business for both in India. We must remember that they were only interested in trade, in buying Indian goods as cheaply as possible and selling them as dearly as possible, so that the shareholders in the Companies would gain a large profit on the monies they had invested. But in the eighteenth century a change took place which turned them into rivals fighting for political power and influence. It began in 1707 when the last of the strong Mogul Emperors died. The great empire which they had erected began to break up, and all over India nabobs and rajahs who had ruled their states as vassals of the Mogul Emperors declared their independence while a great part of the Deccan passed under the control of the Mahrattas, fierce warriors and horsemen who extorted tribute from less warlike tribes. India was in a state of confusion, and in many states whenever a prince died rival claimants struggled for the vacant throne.

Both English and French merchants suffered from this state of affairs, for trade flourishes best in times of peace. Then François Dupleix, who had been in charge of the factory at Pondicherri since 1741, thought he saw a way in which the prevailing disorder might be turned to the advantage of the French East India Company. He raised an army of native troops called *sepoys,* trained them in European methods of warfare, and began to take part in the struggles that were going on. If two princes were fighting for the rule of a state, Dupleix would go to the assistance of one of them and help to put him on the throne. He expected that the grateful prince would then give all the trade of his state to the French, and the English merchants would be at a great disadvantage. An opportunity to put his scheme into operation came with the outbreak of the War of the Austrian Succession, in which England and France were on opposite sides. In 1746 with the aid of a French fleet under La Bourdonnais he captured Madras, but when peace was made between the two countries at Aix-la-Chapelle in 1748 he was ordered to return the post to the English.

The Carnatic : Though Dupleix had received a setback he did not change his policy, and before long a perfect opportunity presented itself for him to put it into effect. In 1749 the ruler of the Carnatic died, and there were two claimants for the vacant throne. This was an extremely important state in south-east India for it contained both the English factory of Madras and the French factory of Pondicherri. If the prince supported by Dupleix, named Chunda Sahib, succeeded to the throne there was a very real danger of the English merchants being expelled from the Carnatic altogether. The English East India Company was consequently forced to embroil itself in Indian politics and decided to support the other claimant for the throne, Mohammed Ali. But the forces which the English merchants were able to enlist were no match for the well trained sepoys of Dupleix. Mohammed Ali was forced to take refuge in the fortress of Trichinopoli, and his capture seemed only a matter of time. That this did not happen was due to a young man in the service of the East India Company who now makes his first appearance in history. His name was Robert Clive.

2. Robert Clive (1725-1774)

Early Life : Robert Clive was born at Market Drayton in Shropshire in 1725, the son of a lawyer and small landowner. His early years were spent with a doting aunt and uncle in Manchester who utterly spoiled him and let him have his way in all things. They attempted to win his favour by giving him small presents from time to time, but this only made him more difficult to control, and by the time he returned to his parents he was completely out of hand, bad-tempered, strong-willed, always up to mischief. Several stories are told of him which give us some indication of his character. It is said that one day, while he was playing " Ducks and Drakes " with some boys, skimming stones on the waters of the River Tern, he remembered having seen a very smooth stone in the mouth of a gargoyle on the roof of the parish church. To the great glee of his companions, but to the consternation of the people of Market Drayton, he climbed upon the roof to get it and crept out on the gargoyle. But his courage was rewarded, and when he reached the ground again he clutched the smooth stone tightly in his hand. This was only one side of his character, however, for he was badly behaved as well. He formed a number of boys into a gang and forced the local shopkeepers to pay them money in return for a promise not to break their windows. His distracted parents were forced to move him about from school to school as their headmasters complained that he was a bad influence on their pupils. Finally when he was seventeen, his father got the chance of a position for him with the East India Company, and, glad to be rid of a son whom he found impossible to control, sent him out to Madras to become a writer in the factory there.

Clive in India (1743-1753) : Clive was very unhappy in his new life. His salary of £5 per annum was totally inadequate; he did not like the climate and was in despair of ever getting accustomed to it; morose and withdrawn, he had no friends and was very homesick. Twice he tried to commit suicide, but each time the pistol failed to fire when he pressed the trigger. The outbreak of hostilities between the English and the French gave him an opportunity to escape from his desk. When Dupleix captured Madras in 1746 he escaped from the station, disguised as a native, made his way to Fort St. David and offered himself as a soldier. From then on he had a career more to his liking.

The struggle for the throne of the Carnatic gave him his first big chance. Mohammed Ali, the English nominee, was being besieged in Trichinopoli, and if Dupleix succeeded in taking the town the English position would be very difficult. Clive suggested that the best way of raising the siege was to take Arcot, the capital of the Carnatic, and thus force Chunda Sahib and the French to try to recapture it. This would relieve the pressure on Trichinopoli and give Mohammed Ali a chance to break out. The plan was accepted, and in 1751 Clive was sent with a small force of two hundred white troops and three hundred sepoys to take the capital. He reached Arcot during a thunderstorm and easily captured it. As he had anticipated, a large army was sent from Trichinopoli, and he had to endure a siege of fifty days. Food was scarce, but the hardy sepoys gave their share of the rice to their white companions and lived on the water in which it had been boiled. The siege ended dramatically when elephants which Chunda Sahib had brought up, carrying battering rams, were terrified by the gun-fire and ran amok, trampling their drivers underfoot. Next day the besiegers moved off, and Arcot remained in English hands. Shortly afterwards Trichinopoli was also relieved, and Mohammed Ali became ruler of the Carnatic. Dupleix was recalled to France in disgrace, but Clive went home to England to be received by the East India Company with great honour, for he had made secure the future of the English merchants in India.

Clive in England : He was now a rich and famous man, and was made welcome in the homes of the mightiest in the land. He lived like an Indian prince, riding about in a magnificent carriage, attended by footmen in glittering livery. He spent money recklessly, taking his parents to London and settling on them an income for the rest of their lives, making gifts to his sister, to his friends, even to his wife's distant relatives. Finally he decided to stand for Parliament, and, after a costly election, had himself returned for the borough of St. Michael in Cornwall, only to be unseated again on a charge of corruption.

Lord Clive, 1725-1774

Within eighteen months of his return to England Clive's large fortune had been spent, and, when the East India Company offered him the position of Governor of Fort St. David and Deputy-Governor of Madras, he was glad to accept it. A week or two later he set out for India.

War in Bengal : Clive reached Madras on May 25, 1756. The Seven Years' War had just broken out in Europe, and once more England and France were on opposite sides. The English and French merchants in India at once began to fortify their stations in case of attack. The ruler of Bengal, a young and unstable prince named Siraj-ud-Dowlah, when he saw the British fortifications at Calcutta and the French fortifications at Chandernagar, ordered these warlike preparations to cease. The French merchants obeyed instantly, but the English tried to explain that they were for the purpose of defence only, not attack. Then suddenly Siraj-ud-Dowlah marched on Calcutta, taking the settlement by surprise. After a brief attempt at resistance the Governor and chief merchants fled down the Hugli, leaving hundreds of men and women to fend for themselves. They appointed one of their number, an Irishman, John Holwell, to be their leader, but they were soon forced to surrender. According to the story later told by Holwell, one hundred and forty-six of them were rounded up and placed in a small guardroom, only eighteen feet square and ventilated by one small iron-barred window. It was a hot June night, and within a short time the prisoners were struggling to reach the window for air, the weak being crushed back or trodden underfoot in the mad scramble. They begged for water and implored the guards to transfer some of them to another room; but Siraj-ud-Dowlah was asleep now, and the guards could not act without his orders. It was not until six in the morning that the doors were opened, and by then only twenty-three of the prisoners were still alive. One hundred and twenty-three men and women had died during the night of June 10, 1756, in " *the Black Hole of Calcutta.*"

Recently there had been disagreement amongst historians as

learn the ap

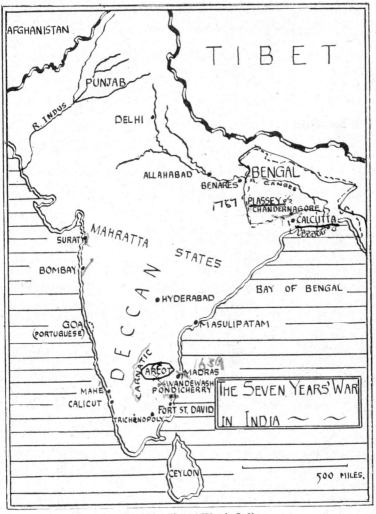

The Seven Years' War in India

to whether this incident ever took place or whether, if it did, it was as bad as the traditional story leads one to believe. Holwell, it has been said, made up much of its horror and it does seem that he was not a very reliable witness. But true or false, the story spread quickly to the station at Madras, and the English there determined to have revenge on Siraj-ud-Dowlah.

The Battle of Plassey (1757) : Clive was chosen to go north to punish the cruel Nabob of Bengal. He was provided with only 3,000 men, but so great was his fame that Siraj-ud-Dowlah immediately expressed his regrets for what had occurred and offered to pay a large sum in compensation to the Company. Clive was not prepared to make peace with him, for he saw that he had a chance not only of punishing the Nabob but also of destroying French influence in Bengal. Accusing the French of conspiring with Siraj-ud-Dowlah he seized their factory at Chandernagar; next he made a secret agreement with the Nabob's chief minister, Mir Jaffir, who promised to desert to the English side if Clive would place him on the throne of Bengal. In these circumstances Clive felt justified in attacking an army of 50,000 men at Plassey, outside Calcutta, in 1757. The battle did not last long. Siraj-ud-Dowlah terrified by the English artillery fire fled in panic, and so did his army. Though the number of casualties was small the battle of Plassey was decisive. Siraj-ud-Dowlah was put to death and Mir Jaffir was placed on the throne of Bengal. But this was not all. The new ruler was only a puppet in the hands of the East Indian Company, which from now on controlled the rich lands of Bengal.

Defeat of the French : Britain and France were still engaged in the Seven Years' War. Thus, while Clive was in Bengal, a large French army and fleet had reached the Carnatic, captured Fort St. David and laid siege to Madras. It was commanded by Count Lally, the son of Sir Gerald O Lally, an Irish Jacobite who had fought for Bonnie Prince Charlie in Scotland and had later settled in France. Lally was a brave soldier but difficult to serve under; he quarrelled with his officers and had nothing but contempt for the sepoy forces. Clive sent Sir Eyre Coote south to deal with him, and in 1760 Lally was defeated in the battle of Wandewash. The French army then retreated towards Pondicherri, but Coote surrounded the settlement by land, while the ships of the Company cut off all hope of reinforcements by sea. When Pondicherri surrendered in 1761, the French dream of an Indian empire was over. By the Peace of Paris 1763, which ended the Seven Years' War, the French were given back their factories at Pondicherri, Mahé and Chandernagar, but they were to be used only as trading posts and were not to be fortified or garrisoned. The English East India Company had now obtained control over Bengal, the Carnatic and Parts of the Deccan. The Directors of the Company had never dreamed, when they had established their trading posts in India, that they would end up with an empire on their hands, larger and wealthier than the home country. The government of such a great dominion was a heavy task for the East India Company, but many years were to pass before the British government could be persuaded to take responsibility for its rule.

The Last Years of Clive : Clive's second visit home in 1760 was even more triumphant than his first had been, and he was hailed everywhere as the victor of Plassey. But his health was still a matter for concern, and within a few weeks of his return he was seriously ill. For nearly a year he hung between life and death but he finally recovered. He entered Parliament as a member for Shrewsbury, the capital of his native county, and was later raised to the peerage.

Meanwhile in India those who had taken his place vied with each other to see who could extort most from the natives, and every kind of abuse and malpractice prevailed. By 1765 conditions were so bad that the Company implored Clive to return. He remained in India for only a year, but during that period he suggested a number of useful reforms. He saw that it was difficult for the Company's servants to be honest and just unless they were better paid, and so he raised their salaries, but he forbade them to take part in private trade or to accept presents from the native princes. In Bengal he introduced the *dual system,* whereby the Nabob carried on the administration while the Company collected the taxes and paid the Nabob a fixed allowance. Clive had correctly diagnosed the causes of trouble in India, but he had great difficulty in having his reforms accepted. The Company's shareholders feared that an increase in salaries would reduce their dividends, while the government was opposed to English merchants getting involved in Indian politics. Clive believed that the government itself should take over the responsibility of administering Bengal, and in a letter to the Prime Minister, Pitt, he expressed the belief that " so large a sovereignty may be an object too extensive for a mercantile company." But the government, just then involved in a dispute with its American colonies, was not prepared to undertake fresh responsibilities, and the suggestion of Clive was ignored.

In January, 1767 Clive left India for the last time. On his return to England his enemies accused him of having enriched himself while acting as a servant of the East India Company. No doubt he had made a fortune in India, and the methods he used were often ones that we would not tolerate today ; but those who attacked him were men who wanted the evils of Indian administration to continue and who were displeased with the reforms which he had suggested. His conduct was investigated by a Select Committee of the House of Commons, which found that he was guilty of fraud and deceit in his dealings with Mir Jaffir, but added " Robert, Lord Clive, had at the same time rendered great and meritorious services to his country." Clive never recovered from the humiliation of the investigation and turned to opium which he took in increasing quantities. In 1774 he died from an overdose of the drug, whether taken deliberately or not it is now impossible to say. His body was taken by his family to a little churchyard near his birthplace where it was buried without even a stone to mark his last resting place.

Though he died in disgrace, Clive's achievement was remarkable. In little more than ten years he had laid the foundations of what was to become the British Empire in India.

Questions and Exercises

1. Draw a large scale map of India. On it mark and name the following:—

   (a) The first trading post of the English East India Company;

   (b) The Carnatic and an important English factory there;

   (c) The place obtained by Charles II on his marriage to Catherine of Braganza (1662);

   (d) The French factories of Pondicherri, Mahé and Chandernagar;

   (e) The town captured by Clive during a thunderstorm (1751);

   (f) The state of Bengal, and the place where a massacre took place in 1756;

   (g) Clive's most famous victory;

   (h) The battle fought between Sir Eyre Coote and the French (1760).

2. Give an account of the early activities of the English East India Company. Describe one of its factories, and draw a map to show the position of the more important English factories in India.

3. What was the scheme of Dupleix for establishing French power in India? Describe the attempts he made to carry it out, and explain why he failed to do so.

4. Outline the career of Robert Clive, and describe the part he played in the establishment of British power in India.

5. Account for British success and French failure in India.

Time Chart: 1714-1760

Reign	Great Britain	Ireland	Empire	Abroad
George I (1714-1727)		1719: Sixth of George I; Toleration Act. 1723: Wood's Halfpence 1724: Drapier's Letters		1715: Death of Louis XIV
	1720: South Sea Bubble 1721: Walpole Chief Minister			
George II (1727-1760)	1733: Excise Bill; Kay's Flying Shuttle		1732: Georgia	1739: War of Jenkins' Ear 1740-1748: War of the Austrian Succession 1743: Dettingen 1745: Fontenoy
	1742: Fall of Walpole		1745: Capture of Louisburg 1746: Loss of Madras	
	1745: Second Jacobite Rebellion 1746: Culloden			1748: Treaty of Aix-la-Chapelle
			1751: Siege of Arcot	
	1752: Calendar Reform		1755: Fort Duquesne attacked 1756: Black Hole of Calcutta	1756-1763: The Seven Years' War.
		1757: Catholic Committee formed	1757: Plassey	
			1759: Quebec	1759: Minden, Lagos Quiberon Bay
		1760: Thurot's Raid	1760: Capture of Montreal and Wandewash	

CHAPTER TEN

General Wolfe and the Conquest of Canada

1. The English in North America

Establishment of Colonies : During the seventeenth century a number of English colonies had been founded along the east coast of North America. The first settlement was made at Jamestown on Chesapeake Bay in 1607, and from it developed the colony of Virginia. Thirteen years later a second colony was founded in the north, when a group of dissatisfied Nonconformists, known as ' the Pilgrim Fathers,' sailed from Plymouth on the *Mayflower,* and, after a voyage lasting ten weeks, landed in Massachusetts Bay. They thus began a great migration of Puritans which went on all through Charles I's reign and brought into being the New England states of Massachusetts, Rhode Island, New Hampshire, Connecticut and Maine. Other religious groups followed the example of the Puritans and found religious freedom across the Atlantic: Lord Baltimore established Maryland as a refuge for Catholics in 1634, and William Penn founded Pennsylvania for the Quakers in 1681. North and South Carolina were settled in the reign of Charles II, who granted this part of the coast to a number of nobles in his court. They established large estates there, on which tobacco and rice were grown and on which most of the work was done by negro slaves.

The only part of the coast in which the English had not settled was that between the Hudson and the Delaware rivers. In 1632 a number of Dutch Protestant refugees had made a settlement there called New Amsterdam, on Manhattan Island, and from it had grown up the colony of New Holland. To the south of it there was a Swedish settlement at Delaware, but it was so small that it had little hope of survival and was finally annexed by the Dutch in 1655. These two settlements separated the English colonies of the south from those of New England, and, when an opportunity arose of dealing with them during the Anglo-Dutch War (1665-1667), they were seized by the British and divided into the three new colonies of New York, New Jersey and Delaware.

Georgia : Thus by the end of the seventeenth century twelve of the thirteen American colonies were already in existence. The thirteenth colony, Georgia, was founded in 1732 by a distinguished English soldier and philanthropist named General James Oglethorpe. At that time people who got into debt were put in prison and kept there until their debts were paid. This brought great hardship on their families, and in some cases meant that the unfortunate debtors were imprisoned for the rest of their lives. Oglethorpe thought that they ought to be given an opportunity to make a fresh start in life and asked George II to grant him territory in North America to make a colony for them. He was given a piece of land between South Carolina and Florida, and there he established Georgia as a home for debtors. It was to be a model colony: negro slavery was forbidden and rum was not to be sold to the settlers. In 1736 a young Church of England clergyman named John Wesley went out to preach to the colonists, taking with him his brother, Charles, to act as his secretary. The venture was not a success, but, while he was in Georgia, John Wesley came into contact with a German denomination, the Moravians, whose example played an important part in turning him into the greatest of the early Methodist preachers and social reformers.

The Settlers : Many of the early settlers were poor people who came to America in the hope of improving their lot; others were men of strong religious beliefs who wished to practise their faith in freedom. Some were criminals fleeing from justice, others were lured by the spirit of adventure. But, whatever their motives for coming, all were tough, courageous and resourceful. They had to be, for only the most daring would undertake the long voyage across the Atlantic in small overcrowded sailing boats or endure the terrible privations involved in starting a settlement. At the beginning the majority of those who made the journey were English, but, during the eighteenth century, increasing numbers began to arrive from Ireland, Scotland, France, Germany and Switzerland. Most of the Irish were Ulster Presbyterians who fled from religious persecution and the rack-rents imposed by greedy landlords. They settled on every part of the coast, but their principal refuge was in Pennsylvania and in the valleys stretching south into Virginia and Carolina. These Ulster settlers may be regarded as typical of the early settler as a whole. Plunging into the forests they built log cabins and cleared the first rough farms, growing corn and wheat among the tree-stumps. Dressed in hunting shirts and deerskin leggings, they made war on the Indians and soon had a reputation for fighting, for boisterous amusements and for a strong attachment to their Presbyterian faith.

By 1750 the thirteen colonies were firmly established and had about one and a half million inhabitants. Each colony had its own distinctive features, but there were already marked differences between the northern and southern settlements. In New England, where the soil was poor and thin and the winters long, life was hard. Farms were small, and many of the settlers grew corn, rye and hay. Others built ships from the plentiful timber supply and fished off the coast for cod, mackerel and herring. New England seamen were renowned for their skill and courage, and traded with England from Boston, Plymouth and other ports. In the southern colonies conditions were entirely different; the summers were hot and long, the farms were large plantations worked by slaves and growing tobacco and rice. Life in the south was more leisurely than in the north and there were fewer towns. The great plantation owners lived in imposing mansions, surrounded by servants, and imported their furniture, furnishings and clothes from England. Between the northern and southern colonies were the middle colonies of which the most important were New York and Pennsylvania. They were inhabited by people from many lands, and already a dozen languages could be heard spoken along the Hudson River. Most of the inhabitants earned their living from trade and had already begun to build New York into the great cosmopolitan city that it is today.

The Government of the Colonies : The amount of control exercised by the mother country over the colonies was small. Each colony had an *Assembly,* chosen by the votes of the settlers, which made laws and levied such taxes as were necessary. There was also a *Governor* appointed from Great Britain who was responsible for the administration and for preserving law and order. He had also, in theory, the power to veto bills passed by the Assembly which conflicted with the laws of England. But, in practice, the Governor's powers were limited by the Assembly's control of taxation, and he was usually forced to give way before the strongly expressed wishes of the settlers. The thirteen colonies were independent of one another, and there was often a good deal of quarrelling among them ; but from the middle of the eighteenth century onwards they were forced to move close together in face of the French scheme for seizing North America which is described in the following section.

2. The French in North America

Explorers and Trappers : The French had reached North America before the English. In 1535 a Breton sailor, Jacques Cartier, had sailed up the St. Lawrence in search of a passage to the East. The Indians whom he encountered told him that

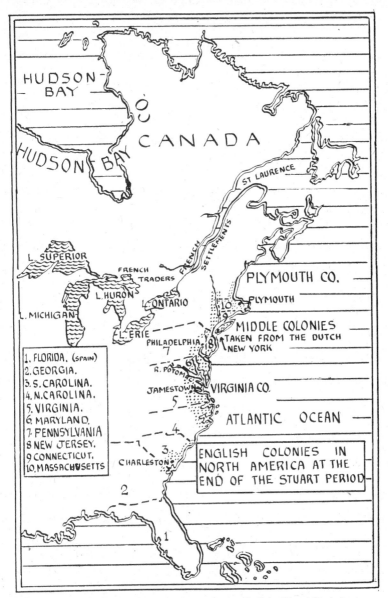

English Colonies in North America at the end of the Stuart Period

the river ran so far inland that no one had ever reached its source, and that on its banks were fabulously rich realms with names like Canada and Hochelega. He sailed on until he reached Montreal, but, before he could go any further, he was frozen in for the winter. For five months he waited for the ice to thaw, during which time his men suffered great hardships and twenty-five died from scurvy. This ended his venture, and he returned home without making a settlement. However, the reports which he brought back of the area led to the development during the sixteenth century of a trade in fur and skins with the Indians who lived near the St. Lawrence estuary. Not until the seventeenth century, however, was a permanent settlement made there. In 1608 Samuel de Champlain persuaded a group of French merchants to finance an expedition up the St. Lawrence. He made a base at Quebec, which he called after an Indian word *kebec* describing the narrowing of the river at this point. From there he continued westwards to explore the region in the vicinity of the Great Lakes and to lay the foundations of a lucrative trade in furs and skins.

The English and French, therefore, began their settlements in North America at about the same time. There was, however, a great difference in the attitudes of the two countries to the new continent. The English settlers had come out to North America to make homes for themselves and had every intention of remaining there for the rest of their lives. They cleared the forest, built houses, cultivated the ground, and hoped to hand on to their children an easier and more comfortable existence than they themselves had enjoyed. In the beginning the French had no interest in settlement at all. They came out in much smaller numbers, and they concentrated on trapping the fur-bearing animals and on trade rather than on agriculture. Thus they pushed westwards into the wilderness, following the great waterways—the St. Lawrence, the Great Lakes, the Wisconsin, Illinois, Wabash and Mississippi. Some were missionaries, like the Jesuits and Franciscans, who sought to convert the Indians to Christianity and made friends with the Huron and Algonquin tribes who lived on the shores of the Great Lakes. If the

French came into conflict with the English at all during this period, it was on the question of forest clearance. As the population of the English colonies increased and more land was reclaimed from the forest, the French (and the Indians also) feared that their fur supplies would be endangered. But the number of French settlers remained small, and when Champlain died in 1635 there were only eighty Europeans in Quebec and the region around it.

New France : In the second half of the seventeenth century things began to change. In 1663 Canada was made a royal province with Quebec as its capital and placed under the control of Colbert, the brilliant minister of Louis XIV. Immigration was properly organised, and shiploads of young women were sent over to marry the many single men. As a result the population began to grow ; some of those who came settled down to a life of agriculture, others established industries such as shipbuilding, tanning, weaving and brewing. At the same time a number of French priest-explorers, pursuing their missionary work, pushed into the heart of the continent. One of them, Marquette, mapped much of the Upper Mississippi valley ; another La Salle, followed the course of the river to its estuary in the Gulf of Mexico, claimed the whole area for Louis XIV, and called it Louisiana in honour of the King. Traders and settlers followed in the wake of the explorers, making a number of settlements on the banks of the great river, and New Orleans was founded at its mouth in 1718.

The English and French Quarrel : Meanwhile the English colonists were also starting to move westwards, and the more enterprising settlers had begun to spill through passes in the Alleghany Mountains into the great plains beyond. Some of the English colonies had been granted royal charters giving them possession of the lands now occupied and claimed by the French. Thus disputes began to occur between the two groups of settlers, and from now on relations between them were anything but friendly. To make matters worse, France and England were frequently at war during these years in Europe. Indeed in the century and a quarter from 1689 to 1815 there were no less than seven wars between them so that the period is sometimes called the Second Hundred Years' War. Each war in Europe had its counterpart in America. During the War of the League of Augsburg (1689-1697) the French, with their Indian allies, destroyed the outposts which the English settlers had built beyond the Alleghanies as a preliminary to their western advance, while the English moved northwards into Canada and made unsuccessful attempts to capture Quebec and Montreal. It was the same during the War of the Spanish Succession (1701-1713), only that this time the French had the assistance of the Spaniards who advanced from Florida against the Carolinas. But in this war England was successful, and the Treaty of Utrecht which ended it gave her a foothold in Canada : she gained Nova Scotia from the French, who were also forced to recognise her claim to Newfoundland and the land around the Hudson Bay.

It is not necessary to describe in any detail the relations between the English and French in North America during the next forty years. One point, however, should be borne in mind. The signing of a peace treaty between the two countries in Europe was not always followed by an end of hostilities in America, for the settlers there had their own reasons for fighting and usually pursued their quarrels without bothering too much about what was happening in Europe.

Fort Duquesne and George Washington : In the middle of the eighteenth century the French in North America produced their master plan. This was to build a line of fortresses along the St. Lawrence, Ohio and Mississippi rivers, stretching from Quebec in the north to New Orleans in the south. A glance at the map on page 215 will show the importance of this decision. If the French succeeded in their scheme, they could shut in the English between the Alleghany Mountains and the sea, and seize all the rest of North America for themselves. Gradually the strong points were built—Fort Frontenac, Fort Niagara, and Fort Duquesne. This last fort, which the French began to erect where the Alleghany and Monongahela rivers join to form the Ohio, provoked the English settlers into action in 1745. George Washington, a young Virginian officer of the militia, was sent by the Governor, Robert Dinwiddie, to ask the French to withdraw, for they were occupying " His Majesty's territory ". The French refused to withdraw and a skirmish took place at a place called Great Meadows. The British were defeated, and the French built Fort Duquesne on the site of the modern city of Pittsburg. The settlers of Virginia then appealed to the British Government for support, and in 1755 General Braddock was sent over from England with two regiments of regular troops. The general, though a brave soldier, had no experience of the methods of guerilla warfare practised by the French and their Indian allies. He marched his army straight into an ambush in which he himself and two-thirds of his men were killed. This defeat exposed the western frontiers of the English colonies to attacks from the Indians and French, and many horrible massacres took place. But, though nobody realised it at the time, the conflict between the two groups of settlers was soon to be merged in a great world war between England and France—the Seven Years' War—out of which Britain was to emerge as master of North America.

3. The Conquest of Canada

Pitt and the Seven Years' War : The War which began in 1756 was the first world war : it was fought in Europe, North America and India as well as on the oceans. In the beginning it went badly for Britain everywhere, and in North America the French general, Montcalm, captured the forts of Oswego and William Henry, thus opening up the way from Canada to New York down the Hudson River. There was an outcry in England at the manner in which the war was being conducted, and, in 1757, William Pitt was made Secretary of State and put in charge of operations. He showed extraordinary ability and self-confidence in the conduct of the war. " I know that I can save the country and that nobody else can," he said. He left the fighting in India to Robert Clive, and sent him out such military support as he required. He strengthened the navy and blockaded the ports of France, so that she had difficulty in supplying her armies scattered over three continents. But where he displayed his greatest ability was in his choice of the two great soldiers—Lord Amherst and James Wolfe—whom he placed in charge of the armies in North America. Wolfe in particular became a national hero, and he will always be remembered for the capture of Quebec.

James Wolfe (1727-1759) : Wolfe was born into a military family that had originally come from Ireland, but in his youth he was tall and thin with none of the robust health one usually associates with a soldier. Nevertheless, before he was fifteen he followed his father into the army and saw service at the battle of Dettingen in the War of the Austrian Succession. Three years later he took part in the campaign against " Bonnie Prince Charlie " and was present at Culloden when the Jacobite dream was ended. Promotion came rapidly : at twenty-three he was a lieutenant-colonel and was regarded as one of the ablest officers in the British army. Like Pitt he was self-assured almost to the point of arrogance, and this did not help to make him popular with some of his colleagues. The Duke of Newcastle is said to have told George II that Wolfe was mad. " Mad, is he ? " barked the King, " then I hope he will bite some of my other generals." He first attracted Pitt's notice by the courage and initiative he displayed in a raid on the French coast, and so, when the British minister formulated his scheme for driving the French out of Canada, he chose Wolfe as one of the generals to put it into effect.

Pitt's Plan : Pitt believed that, if Montreal and Quebec could be captured, it would be possible to expel the French from North America altogether. In preparation for this, he decided to clear them out of the other areas they occupied, so that the entire French forces should be forced to fall back upon these two centres. In 1758 he put his plan into operation. An army under General Forbes moved down the Ohio valley, captured Fort Duquesne which was later renamed Pittsburg. Two other armies swept the enemy before them from the area around the Great Lakes and the New York-Montreal Valley, and laid siege to the French fortresses of Crown Point and Ticonderoga. It was only when they were captured that the final stage of Pitt's plan could go into effect : a fleet of British ships was to move down the St. Lawrence, so that the French would be caught in a " pincer movement " and be forced to surrender. Amherst and Wolfe were put in charge of this important operation. It opened with the capture of Louisburg on Cape Breton Island in July, 1758, which allowed British ships to sail freely up the great estuary, and Amherst and Wolfe prepared to advance. Before they could do so, however, Pitt withdrew Amherst and put him in charge of the operations against the French strongholds of Crown Point and Ticonderoga. Wolfe was thus left in sole charge of the advance up the St. Lawrence, though it was hoped that, by the time he reached Quebec, Amherst would be ready to join him. Actually the later took so long to overcome the French that Wolfe was left to capture Quebec on his own. How he did so is one of the best known stories in history.

The Capture of Quebec (1759) : Quebec stood on a high cliff overlooking the St. Lawrence and at first sight seemed almost impregnable. In addition the garrison was commanded by Montcalm, the great French general. For some time Wolfe did nothing as he waited for reinforcements to come from Amherst, until the months of summer passed, and the time approached when the river would freeze over. Then at last, in September, 1759, he decided that, if Quebec were to be taken before winter came, he would have to act at once. His plan was a desperate one. Some of his ships had discovered a little cove just west of Quebec, from which a path led to the towering Heights of Abraham above. The French were aware of this path, and

Montcalm had placed sentries to guard it. Nevertheless Wolfe decided to chance an attack. Some of his ships were sent up the river well beyond Quebec, and then, on the night of September 13, 1759, men from these were floated downstream to the little cove where the pathway began. Luck was with Wolfe, for the French had arranged to run a convoy down the river on that night with supplies for the garrison. Thus, when the British ships were challenged by a sentry, a Scottish officer answered him in French, and they were allowed to pass with a close inspection. Landing under cover of darkness, the British troops overpowered the guards and clambered silently up the path, until Wolfe had four thousand men drawn up on the Heights of Abraham. When dawn broke, Montcalm was so taken by surprise that he had no time to make proper preparations for battle. He came with what forces he could gather, but they were no match for the British, and the battle did not last very long. Wolfe was mortally wounded in the hour of victory. As he lay dying, word was brought to him that the French were in retreat. " God be praised, I die happy " were his last words. Montcalm was also killed, and on September 18 Quebec surrendered to the British.

End of the War : The fall of Quebec did not immediately lead to the end of the war. The French rallied, and General Murray who was now in command of the British forces, had great difficulty in holding the city. Provisions were short, and the fate of Canada depended on whether British or French foodships should first arrive when the St. Lawrence thawed in the following spring. On May 9, 1760 the weary months of waiting ended, when a British fleet sailed up the river. Lord Amherst captured Montreal, and all the remaining French troops surrendered. The conquest of Canada was complete.

The Seven Years' War decided the struggle between Britain and France for North America. By the Treaty of Paris Britain got Canada and all the territory south of it between the Alleghany Mountains and the Mississippi. In return for this,

The taking of Quebec, 1759

[*The Parker Gallery, 2 Albemarle Street, London*]

the French were granted fishing rights off the coast of New-foundland and allowed to use the islands of St. Pierre and Miquelon as depots. The lands beyond the Mississippi were given to Spain to compensate her for the loss of Florida, which was ceded to Britain who now controlled the whole Atlantic coast of North America.

The Seven Years' War was a turning point in history. Britain had gained territory in India, in Africa and in the West Indies as well as in North America, and had thus begun her career as a colonial and naval power. For the American colonies the war was also important : it removed the menace of French domination and opened the way for expansion into the rich lands of the Mississippi Basin. But it also, as we shall see, cleared the way for a dispute between the British settlers and the mother country which terminated in the American War of Independence.

Questions and Exercises

1. Trace a large scale map of North America.

   (a) On it show the following physical features : the Alleghany Mountains, Hudson Bay, the Great Lakes, the St. Lawrence, the Ohio, the Mississippi, the Hudson river, Newfoundland.

   (b) Show the position of the English colonies, indicating by different colours (i) New England, (ii) the middle colonies, (ii) the southern colonies.

   (c) Mark by a broken line the French advance down the St. Lawrence, Ohio and Mississippi rivers, and name the forts of Ticonderoga, Crown Point and Duquesne.

   (d) Mark and name Montreal and Quebec.

   (e) Indicate the area with which the Hudson Bay Co. traded, and print in the principal commodities of its trade.

2. Describe the establishment and development of the English colonies in North America during the seventeenth century, and add a short note on the relations between them and the mother country.

3. Outline the career of General Wolfe, and describe the part he played in the conquest of Canada.

4. How would you explain the victory of the British over the French in North America during the eighteenth century ?

CHAPTER ELEVEN

John Wesley and
The Methodists

Early Life : John Wesley was born in 1703 at Epworth in Lincolnshire, where his father was rector of the Established Church. His mother, Susannah, was the daughter of a Nonconformist minister, who had been deprived of his living in 1662 because he would not accept the Prayer Book. She was a woman of strong character, who brought up a large family strictly and accustomed her children to a life of unremitting study and prayer. "None of the children," she tells us, " were taught to read until they were five years old. One day was allowed the child wherein to learn his letters ; and each of them did in that time know all his letters, great and small, except Molly and Nancy, who were a day and a half before they knew them perfectly ; for which I thought them very dull." They were kept at work from nine until twelve in the morning and from two until five in the afternoon. " It is almost incredible," writes Mrs. Wesley, " what a child may be taught in a quarter of a year, by a vigorous application, if it have but a tolerable capacity and good health."

After a few years of this stern grind young John was sent to school at Charterhouse, and later to Oxford, where he was entered at Christ Church in 1720. We know little of his life as an undergraduate, but he was probably a serious student, for he was elected a Fellow of Lincoln College at the age of twenty-

John Wesley, 1703–1791

three. His old father, who had gone into debt to keep his son at the university, was overjoyed at the news. " What will be my fate only God knows," he wrote. "Wherever I am, my Jack is Fellow of Lincoln."

The Methodists : By that time Wesley's younger brother, Charles, had come up to Oxford, and these two, along with a number of other men, used to meet in each other's rooms for prayer and meditation. They resolved to improve their lives and to give a good example to those around them. They took their studies seriously, received Holy Communion every Sunday in the college chapel, and visited the sick and the poor. But the other undergraduates were only amused by their pious practices and hurled all kinds of nicknames at the group. The one which persisted was that of *Methodist*. It was a jeering student who first shouted it after them, as they passed to church, and it was very apt for they did try to order their lives by rule or method. The name has survived to the present day, and is now used to describe one of the largest of the Protestant denominations.

Wesley in Georgia : In 1732 General Oglethorpe had founded the colony of Georgia, where poor people who had been imprisoned for debt might be given an opportunity of making a fresh start in life. He also hoped that the American state might become a refuge for persecuted Protestants in Europe, and invited a group of Moravians to settle there. In 1735 John Wesley, who was now ordained, decided to emigrate to the colony not only to minister to the English who were making new homes there but also to carry out missionary work among the Indians. A worse choice for the task it would be difficult to imagine. Wesley was at that time an uncompromising Anglican, with strict views on matters of ritual and Church discipline. The community he had to deal with was a motley crew of debtors and criminals, turbulent Scottish Highlanders and saintly Moravians. He tried to insist on baptism by immersion, expected his flock to attend church regularly, and would not allow the ladies to wear rich dresses or gold ornaments when they were present at his services. As might be expected, Wesley was soon extremely unpopular. With the Indians he had no greater success. Apart from the fact that they were too busy fighting to listen to his message, they were not very impressed by the Christians that they saw around them. Tomochichi, a chieftain, said to Wesley : " Christians lie, Christians steal, Christians beat me. Me no Christian."

Finally in despair, he returned to England, sick and depressed because of his failure.

Conversion : Shortly after his return Wesley came under the influence of a young Moravian minister named Peter Böhler, and began to attend meetings of the denomination at Aldergate Street in London. He was at this stage tortured by doubts about the reality of his faith (" a fair summer religion " he called it), and sought deliverance from " this evil heart of unbelief ". This condition did not last long, however. On May 24, 1738, while attending a Moravian meeting, he underwent a great emotional experience, which is usually described as his conversion. " I felt my heart strongly warmed," he wrote in the Journal which he kept of his life. " I felt I did trust Christ alone for salvation; and an assurance was given me that He had taken my sins, even mine, and saved me from the law of sin and death." This feeling remained with Wesley, and he determined to devote the rest of his life to preaching the doctrine of justification by faith to the people of England.

Some months after this he received an invitation from George Whitefield, one of the friends of his Oxford days, to come to help him with open-air preaching to the coal-miners of Kingswood, near Bristol. For a time Wesley hesitated about accepting, for field-preaching was frowned upon by the Church as irreverent and undignified. On the other hand the Kingswood miners had no church, and ministers never bothered about them. Eventually he decided to go, and on April 2, 1739 he preached to three thousand black-faced miners and labourers from a hill outside the town.

John Wesley had found his life work. For the next fifty years he travelled on horseback along the roads of England, Ireland, Scotland and Wales, preaching, teaching and organising. During that time he is said to have covered nearly a quarter of a million miles and to have preached over forty thousand sermons. As an example of physical endurance alone, Wesley's career is remarkable.

Wesley and the Church of England : Wesley did not intend to form a new religious body. A loyal member of the Church of England, he was careful not to hold his meetings in a parish at the time of the service in the local church. But the ministers were shocked by the manner of his preaching and by the weeping, shouting and hysteria which it caused. One by one they closed their doors against him, and so Wesley was forced to hold all his meetings in the open air. This was a blessing in disguise, for it brought him into contact with thousands who would never have entered a church.

Persecution : In the beginning Wesley was handicapped by a lack of helpers. At first he had only two : his brother Charles, who wrote hundreds of hymns for the movement, and George Whitefield, a preacher of rare eloquence, who contributed a great deal to the success of " the revival " in its early years. In 1741 a number of lay preachers were engaged, and, from then on, itinerant missionaries were to be found in the most out of the way places, making impassioned appeals to the crowds in market places, in wrestling booths and on the race tracks. This brought them into contact with some of the roughest elements in the country, and they were frequently heckled, abused and forced to flee for their lives. Every kind of intimidation was tried. In hostile areas innkeepers often refused to give them lodgings ; farmers would not allow labourers to attend their meetings ; even clergy were prepared to hire gangs to attack them. When Wesley proposed to visit the town of Colne in Lancashire, the following notice was posted up in the parish church :

" If any man be mindful to enlist under the command of

the Rev. George White for the defence of the Church of England, let him repair to the cross where he shall have a pint of ale and other proper encouragements."

Wesley and his disciples were not daunted by threats like these, and gradually the number of Methodists increased, especially among the poor and the uneducated. Gradually chapels sprang up where they congregated for prayer and hymn singing and to listen to the exhortation of visiting preachers. Periodically they were visited by Wesley himself, and every year the local societies sent delegates to the Annual Conference, where the founder addressed them.

Separation: Despite the opposition which he met from bishops and clergy up and down the country, Wesley retained to the end a deep affection for the Church of England and forbade his followers even to consider the question of separation. Yet it was his own actions that caused the division which eventually took place.

In the American War of Independence the Anglican ministers had taken the British side against the colonists. When the war ended, they were no longer welcome in America, and the majority of them returned home. This created problems, and it was scarcely possible to receive Communion from an ordained person in the whole of the United States. Wesley was concerned about this situation for he had many followers there. He tried to persuade the Bishop of London, in whose diocese America was placed, to ordain ministers for him, but, when the bishop refused, Wesley carried out the ordinations himself. He went even further and conferred episcopal powers on Dr. Coke whom he made bishop of the American Methodists. The Church of England, of course, did not recognise these orders as valid, and Methodism was on its way to become a separate Church. Against this Wesley made a heartfelt appeal just a year before his death in 1791. " I never had any design of separating from the Church; I have no such design; I do not believe that Methodists in general design it . . . I declare, once more, that I live and die a member of the Church of England and that

none who regard my judgment will ever separate from it."
Wesley's appeal did not succeed, and shortly after his death
the separation took place. Now there are welcome signs of the
two Churches coming together again in the more friendly
atmosphere prevailing today.

Importance of Wesley's Work : John Wesley was one of the
great men in British history, and it would be difficult to exaggerate the good effects of his work. He brought about a
religious revival. In the eighteenth century the Church of England was not in a healthy state. Of course, there were good
bishops who worked zealously for their people, but the majority
were careless and absented themselves from their dioceses for
months on end. They thought that they had done their duty
if they appeared in their cathedrals once or twice a year. They
never mixed with the people, rarely preached to their flocks,
and had no contact at all with the new mining and manufacturing villages that were springing up in the North and Midlands.
Many of the parish clergy were no better and gave their time
to hunting, shooting, fishing and drinking with the local gentry.
The result was that there were thousands of poor who never
went to church or listened to the word of God.

John Wesley went out into the slums and mining villages to
contact these people, and was horrified by the squalor and
wretchedness of their lives. To them he brought consolation
and hope, and as a result of his preaching there must have
been very many who tried to lead better lives. Even the Church
of England benefited from his mission, and, after he had
visited a place, there was invariably an increased attendance
at the parish church. The majority of Anglican clergy bitterly
opposed him, but there were many who were stirred into action
by his example and the religious life of the country improved
enormously.

Wesley had a great love for the poor and the under-
privileged, and did not spare himself in his efforts to remove
the social evils of his time. His book " Thoughts upon Slavery ",
published in 1774, was the first reasoned attack upon this

institution by a man of influence. He founded schools for the poor in many places and encouraged others to do the same ; he visited gaols and poor-houses up and down the country, and agitated for the improvement of conditions there ; he opened a dispensary at his London headquarters where the poor could get advice and free medicine. He distributed his money generously to all in need, and at his death could say in his will, " I leave no money to anyone because I have none."

Questions and Exercises

1. Give an account of the career of John Wesley and indicate the importance of his work.

2. Imagine you are an early Methodist preacher. Write a report to John Wesley describing a visit to a town in Lancashire.

CHAPTER TWELVE

Captain Cook and the Settlement of Australia

1. The Pacific Ocean

Ferdinand Magellan : The first man to sail across the Pacific Ocean was Ferdinand Magellan, a Portuguese sea-captain in the service of Spain. Leaving Seville in 1519, he followed a south-westerly course across the Atlantic until he reached Brazil, and then moved southwards along the coast of South America. He had made a close study of maps and charts before leaving Spain and was convinced that there was a channel through the continent about 40° South Latitude, which would lead him from the Atlantic to the seas beyond. But carefully though he searched he failed to find it and was forced to spend a long, hard winter in the stony desert of Patagonia. Eventually he did discover the strait which now bears his name between South America and the island of Tierra del Fuego. For five weeks he struggled against wind and rain through the strait until at last he reached the open sea again. All was calm and peaceful there, and he called it the **Pacific Ocean**.

The first stage of Magellan's journey had been successfully accomplished, and he expected that in a short time he would reach the Moluccas or the Spice Islands, which were his real objective. His ships were carried up the west coast of South America by the Chile and Peruvian current until they reached

the latitude of the Trade Winds. Then, with these winds filling
their sails, they were blown across the Pacific towards the
Philippine Islands. It was a terrible journey: the food was
done, the water had gone foul, and the sailors were driven to
chewing sawdust and the hard leather casing of the masts. Then
scurvy broke out, and one-third of the crew perished in a
voyage that took three months and twenty days. But despite
his heroic leadership Magellan was not to return home. In the
Philippines he got involved in a war between the kings of
neighbouring islands, and some of the natives put him to death.
One of his captains, Sebastian del Cano, then took command
of the expedition, and succeeded in bringing a single ship, the
Victoria, back to Spain around the Cape of Good Hope. They
arrived back in 1522, having taken three years to sail round
the world.

The voyage of Ferdinand Magellan has been described in
some detail, because it had a number of important consequences.
For one thing it proved that the earth was a globe; for another
it revealed to men for the first time the enormous extent of the
Pacific Ocean. In addition, since it was now known that there
was a great land-mass consisting of Europe, Asia and North
America to the north of the equator, men were convinced that
there must be a great undiscovered continent in the southern
hemisphere that helped to keep the earth in balance. This
continent they called the Terra Australis Incognita or the
Great Unknown South Land.

Terra Australis Incognita : It might be thought that sailors
would have been tempted to search for this continent, but for
many years no one seems to have made the attempt. The hardships which Magellan's crew had endured (out of 265 men
only 18 had returned alive) had created a fear of the Pacific
Ocean, and every subsequent sea-captain who crossed it followed
closely the route which Magellan had marked out. Large areas
of the ocean were thus unknown, and the most fantastic ideas
were held concerning it. Some sixteenth century cartographers
showed a great continent stretching across the bottom of their

maps, decorated with fabulous beasts and sea-monsters or strange men with huge feet who, when they wanted to lie in the shade, simply raised a foot to serve as an umbrella over their heads. Though other parts of their maps might be accurate enough, in the South Seas fancy had to take the place of fact.

The Dutch and New Holland: At the beginning of the seventeenth century a number of European sailors made voyages into the Pacific Ocean, but so jealous were the maritime powers of each other that any information which they discovered was kept a closely guarded secret. The first of these voyages was in 1605, when a Dutch fleet under Willem Janszoon, sailing from Java in the East Indies, reached the north coast of Australia and the Gulf of Carpentaria. In the following year a Spanish sailor, Luis de Torres, on a voyage from South America, traversed the strait which now bears his name between New Guinea and Australia ; he thus proved that the former was an island and not part of the Southern Continent as men had supposed. But it was not until a hundred and fifty-six years later, when the British captured Manila in the Philippines and found among the Spanish archives a map on which the Torres Strait was clearly marked, that the information became generally known.

Towards the middle of the seventeenth century the Dutch learned more about the west coast of Australia. Seamen in the employment of the Dutch East India Company discovered that the easiest and fastest way of reaching Java, after rounding the Cape of Good Hope, was to sail before the strong west winds of the Southern Hemisphere and then turn northwards for the East Indies. Captains who did not alter course soon enough were sometimes driven onto the west coast of Australia. The first to suffer this fate is said to have been Dirk Hartog in 1616, but he found the area so inhospitable that he did not remain for long. Other sailors had a similar experience, and gradually the west coast of what came to be called *New Holland* was quite well known—though nobody knew for certain whether it was part of the Great South Land or just another island. It was in the hope of solving this problem that Anton Van Dieman, the Governor of Java, sent Abel Tasman on a voyage of discovery in 1642.

Tasman's Voyage: Abel Tasman ventured farther south along the west coast of New Holland than anyone had done before him. He then turned eastwards and reached the island of Tasmania, which is now named after him, though he called it Van Dieman's Land in honour of the Governor. He remained there for several days before continuing his voyage but did not realise that he was on an island and not on the mainland of Australia. He then sailed northwards along the west coast of New Zealand, and proceeded via Tonga and the Fiji Islands back to Java from which he had set out. As a result of his voyage Tasman was convinced that New Guinea, Australia and Tasmania were part of one great island and did not stretch away to the South Pole as people had believed. He had missed completely the east coast of Australia, and thus the reports which he brought back about the area were anything but favourable : the only natives he had seen were primitive savages without capacity for work or trade, and the country did not appear to have any mineral or vegetable resources. The Dutch thus made no attempt to claim the area, and their voyages of discovery ceased.

William Dampier : The only Englishman to venture into the South Seas in the seventeenth century was a buccaneer, William Dampier, who has been described as " the mildest mannered man that ever scuttled a ship or cut a throat ". In 1688 he visited the north coast of Australia, and the description he gave of the land was no more attractive than that given by Abel Tasman:

" *The inhabitants of this country are the miserablest people in the world . . . Their hair is black, short and curled, like that of the negroes . . . The colour of their skins is coal-black, like that of the negroes of Guinea. They have no sort of clothes, but a piece of rind of a tree tied like a girdle round about their*

waists. They have no houses, but lie in the open air without
any covering, the earth being their bed and the heavens their
canopy. . . . Their only food is a small sort of fish. . . . There
is neither herb, root, pulse nor any sort of grain for them to eat,
that we saw ; nor any sort of bird or beast that they can catch,
having no instruments wherewithal to do so."

But on the great question as to whether there was still an
undiscovered continent in the South Seas Dampier had little
help to give. His final conclusion about Australia was : " It is
not yet determined whether it is an island or a main continent ;
but I am certain that it joins neither to Asia, Africa nor
America."

It is against this background of uncertainty that the voyages
of Captain Cook must be studied.

2. Captain Cook's Voyages (1768-1779)

Early Life : James Cook was born at Marton in Yorkshire in
1728. His father was a farm labourer, and, after he had left
school, the young James drifted into the same occupation.
Farming had little attraction for him, however, and, after a few
years, he began to look around for a career that would be more
exciting or more rewarding. His first change was not very successful. At the age of sixteen he went to work in a grocer's shop
at Staithes, a small fishing village on the Yorkshire coast. His
life was extremely hard : the hours were long, the food poor,
and he had to sleep under one of the counters at night. One is
not surprised to learn that, after two years of this treatment,
Cook ran away to sea, joining a collier that carried ' sea-coal '
from Whitby to London. He settled into the life at once, and
the ship's captain was impressed by his intelligence and devo-
tion to duty. At the captain's suggestion the shipowners decided
to take Cook into their service as an apprentice in order to
train him in navigation and seamanship. His progress was

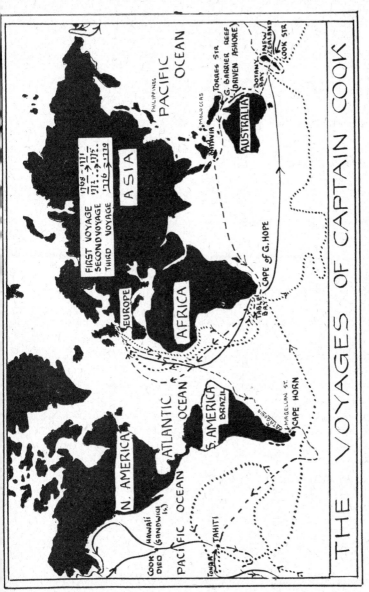

The Voyages of Captain Cook

remarkable. It was customary then for coasting vessels to be laid up for the winter, and Cook devoted these months to the study of books and charts that were likely to make him expert in his new occupation. Promotion came rapidly, and, in 1755, the owners offered him the command of their newest vessel, the *Friendship*. To their disappointment, however, Cook refused the offer. The Seven Years' War was about to begin, and so he enrolled as an able seaman on H.M.S. *Eagle* at Portsmouth.

With Wolfe in Canada : Cook had a great deal more knowledge and experience than the rest of the crew that had been collected by the press gang, and he was soon rated as a master's mate. His first two years of the war were not very exciting, for the *Eagle* was principally engaged in patrolling the south-west of Ireland and the French coast. Eventually Cook was made a master, transferred to a new ship, the *Pembroke,* and given the task of surveying and charting the St. Lawrence estuary, in preparation for an attack on the French possessions in Canada. Night after night he and the other masters moved quietly about the estuary, taking soundings and marking out a channel for the fleet. He took no part in the landing which led to the battle on the Heights of Abraham, but he had made a great contribution towards Wolfe's victory.

After the fighting was over, Cook remained in Canada to complete his survey of the St. Lawrence and of several other important waterways. This work occupied him for a number of years, and during it he gained the reputation of being the most skilful navigator in the Royal Navy. When an eclipse of the sun took place in 1766, he made a number of observations, and submitted an account of the event to the Royal Society. So impressed were they that they decided to publish his findings, and Cook thus won fame as an astronomer as well as a navigator.

Cook's First Voyage : Half a century earlier Edmund Halley had predicted that on June 3, 1769 one of the planets, Venus, would pass across the sun and that this event would enable scientists to calculate the distance of the earth from the sun. To obtain the best results, observations would have to be taken from widely separated parts of the world, and the Royal Society petitioned the government to fit out an expedition to the South Seas. The government agreed to do so, and invited Cook to take command of the *Endeavour* with a crew of 84 officers and men. His instructions were in two parts. In the first he was ordered to receive on board a number of scientists, including the naturalist Joseph Banks, and to proceed to Tahiti " to observe the passage of the planet Venus over the disk of the sun." When this was completed, he was to put to sea and to carry out the " additional instructions contained in the enclosed sealed packet."

On August 25, 1768 the expedition left Plymouth and sailed by way of Cape Horn to the Pacific Ocean. After a voyage of eight months they reached Tahiti, and on June 6, 1769 the transit of Venus was witnessed and recorded. But it was only when Cook opened his second set of instructions that the *real* purpose of the voyage became apparent. He was to search for the Southern Continent, and, if he found it, to " take possession for His Majesty by setting up proper marks and inscriptions, as first discoverers and possessors."

On August 9, 1769 Cook left Tahiti and sailed into the southern seas. He reached latitude 40° without meeting land, and so he altered course for New Zealand, which had not been visited since the time of Abel Tasman. It had been believed that this was part of the continent, but Cook showed that it was in fact two islands separated by a narrow passage—Cook Strait. He mapped the coastline of both islands, and on January 31, 1770 hoisted the Union Jack and took possession of New Zealand in the name of George III.

By this time Cook had come to doubt the existence of Terra Australis Incognita, and so he decided to return home by way of the East Indies and the Cape of Good Hope. On his way northwards to Java he unexpectedly sighted the east coast of Australia and landed at Botany Bay, a few miles south of the modern Sydney. As in New Zealand, Cook claimed the land for Britain and made markings on the trees to prove his discovery.

After a week there he continued northwards, exploring and
mapping the coast as he went. Then unexpectedly the
Endeavour ran aground on the Great Barrier Reef. For the
first time on the voyage there was panic on the ship : they were
thirty miles from land, and there were not enough boats to take
off all aboard. Worse still the provisions were nearly done. But
Cook remained calm and used all his skill to have the ship
refloated. Eventually he succeeded; the ship was repaired and
able to put to sea again. Cook then set out on his homeward
journey, sailing through Torres Strait and calling at Batavia
on the island of Java, where he remained for two months while
the *Endeavour* was being repaired. So far, Cook had lost only
eight of his crew, not one of them from illness, but in Batavia
malaria and dysentery were rampant, and men who had survived
two years of hardship at sea were struck down at once. After
two months in the port, Cook had scarcely enough healthy men
to work the ship as he set out for the Cape of Good Hope.
When at last he reached England, in July 1771, only half of
the original crew and four out of the eleven passengers were
still alive.

The most important voyage in the history of southern
exploration had thus been completed. Cook had shown that
Australia and New Zealand were two separate land masses, and
he had mapped the entire coastline of New Zealand and the
east coast of Australia. He did not believe that there was a
Southern Continent, apart from these, but as he had left large
areas of the seas unexplored he could not be sure. However, to
settle the question once and for all, he volunteered to undertake
a further voyage of discovery.

Cook's Second Voyage : The old ship, *Endeavour,* was in no
condition to stand up to another voyage. Instead Cook was
provided with two new vessels, the *Resolution* and the
Adventurer, and promoted to the rank of commander. This
time he planned to sail southwards in the Atlantic as far as
climatic conditions would allow. Then he would circumnavigate
the globe, and he was certain that, if the continent existed, he

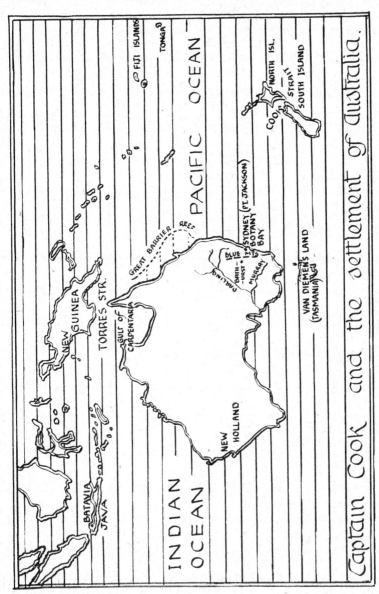

Captain Cook and the Settlement of Australia

must find it. The expedition set out on July 13, 1772, and the two ships were driven southwards by a steady breeze. By November they had passed the Cape of Good Hope, but shortly before Christmas great masses of ice barred their way. Cook decided to remain in the area to allow the men to celebrate the festival in the traditional manner. He entertained the officers to dinner in his cabin, while the crew was given an extra allowance of rum. Early in February, 1773 a dense fog came down and the two ships lost contact, but Cook decided to make a last attempt to force his way past the ice-pack. He sailed the *Resolution* across the Antarctic Circle but had to admit defeat, and so he steered a north-east course towards the Pacific Ocean. In the last week of March, 1773 he reached Dusky Bay on the south-west coast of New Zealand, and there he remained for a short time to allow his crew to recover from the effects of their long voyage. With the return of summer he sailed south again, making a last effort to discover the southern continent. This time he reached the latitude of 71° 10′ south—the highest that any ship had ever attained—but once more the icefields barred his way. By now Cook's health was beginning to break under the strain, and he tells us in his Journal : " I, who had ambition not only go further than anyone had been before but as far as it was possible for man to go, was not sorry at meeting with this interruption." After sailing from New Zealand to Tierra del Fuego, in order to ensure that the continent did not lie in the South Atlantic, he decided to return home. " If I have failed in discovering a continent," he said," it is because it does not exist in a navigable sea, and not for want of looking after."

On July 30, 1775 Cook returned to England after a voyage of three years. Though he had been at sea longer than any man in history, he had not lost a single member of his crew from scurvy. This he regarded as the greatest achievement of his second voyage. In his opinion it was due to the rigid rules for cleanliness on board. The crews were properly fed and given fresh vegetables when obtainable or orange and lemon juice. The Royal Society awarded him the Copley Medal for his contribution to the advancement of medicine and made him a Fellow. He was now famous, and George III presented him with a jewelled sword, while the Royal Navy promoted him to the rank of captain. It might have seemed that Cook had enough of adventure to do for a lifetime, but, within a year, he was off once more, this time to the northern seas.

Cook's Third Voyage: One evening when Cook was having dinner with Lord Sandwich, First Lord of the Admiralty, the conversation turned to the North-West Passage from the Atlantic to the Pacific Ocean, for which Frobisher, Davis and Hudson had searched in vain. Parliament had just offered £20,000 to the first man to discover it, and as the conversation developed, Cook became more and more enthusiastic. Finally he volunteered his services to lead an expedition up the west coast of North America to search for an opening from the Pacific to the Atlantic to the north of Canada. His offer was accepted as soon as it was made, and just one week after the Declaration of American Independence he left England on the *Resolution* once more (July, 1776). He rounded the Cape of Good Hope and sailed eastwards for Tasmania and New Zealand. From there he moved on to the Hawaiian islands in the Pacific, which he called the Sandwich Islands in honour of the First Lord of the Admiralty. The natives looked upon him as a god and bowed down before him when he landed. He stayed a month with them, before continuing his journey northwards to search for the Passage. Eventually he reached an inlet which gave promise of what he was seeking. It was in fact the estuary of the Cook River, and he sailed almost a hundred miles up it before realising his mistake. As he continued northwards fog and snow obscured the coast, and, had it not been for the plentiful supply of fish, their provisions would soon have been exhausted. Eventually north of Bering Strait the ice closed in on him, and he decided to return to Hawaii until weather conditions allowed him to try again. At first the islanders welcomed the two ships and prepared elaborate feasts for the crews. Then suddenly their attitude changed, and they began to steal from the boats. When Cook learned of this he was very angry and decided that the king should be held as a hostage until the property was restored. When he went ashore to make the arrest, a skirmish took place with the natives, in course of which the guns of the *Resolution* opened fire. Cook turned his back to the islanders to order the guns to cease fire, and, as he did so, the natives over-powered him and clubbed him to death. The date was February 14, 1779.

Cook's men were shocked by the tragic happening. One of them said : " We all felt we had lost a father." Negotiations were begun with the king of the island, and eventually the great explorer's mutilated body was handed over to Captain Clark who was now in command. The decks of both ships were lined with officers and men, and the flags were flown at half-mast. The body was placed in a coffin; the commander read the funeral service, and James Cook was laid to rest at sea, where so much of his life had been spent.

Cook was one of the greatest of British explorers. He mapped the coasts of New Zealand and Eastern Australia, and disproved a whole host of myths about the Southern Seas. He discovered and named many islands of the Pacific Ocean. He crossed both the Arctic and Antarctic Circles and twice sailed round the world. In addition he contributed to our knowledge of astronomy, prepared detailed and accurate navigational charts for the Royal Navy, and proved that the dreaded scourge of scurvy could be avoided at sea. These were remarkable achievements for one man, and entitle Cook to a place among the greatest sea-captains that the world has known.

3. The Early Settlement of Australia (1788-1815)

A Penal Settlement : Until the Americans rebelled in 1775, Britain had been accustomed to shipping her criminals to the colonies where the settlers used them for work in the plantations.

The Death of Captain Cook at Hawaii, 1779

[*National Maritime Museum, Greenwich Hospital Collection*]

After they had asserted their independence, however, the Americans refused to accept any more convicts, and the British government was forced to find an alternative dumping ground. Sir Joseph Banks, a scientist who had accompanied Cook on his first voyage, recommended Botany Bay as a suitable site for a penal settlement, and, after some delay, his suggestion was accepted. In May, 1787 a fleet was sent out under the command of Captain Arthur Phillip with over seven hundred convicts and two hundred marines aboard. After six months the expedition reached Botany Bay, but Phillip did not consider it suitable for his purpose and moved to Port Jackson, a few miles away. There the first permanent settlement in Australia was made, and called Sydney in honour of the Home Secretary. As with the early colonies in North America, it was expected that the settlers in time would become self-supporting, but in order to start them off properly Captain Phillip had been provided with seeds, tools and other equipment. But many of the settlers had no knowledge of agriculture, while others were hardened criminals who refused to work or obey orders. For a time the colony seemed doomed to failure, but then slowly it began to develop. Criminals who had completed their sentences were encouraged to remain, and, by degrees, people were induced to come from Britain and were given farms on which to settle. Captain Phillip remained in control until 1792, and, despite all his efforts, the settlement was on many occasions on the verge of starvation.

Sheep rearing : One development took place during these years which was of great importance for the future prosperity of Australia. John MacArthur, a retired soldier who had volunteered for police duty in the new colony, conceived the idea of developing a pastoral industry. The story of how the venture began can best be told in his own words :

" In the year 1794 I purchased from an officer sixty Bengal ewes and lambs, which had been imported from Calcutta, and very soon after I procured———two Irish ewes and a young ram. The Indian sheep produced coarse hair, and the wool of the Irish sheep was then valued at no more than 9d the lb. By crossing the two breeds I had the satisfaction to see the lambs of the Indian ewes bear a mingled fleece of hair and wool —this circumstance originated the idea of producing fine wool in New South Wales."

Some years later MacArthur imported merino sheep from the Cape of Good Hope and by careful breeding created a flock which produced wool of the highest quality. In 1801 he took specimens of this to England, and, so impressed were the experts by his achievements that the government granted him five thousand acres of the best pasture land on condition that he continued to produce wool and export it to England. Other men followed his example, and before long the area between the Blue Mountains and the east coast was dotted with sheep-runs.

Development of Australia to 1815 : So far, settlement was confined to the area around Botany Bay and Port Jackson, and the rest of the continent was a great blank about which nothing was known. The first attempt to move into the interior was made in 1813, when Gregory Blaxland led an expedition through the Blue Mountains and discovered the great grazing lands beyond. The Governor, Lachlan Macquarie, was quick to see the value of this discovery. He had a road constructed through the mountains so that people could move westwards easily from the over-crowded coastal plain to the empty lands beyond. He surveyed the land and encouraged settlement, and selected a site for the town of Bathurst. His task was made easier by the fact that, after the Napoleonic War, some of the disbanded soldiers, unable to find work at home, were prepared to try their luck in Australia. Six years later, in 1821, all restrictions on the emigration of free settlers to the colony were removed, and what had begun as a penal settlement gradually during the nineteenth century became one of the most prosperous parts of the British Empire.

Questions and Exercises

1. Trace a large map of the world. On it mark in different colours each of Captain Cook's voyages, showing the places he visited and the islands he discovered.

2. Write a short essay on the history of exploration in the Pacific Ocean before the time of Captain Cook.

3. Draw a map of Australia. On it mark and name the following:—

    (a) the areas visited by the Dutch sailor, Janszoon, in 1605;

    (b) the strait between Cape York and New Guinea named after a Spanish sea-captain;

    (c) the island visited by Abel Tasman in 1642. What did he call it?;

    (d) the area where Cook's ship ran aground on his first voyage;

    (e) Port Jackson and Sydney, where the first settlement was made in 1788.

4. Outline the career of Captain Cook, and give an account of one of his voyages.

5. Trace the development of the British settlement in Australia from 1788 to 1815.

SECTION THREE

The Age of Revolutions
1763-1815

Time Chart: The Reign of George III (1760-1820)

Great Britain	Ireland	Empire	Abroad
1761: Brindley's Canal			1763: Peace of Paris
1764: Hargreaves' Spinning Jenny		1765: Stamp Act	
1765: Watt's Condenser		1767: Townshend's Duties	
1769: Arkwright's Water Frame		1773: Boston Tea Party	1768–1779: Cook's Voyages
		1775: Lexington; Bunkers Hill	
1776: *Wealth of Nations* published		1776: Declaration of American Independence	
		1777: Saratoga	
1779: Crompton's "Mule"	1778: Irish Volunteers; Catholic Relief Bill	1781: Yorktown	
1780: Gordon Riots	1780: Free Trade; Repeal of Test Act	1783: Treaty of Versailles	
	1782: Legislative Independence; Catholic Relief Bill	1784: India Act	
1784–1793: Pitt's Reforms	1784: Foster's Corn Law		1789: French Revolution
1790: Burke's *Reflections on the French Revolution*	1791: United Irishmen		1793: Outbreak of War
1795: Speenhamland System	1795: Fitzwilliam Episode		1798: Battle of the Nile
1797: Spithead and Nore	1798: Rebellion in Ireland		
1799: Combination Acts	1800: Act of Union		1801: Copenhagen
			1802: Treaty of Amiens
			1805: Trafalgar
1806: Death of Pitt			1807: Berlin Decrees
1807: Orders in Council		1807: Abolition of Slave Trade	1808–1814: Peninsular War
			1809: Corunna
			1812: Moscow Expedition
			1813: Leipzig
			1815: Waterloo

CHAPTER THIRTEEN

The American Revolution

The conquest of Canada and the expulsion of the French from North America was a great triumph for the British and seemed to make secure for many years to come their empire across the Atlantic Ocean. Yet the Seven Years' War was hardly over before Britain and the colonies began to quarrel, and, only twenty years after her victory over the French, she was herself compelled to withdraw from the continent and to recognise the independence of the thirteen states which lined the east coast of America from New England to Georgia. Changes of this kind may occur suddenly, but they usually have causes that go far back into history. What these causes were and how the separation took place is explained in the following sections.

1. The Quarrel between Britain and her Colonies

The Old Colonial System: From the very beginning Britain had tried to control the trade of her American colonies. In this she resembled other European countries that had overseas possessions, for it was then generally assumed that colonies existed for the benefit of the mother country, by supplying her with raw materials which she could not supply for herself, and by purchasing her manufactured goods. In the seventeenth century a number of laws were passed, called Navigation Acts, ordering that all goods passing to and from America should be carried in British or colonial ships. The products of America such as tobacco, sugar and cotton could be exported only to Britain ; and the colonists were not allowed to have manufacturing industries in case they should compete with those of the mother country. Considering the sort of vigorous and enterprising men who had settled in America, one may wonder why they were prepared to tolerate this strict control of their trade. One explanation is that, while they feared the French, they could not afford to quarrel with the British as they might need their help. In addition, while laws in restraint of trade were passed by Parliament, they were not as a rule very strictly enforced, and thus the colonists ignored those that they found inconvenient. The Molasses Act of 1733 put a duty of sixpence a gallon on molasses imported into the colonies from the French West Indies; but the law was openly flouted and some of the wealthiest and most influential families in New England made their fortunes from smuggling.

When the Seven Years' War ended in 1763, things began to change. George Grenville, who became Prime Minister of Britain in 1763, was determined to enforce the trade laws as a means of compelling the Americans to contribute something towards the cost of defeating the French. He imposed a new tax of threepence a gallon on imported molasses and employed more customs officers to see that the law was obeyed. Vessels engaged in smuggling were stopped by British warships, and ' writs of assistance ' were issued to royal officials to enable them to search houses suspected of containing smuggled goods. The New England merchants and shipowners were furious—not because a new commercial system had been created, but because the old one was being strictly enforced for the first time.

The Western Lands : There was worse to come. The population of the colonies had grown steadily all through the eighteenth century, and land was becoming scarce on the eastern seaboard. Consequently the more ambitious and enterprising settlers began to move westwards through the passes of the Alleghany Mountains to found new homes on the plains beyond. When the French tried to stop this movement by building a chain of frontier forts along the rivers St. Lawrence, Ohio and Mississippi, they caused the Seven Years' War. Governor Dinwiddie had promised large estates in the Ohio Valley to those who would enrol in the militia, and, at the end of the war, companies were formed to supervise the distribution of the land. It is thus easy to understand the colonists' anger, when, in 1763, a proclamation was issued forbidding any settlement west of the Alleghany Mountains and reserving all lands beyond them as a Crown domain. We know now that the British government was concerned for the safety of the Indian tribes that inhabited the area, and wanted time to plan the settlement of the western lands in such a way that they would not suffer. But to the colonists it seemed that the British government was no better than the French : in colony after colony they decided to defy the proclamation, and land-hungry men like the famous Daniel Boone settled on the rich lands of the Ohio Valley.

The Stamp Act (1765) : But the action which caused most resentment amongst the colonists was the attempt to impose direct taxation in America. The British government had decided to keep a garrison of 10,000 soldiers there partly as a safeguard against a French war of revenge, partly in order to protect the settlers from the Indians. George Grenville thought that it was not unreasonable to expect the colonists to contribute towards the cost of the garrison and proposed raising £360,000 a year in the colonies. The Prime Minister suggested that this sum might be raised by means of a stamp duty levied on legal documents (licences, wills etc.) and on newspapers, but said that, if the method suggested was unacceptable to the Americans, he was prepared to introduce an alternative scheme. When no suggestions were forthcoming, Grenville passed his Stamp Act 1765. The reaction in America was violent. An organisation known as the ' Sons of Liberty ' was formed, and agitators like Samuel Adams of Boston excited the people by their inflammatory speeches against the British government. Before long, mobs were in the streets, attacking officials and burning down the houses in which the stamps were stored. The merchants, in their turn, resolved to import no more goods from Britain; while representatives of nine colonies met in New York and repudiated the right of the British Parliament to tax the Americans without their own consent.

Townshend's Duties : The government was shocked by the violence of the American protest, and it soon became obvious that the situation would require careful handling if the colonists were not to be driven into revolt. Two of the wisest statesmen of the day, William Pitt, who was now Earl of Chatham, and Edmund Burke advised the government to give way. Chatham did not believe Britain had the right to impose taxation on the colonists in this way. " We may bind their trade, confine their manufactures and exercise every power whatever," he said, " except that of taking their money out of their pockets without their consent." Burke argued that, even if Britain had the right to tax the Americans, it would be most unwise to do so at the present time, for it would probably lead to the loss of the colonies.

Before the government could decide how to tackle the problem, George Grenville and the King had quarrelled, and the Prime Minister was forced to resign. His successor, Lord Rockingham, decided to repeal the Stamp Act, but destroyed the good effect which this might have had by passing a Declaratory Act, saying that Britain had the right to tax her colonies if she wished. Peace was restored, but relations between Britain and her colonies could never be the same again, and from now on the Americans viewed every action of the government with suspicion.

In 1767 Charles Townshend, the Chancellor of the Exchequer, was short of money and succumbed to the temptation of trying to raise some of it in America. The colonists had always admitted the right of Britain to regulate their trade, and consequently Townshend proposed to impose duties on paper, glass, tea and paints imported into America. The colonists protested angrily that the new legislation was not for the purpose of regulating trade but for raising revenue, and they would not accept it. Once again there were meetings, riots and a boycotting of goods on which the duty had been paid. Once more the British Government yielded to the fury they had aroused, and Lord North, the new Prime Minister, repealed all Townshend's duties except that on tea.

The Boston Tea Party (1773) : Five years earlier the government's decision might have been acceptable to the colonists, but not now. On the same day as Lord North made his announcement in Parliament the first shots of the American Revolution were fired in Boston. On March 5, 1770, a party of British soldiers on duty outside a customs house were jeered at by a mob and pelted with snowballs. Eventually, losing patience, the soldiers opened fire on the crowd and killed several civilians. The 'Boston massacre' made reconciliation impossible, for the Americans had their first martyrs.

Tea drinking had practically ceased in the colonies, and, partly because of this, the East India Company was in financial difficulties. In order to help it, the government decided to allow the Company to send the tea direct from India to North America without calling at English ports as was the practice under the old colonial system. The result of this would be that, though the Americans would have to pay the duty of threepence a pound which had been imposed, they would get their tea at a lower price than they had previously paid. But the colonists were not impressed by this argument and regarded it as an attempt to persuade them to abandon their political principles. When the ships carrying tea reached North America, one port after another refused to allow them to unload their cargoes. In Boston, as usual, excitement was high, and on the night of December 16, 1773 a number of young men of the town, dressed as Red Indians, boarded the ships and dumped the tea in the harbour. This is the episode which is known in history as "The Boston Tea Party."

The Drift Towards War : No government could ignore such actions if it were to continue to rule. " The die is cast," wrote George III to Lord North. " The colonies must either triumph or submit." Parliament acted promptly, and a number of Acts were passed to punish the people of Boston. The port was closed to shipping until the tea, which had been destroyed, was paid for; Massachusetts lost the power of governing itself and was put under the control of General Gage, the British commander in North America, and it was decreed that certain offenders might be sent to England for trial. At once the other colonies sprang to the aid of Massachusetts, and arrangements were made for the holding of a meeting in Philadelphia in order to decide how to protect their liberties. All the colonies, except Georgia, were represented at this meeting of the Continental Congress on September 5, 1774, in the famous Carpenter's Hall at Philadelphia. The meeting expressed approval of the recent actions of the people of Boston and declared that, if force were used against them, " all America ought to support them." A boycott of British goods was ordered, and arrangements were made for the Congress to re-assemble in May, 1775, unless their grievances had previously been remedied. But before that date General Gage had clashed with the colonists at Lexington, and the War of Independence had begun.

2. The War of American Independence (1775-1783)

The Beginning of the War : The Assembly of Massachusetts continued to meet in defiance of the law. It organised an army of " minute men " (so called because they were ready for service at a minute's notice), and began to collect what arms and ammunition they could find. General Gage was worried by these preparations and believed that, if they were not stopped, the colonists would soon be in a position to attack. On the night of April 18, 1775, he sent a detachment of troops towards Concord, a town about twenty miles from Boston, to seize the arms

The American Revolution

that had been gathered there. The colonists soon learned of his plans, and one of them, Paul Revere, rode off through the countryside to raise the alarm. When morning broke, the British troops entered the village of Lexington to find a group of " minute men " barring their way. There was a moment of hesitation, and then a shot was fired. More followed, and, when the Americans retreated, they left eight of their companions dead behind them. The British troops continued their journey to Concord and destroyed what military stores they could find before they returned to Boston. But it was plain that war was now at hand. Volunteers from neighbouring colonies poured into Boston, and an army three thousand five hundred strong took up its position on Bunker Hill overlooking the town. Gage decided to disperse them before the army got any bigger, and made a frontal attack on the hill. The colonists stood bravely and held their fire until the British were only forty yards from their lines. They then opened fire and repulsed the soldiers with terrible effect. Three times did Gage send his men forward before the Americans retreated. Bunker Hill was captured by the British, but the engagement encouraged the Americans as much as victory.

The Declaration of Independence (1776): Meanwhile the second Continental Congress had met in Philadelphia on May 10, 1775, and appointed George Washington commander-in-chief of the American forces. Even yet many of its members were not prepared for complete separation from England and persuaded themselves that the war which they were beginning was being fought for the rights of Englishmen. But in the months that followed it became more and more difficult to keep up this pretence : in August, 1775 George III issued a proclamation declaring the colonies to be in a state of rebellion, and in the following month an army of twenty thousand German mercenaries arrived to crush the revolt. Finally on July 4, 1776, Congress took an important decision and issued the Declaration of Independence. It was drawn up by Thomas Jefferson, and in memorable words asserted the right of all men to choose their own form of government.

"*We hold these truths to be self-evident, that all men are created equal; that they are endowed by their creator with certain unalienable rights; that among these are life, liberty and the pursuit of happiness. That to secure these rights, governments are instituted among men, deriving their just powers from the consent of the governed; that whenever any form of government becomes destructive to these ends, it is the right of the people to alter or abolish it, and to institute a new government, laying its foundations on such principles, and organising its powers in such form as to them shall seem most likely to effect their safety and happiness.*

We, therefore, the representatives of the United States of America in General Congress assembled, appealing to the Supreme Judge of the World for the rectitude of our intentions, do, in the name, and by the authority of the good people of these colonies, solemnly publish and declare that these United Colonies are, and of right ought to be free and independent states; that they are absolved from allegiance to the British Crown, and that all political connection between them and the state of Britain is and ought to be totally dissolved."

This declaration made the break with Britain final, and today the date of its publication is celebrated as American Independence Day.

The Surrender at Saratoga (1777): The British commander, Howe, who had replaced Gage, moved his headquarters from Boston to New York, a more central position for the conduct of the war. In the beginning he had great success. Washington was defeated at Manhattan and White Plains; his army deserted him in droves, and only his brilliant little victory at Trenton saved him from total annihilation. But in 1777 the tide began to turn. Lord George Germain in London had devised a plan for ending the war. He proposed to send an army, under General Burgoyne, south from Canada towards New York and ordered Howe to march up the Hudson valley to join him. In this way it was hoped to cut off New England, the real centre of the rebellion, from the rest of the colonies, where there were still many settlers who were loyal to Britain. The scheme was a good one and would probably have succeeded had Howe carried it out as planned. But, thinking that he had plenty of time on his hands, the British commander decided to deal with Washington first. Instead of advancing up the Hudson he marched south into Pennsylvania, defeated Washington at Brandywine and occupied Philadelphia. Howe's delay was fatal for the success of the plan. Burgoyne had moved south from Canada, expecting to meet him. Instead he met a hostile population and an American army, under General Gates, much larger than his own. On October 17, 1777 he was surrounded at Saratoga and forced to surrender.

Intervention of France and Spain : The surrender of Saratoga was the most decisive event of the war. Nearly a quarter of the total British troops had been captured, and the Hudson was placed permanently under American control. George Washingon encamped at Valley Forge with what a contemporary writer called his " ragged, lousy, naked regiments " was given new hope of victory. Most important of all, it led to the intervention of France and Spain. Ever since their defeat in the Seven Years' War, the French had been waiting for an opportunity to get revenge on Britain. They had already been sending " unofficial " help to the colonists ; now they decided to come into the open, and in February, 1778 they entered the war. Spain and Holland followed their example shortly afterwards, while the northern powers of Europe—Russia, Denmark and Sweden—formed a league to resist British attempts to stop their trade with America. This changed the whole character of the war : faced with such an array of enemies Britain lost control of the sea and had difficulty in supplying her forces in North America. It was this loss of sea-power which made her defeat inevitable.

Washington giving last orders for the attack on Yorktown, 1781

[*The Parker Gallery, 2 Albemarle Street, London*]

Surrender of Yorktown (1781) : Sir Henry Clinton, the new British commander, made strenuous efforts to stave off disaster as long as possible. Concentrating on the more loyal southern colonies, he captured Charleston and occupied the greater part of Carolina. Then he marched northwards towards New York, leaving Lord Cornwallis to continue the campaign in the south. But Cornwallis allowed himself to be trapped in Yorktown on Chesapeake Bay by Washington, just at the moment when a French fleet under de Grasse gained control of the sea off the American coast. Cut off by land and sea, the position of Cornwallis was hopeless, and on October 19, 1781 he surrendered with eight thousand men.

The war continued in name for two more years, but Britain had lost all hope of victory. She did recover command of the sea when Admiral Rodney triumphed over the French at the Battle of the Saints in the West Indies in 1782, but this did not prevent her defeat. When peace was signed at Versailles in 1783, she recognised the independence of the thirteen colonies, and the United States of America began their history.

Causes of British Failure : The colonists might have been defeated in the opening stages of the war, if Britain had been able to employ large military forces against them. But America was six weeks' journey away, and officials at the War Office appear to have been ignorant of even the elementary geography of the areas where the fighting was going on. Many of the troops employed were not British but mercenaries hired from Germany, and they were placed under commanders who were accustomed to European methods of warfare and who found it difficult to adjust themselves to the guerilla tactics employed by the Americans. Howe, in particular, has come in for much criticism for his failure to carry out Lord Germain's plan. His delay was responsible for the surrender of Saratoga and for the intervention of France and Spain. These were the two decisive events in the war, for Britain could no longer concentrate her efforts on America, but had to fight in Europe and on the ocean as well. In spite of this, she might still have won had she not lost control of the sea ; but the Government had allowed the navy to fall into decay and paid dearly in defeat. Finally in George Washington the rebels possessed a leader of iron courage, who refused to give up when lesser men would have acknowledged defeat, and to him more than to any other single factor the victory of the colonists was due. The Americans showed their recognition of this fact by making Washington the first President of the U.S.A.

Questions and Exercises

1. Trace a large map of North America. On it mark and name the following :

   (a) The mountain range beyond which settlement was forbidden by the Proclamation of 1763.

   (b) The place where a famous 'tea party' was held in 1773.

   (c) The village in which the first shots of the War of Independence were fired.

   (d) The town in which the Declaration of Independence was adopted on July 4, 1776.

   (e) Saratoga where General Burgoyne surrendered.

   (f) Two defeats sustained by Washington and a victory which he won.

   (g) The town at which Lord Cornwallis surrendered in 178_

2. Make a time chart to illustrate the history of the British colonies in North America, 1607-1783.

3. Describe the causes of disagreement between Britain and her American colonies, 1763-1775. Could the war have been avoided ?

4. Trace the course of the War of American Independence, 1775-1783. Why did Britain lose ?

CHAPTER FOURTEEN

The Agrarian Revolution of the Eighteenth Century

During the years when Britain was at war with her American colonies and, later when she was engaged in a great struggle with Napoleon and France, significant changes were taking place in the economic and social life of the country—in the ways in which people lived, worked and travelled. For a long time historians were accustomed to refer to those changes as **revolutions**—the Agrarian Revolution, the Industrial Revolution, the Revolution in Transport—but more recently these terms have come in for a good deal of criticism. The word 'revolution' suggests a violent or sudden upheaval, a break with the past. Modern historians say that this did not happen. Change is continuous in history, and many of the developments in agriculture and in the manufacture of textiles, that are ascribed to the Agrarian and Industrial Revolutions, were already taking place before 1760. From the middle of the eighteenth century onwards these processes were accelerated to meet the needs of the time. We need not concern ourselves with these controversies, but it is well to remember that many of the subjects dealt with in this and the following chapter are being argued about by historians, and it is unlikely that there will ever be absolute agreement about them.

222

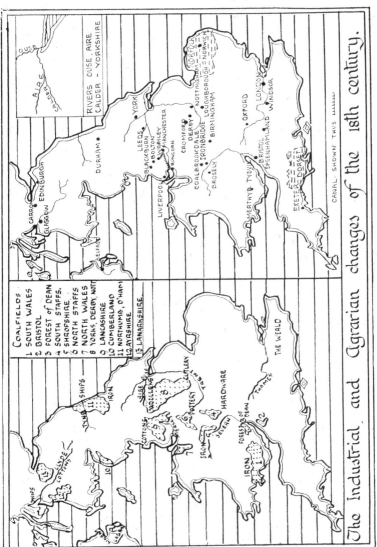

The Industrial and Agrarian Changes of the 18th Century

1. Population

Increase of Population : One subject on which there is no disagreement is the sudden rise in the population of England and Wales towards the end of the eighteenth century. The first official census was not taken until 1801, and so for the earlier periods we have to rely on estimates made by contemporaries. One of the most reliable of these was Gregory King, who calculated that the population of England and Wales in 1695 was five and a half millions. In 1801 it was nearly eleven millions, having doubled in the eighteenth century. Why did this increase take place ? There are two ways (apart from immigration) in which the population of a country may grow : one is by an increase in the *birth rate*, (i.e. more children are born each year), another is by a decrease in the *death rate*, (i.e. people live longer). We have not a great deal of information to go on, but what we have suggests that, of the two, the falling death rate was probably the principal means whereby the population grew. Better medicine, nursing and sanitation contributed in some measure, though doctors had still a great deal to learn about hygiene and surgery. The ' Great Plague ' of Charles II's reign was the last in British history, and the disappearance of the black rat after the ' Fire of London ' must have helped to reduce the death rate. Early in the eighteenth century cheap gin had been sold in London and brought squalor and death to the city slums. But in 1751 the Government increased the duty on spirits with noticeable improvements in the habits and health of the poorer classes. Another highly important factor was the better food supply which resulted from the great changes in agriculture that are described in the following sections. The people were freed from the monotonous diet of salted meat during the winter months, and the bread was finer, more wholesome and more abundant. Some changes in industry, such as the production of cheap cotton cloth and plentiful supplies of soap, must have been beneficial also, for the heavy woollen and leather garments that the people wore were often the breeding ground of germs and vermin.

Distribution of Population : England was still a country place, and, apart from London and a few other towns such as Bristol, Norwich, Exeter and York, the overwhelming majority of people lived in villages. Most of these were in the south and midlands, where the richest and most easily cultivated lands were. From about 1760 onwards, however, the population of the north began to increase, as wasteland was brought under cultivation, and as new textile manufacturing centres grew up in Lancashire and Yorkshire. The early factories were driven by water-power, and so were placed wherever there were fast running streams. Later, when steam had replaced water-power, the mills moved into the coalfields, and the great ugly towns of Lancashire, Yorkshire and the Black Country developed at an astonishing rate.

Where did the population of these new towns come from ? The important thing to remember is that there was no large-scale migration from the south to the north. As we shall see, some people did move from their villages after the farm land was enclosed, but they did not move far and usually settled in a nearby town. The stage-coach was not a cheap means of travel, and long journeys on foot would usually be confined to workers who had no families and few belongings. The new industrial towns of the north—Manchester, Leeds, Birmingham, etc.—recruited their inhabitants from the surrounding country-side and, in the case of Lancashire, from Ireland. The popula-tion of Ireland was growing rapidly at this time also, and a large number of people migrated to Britain in search of work and opportunity.

The growth of population meant that there were more people to feed, and this was achieved by bringing more land under cultivation and by introducing the new and more efficient methods that are described below.

2. Consolidation and Enclosure

The Open-Field System : Until the middle of the eighteenth century probably as much as half of the arable land of England was still being cultivated according to the open-field system. Under it, the arable land of a village was apportioned in three large fields, each of which was divided into acre or half-acre strips. Every landowner held a number of these strips, but they were widely scattered through the three fields in order to ensure a fair distribution of good and bad land. These fields were very much bigger than any that we have today, and with their ploughed strips running in all directions they must have looked like a huge patch-work quilt. Only two of the fields were cultivated at a time, and thus each field was idle (or fallow) every third year. A traditional pattern of cropping was followed, which had not changed much for hundreds of years.

Field	1st Year	2nd Year	3rd Year
A	Wheat	Barley	Fallow
B	Barley	Fallow	Wheat
C	Fallow	Wheat	Barley

A man had to farm in accordance with the custom of the village, sowing and harvesting the same crops at the same time as his neighbours. A group of villages would combine to provide a plough team or implements, but each farmer kept what grew on his own strip.

Apart from the arable land, each village had a large stretch of common pasture on which the inhabitants grazed their animals, and meadow-land which provided the fodder for winter use. Surrounding the village was a great stretch of waste and forest from which the farmers obtained timber for fuel and for building purposes, and in which the pigs sometimes grubbed for roots, nuts and acorns under the trees.

Changes in the System : Open-field farming was widely practised in England up to the middle of the eighteenth century, but it was not universal. Other systems were followed in the north-west and south-west, while large tracts of northern England were so thinly populated that there was little cultivation at all. Even in some areas where open-field farming was practised, the system was modified as villagers exchanged strips to get all their land together in one piece. The land was then generally enclosed or fenced, and thus the name *enclosure* was given to this method of changing the open-field system.

In the fifteenth and sixteenth centuries enclosures on a large scale took place for sheep rearing. There was a great demand abroad for English wool, and so in those areas where climatic and soil conditions were suitable the large farmers converted their arable land into pasture. The area principally affected was a wide belt stretching from Lincoln through Northampton and Leicester to Warwick, and then south to include Bedford and Buckingham. The Tudor Government were opposed to this movement and passed laws to prevent it, but they had not a great deal of success, and enclosure for sheep rearing went on until the end of the sixteenth century.

After the Restoration the attitude of the Government to enclosure began to change. This was mainly because enclosure was now being made for the purposes of improved agriculture, and the authorities were prepared to support any change that would provide more food for the growing population. On these enclosed lands farmers were no longer bound by the custom of the village, but could experiment with new methods and new crops. One example of this was the field cultivation of turnips. At the end of the Tudor period these had been grown in some gardens, but they were regarded as delicacies and were not cultivated on a large scale. After the Restoration Sir Robert Weston, who had been a refugee in Flanders, published a *Discours on the Husbandrie used in Brabant and Flanders,* in which he praised the methods of the Flemish farmers, especially their large scale cultivation of turnips and clover. Some English landowners followed his advice, and Lord Townshend (1674-1738) developed a four year rotation (usually called the *Norfolk rotation*) of turnips, barley, clover, wheat, which successfully eliminated the fallow-field. In other areas, too, and, especially in Kent and Essex which catered for the London market, farmers began to specialise in such commodities as milk, meat, fruit and vegetables.

These developments are dealt with at some length because it is too often taken for granted that all the great improvements in English agriculture took place during the reign of George III (1760-1820), and not enough credit is given to the pioneers. They were exceptions, of course, and the majority of farmers were satisfied to use their land as their ancestors had done before them.

Defects of the Open-Field System : By the middle of the eighteenth century the open-field system still survived in a broad belt stretching up the centre of England from Dorset in the south to Yorkshire in the north. This contained some of the most fertile land in the country, but it was not producing all the food it was capable of, and, as the population increased, the defects of the open-field system of agriculture became more obvious. It was wasteful of land : one third of the arable land was not producing crops at a time when there was a scarcity of food. It was wasteful of time, for a man's strips were often widely scattered through the open fields. If he had a careless neighbour, he found it almost impossible to keep his land free from weeds. Thirdly, it was impossible to rear good cattle and sheep, partly because all the animals of the village grazed together on the common and disease passed rapidly from herd to herd ; partly because there was always a great shortage of hay for winter fodder. In the autumn most of the cattle and sheep were slaughtered, and their carcases were salted and stored in barrels for human consumption. But the greatest defect of all was that every farming operation was determined by the custom of the village : the cropping of the fields followed a traditional pattern, and thus it was impossible for a farmer to experiment with any of the new crops or rotations that were being used in other areas.

Causes of Change : Scarcity of food naturally produced a rise in prices. Wheat, which had averaged 30s. a quarter in the 1730s, sold for over 50s. a quarter in the 1780s. When war broke out with France, this price rise was intensified, and even the most old-fashioned farmer was tempted to change his methods in the hope of making money. Where all the land-owners of a village were agreeable, the land was redistributed, and each farmer was given a compact farm equal in area to the scattered strips he had held in the open fields. But this did not happen often, and, in the majority of cases, it was necessary to coerce at least a minority of landowners into agreement. The Government was now in favour of enclosure and sanctioned the break-up of the open-field system in every case in which the owners of four-fifths of the strips were in its favour. They, of course, might amount to only three or four large landowners, while the remaining one-fifth of the strips might be occupied by a hundred or more small farmers. The enclosures were consequently often highly unpopular, but the poorer villagers could do little to stop them.

Method of Enclosure : There was a separate enclosure act for each village, and, once it was passed, commissioners were appointed to redistribute the land in compact farms. Their first duty was to determine the amount of land held by each villager in the open fields, and to enquire into all other rights that he might claim. They recognised only legal rights and paid little attention to custom. This was very hard on the *squatters,* the landless labourers who had built cottages for themselves on the waste and who were usually permitted to graze their few animals on the village common. What remained after all legal claims had been met was given to the local squire or lord of the manor, who as a result became enormously wealthy. Many farmers felt that they had been cheated, and a rhyme popular at the time was

> " The law arrests the man or woman
> Who steals the goose from off the common

But leaves the greater rascal loose
Who steals the common from the goose."

Enclosure was an expensive business, and the landowners of a village had to meet its entire cost. This included the expense of getting the Bill passed through Parliament, the fees and expenses of the commissioners, the cost of the survey and the preparation of maps. And this was only a beginning. If the farmer wished to make the best use of his holding, he had to enclose it with hedges and fences, build new barns and sheds, and introduce new stock, seeds and equipment. Many of the smaller farmers found these costs beyond them and were forced to sell their property to their wealthier neighbours. This accelerated a process which had been going on in England from the seventeenth century, whereby the farmland was passing into fewer and fewer hands. But it would be a mistake to assume, as some historians have done, that these " dispossessed yeomen " all moved into the towns. Some of them did so, of course, but a considerable number of them leased new farms from the great estate owners, and, using their money as capital, began to introduce the agricultural improvements that are described in the following section. Others, less enterprising, frittered away their money and sank into the position of landless labourers.

End of the Enclosure Movement : We have seen that enclosure was not a new phenomenon and had gone on quietly all through history. But whereas the earlier enclosures had been usually carried out in defiance of the law, those of the eighteenth century had the sympathy of Parliament which did everything to help them. The result was that the number of enclosures increased steadily : in George I's reign sixteen enclosure acts were passed, in George II's reign two hundred and twenty-six, in George III's reign nearly two thousand. The population of the country was continuing to increase, and more food was needed to feed them, especially in the new manufacturing towns that were springing up in the north and midlands. This was the great stimulus to enclosure, for it was obvious that heavier and better crops were being produced on the new farms. In 1801 a General Enclosure Act was passed simplifying the procedure, and so, by the end of the first quarter of the nineteenth century, the open-field system had practically disappeared. Today only the village of Laxton in Nottinghamshire retains the system, and it is being kept alive there by the Ministry of Agriculture as an example of England's agrarian past

3. Improved Methods of Agriculture

More Food : One immediate effect of enclosure was an increase in the output of agricultural produce. The fallow field was eliminated and the rotation of root crops with cereals, which had been first popularised by Lord Townshend in Norfolk, was adopted by the country as a whole. It was soon generally realised that the farmer, by growing turnips and clover, could restore the fertility of the soil sufficiently to put an end to the traditional year of rest. This led to a huge increase in the area of land under crops, but it did more : The turnips could be used as fodder for the cattle during the winter, and it was no longer necessary to slaughter so many of the animals at the end of autumn. This helped to make fresh meat more plentiful.

Improving Landlords : There were improvements, too, in implements and machinery and in the way of sowing seed. The traditional method of sowing corn was for the farmer to scatter the seed by hand on either side of him as he walked about his fields, in the way that is described in the Parable of the Sower. As early as 1701 a Berkshire man, Jethro Tull, had invented a machine called a 'drill', which sowed the seeds in rows and covered them over with soil, so that the farmer was able to grow crops twice as heavy as before, using only one-third of the seed. Thirty years later Tull published a book called *"Horse-hoeing Husbandry"* in which he stressed the value of hoeing between the rows of growing plants, but the methods which he advocated could not be easily used in the narrow strips of the open fields and had to await the coming of compact farms.

Another great improving landlord of the period was Thomas Coke of Holkham, later Earl of Leicester. When he inherited the family estate in 1776, one of his witty friends told him that he would find " one blade of grass and two rabbits fighting for it ". Coke changed all this. He enriched the soil by a process known as marling (that is by adding lime and clay to the sand), and was soon growing wheat as good as any in the country. He was one of the first Englishmen to study systematically the growing of nutritious grass, and in this way he continuously increased the number of animals his acres would support. He encouraged his tenants to imitate his methods, and every year he distributed prizes to the farmers who obtained the highest yields. Soon visitors from all parts of the country and from Europe were coming to study his methods, and his annual sheep-shearing ' festivals ' were attended by huge crowds. When he succeeded to the estate, it was worth £2,200 a year; when he died in 1842 at the age of ninety, he had a rent income of £20,000, which gives an indication of the value of the new methods of farming.

Stock Breeding : Under the old open-field system farm animals had been of poor quality. Cattle were thin, long legged and bony, valued for their pulling power rather than for their meat; sheep were small and produced a very light fleece. No care was taken in the selection of animals for breeding, and, as the cattle and sheep of a village grazed together on the common, it was impossible to check or eradicate diseases. In the eighteenth century a number of farmers turned their attention to this problem. Chief among them was Robert Bakewell, who farmed an estate at Dishley, near Loughborough in Leicestershire, and specialised in the breeding of cattle and sheep. He was particularly successful with his sheep and produced a new breed of " Leicestershires ", which were famous for their mutton as well as their wool. As a result of Bakewell's work and that of other stock-breeders, such as Charles and Robert Colling of Durham, there was a remarkable improvement in the weight of cattle and sheep sold in the Smithfield market in London during the eighteenth century, as the following figures show :

	Cattle	**Calves**	**Sheep**
1710	370 lbs.	50 lbs.	38 lbs.
1795	800 lbs.	150 lbs.	80 lbs.

Arthur Young : But the knowledge of improved methods possessed by a few enlightened men was not sufficient to cause a revolution in agriculture. Information travelled slowly in the eighteenth century, and news of what we have been describing took a long time to reach isolated parts of the country. Even then many farmers were reluctant to try out new ideas. One of the first to realise the need for propaganda and instruction was Arthur Young. Starting in 1767, he travelled up and down the country, passionately urging the need for enclosures as a first step to better farming. His industry was immense. In every district which he visited he carefully noted the methods that were used, and in 1784 he began the publication of the *Annals of Agriculture* in order to circulate information. He helped to found farmers' clubs and agricultural societies, and sponsored ploughing matches and competitions. Finally in 1793 Young persuaded the Government to establish a Board of Agriculture (not a government department but a national society), and he became its first secretary. Another factor which helped to make the new farming popular was the patronage of the King. George III established a model farm at Windsor and took a personal interest in its management. The aristocracy imitated the King, and it was fashionable to be an up-to-date farmer.

Prosperity and Poverty: After war had broken out with France in 1793, Britain had to depend on her own food supplies. These were not sufficient, even with the new methods of cultivation, and bread was scarce and dear. Corn cost two or three times

Arthur Young

[*National Portrait Gallery, London*]

as much as in the pre-war years, and this encouraged farmers
to concentrate on the growing of cereals. It also stimulated
land enclosures in the remaining open-field villages. Land of
every description was brought under the plough, and the
incomes of the larger farmers soared. Rents rose also for those
who had leased their lands from the estate owners, but these
were cheerfully paid by men who were making large profits.

The farm labourers did not share in this prosperity. Their

wages rose but did not keep pace with the rising cost of food, and soon men, who had never been fairly paid, were in a desperate plight. Many drifted into the towns to work in the mills, but some refused to leave the country and sank deeper and deeper in poverty. Eventually something had to be done, and, on May 6th, 1795 the Berkshire magistrates met at the Pelican Inn of Speenhamland, near Newbury, to consider " the insufficiency of the labourers' wages ". Our method of dealing with this problem would be to fix a just wage and compel the farmers to pay it to their workers. But the magistrates decided to pay an allowance from the poor rate to bring up a labourer's income to a living wage. The allowance paid depended upon the size of the labourer's family and on the price of bread. The magistrates meant well, but their action had disastrous consequences. Their scheme was adopted by nearly every county in the south and midlands of England and was known as the *Speenhamland System*. Farmers did not now care whether they paid their labourers a living wage or not; they knew that the magistrates would make up their wages to an adequate amount. Indeed a labourer often found that he could not get work unless he first became a pauper. The poor rate was very heavy, for the ratepayers had to meet part of the farmer's wage-bill. Worst of all were its effects on the worker. A man likes to feel that by his own efforts he can support his wife and family, but no matter how hard he worked he was a pauper, depending on the poor rate for part of his income. Despite its many defects, however, the Speenhamland System remained in operation in England until 1834.

Questions and Exercises.

1. Discuss the factors which affected (a) the growth and (b) the distribution of population in England during the second half of the eighteenth century.

2. Describe the land arrangement of an open-field village, and give an account of its system of farming.

3. What were (a) the good effects and (b) the bad effects of the eighteenth century enclosure movement ? How did it differ from earlier enclosure movements ?

4. Describe the part played by each of the following in the making of a better system of agriculture : Lord Townshend ; Robert Bakewell ; Arthur Young.

5. Write informative notes on two of the following :
(a) Jethro Tull ; (b) Coke of Holkham ; (c) the Speenhamland System.

CHAPTER FIFTEEN

The Revolution in Industry and Transport

1. Textiles: Wool and Cotton

Woollen Cloth: Apart from agriculture, the principal English industry was the manufacture of woollen cloth. The cloth was not made in large factories as it is today, but in the homes of country people. Originally it was not intended for sale but to supply the needs of the household, and every member of the family took part in its manufacture. When a farmer sheared his sheep, the wool was washed to remove the dirt and grease, and the children " carded " it with metal combs to disentangle the fibres. His wife and daughters next spun the wool into yarn, and finally the farmer himself wove the yarn into cloth on his handloom. At first the cloth was coarse and unattractive, but gradually its quality began to improve. This was partly due to the increasing skill of the textile worker, but more to the large number of Flemish and French Huguenot weavers who settled in England in the sixteenth and seventeenth centuries. These devoted all their time to the industry and introduced new techniques and machines. At first the manufacture of woollen cloth was carried on in all parts of the country, but some areas began to specialise. Fine cloth was made in the West Country and exported through Bristol and Exeter ; East Anglia concentrated on hard-wearing worsteds ;

the Aire and Calder valleys of the West Riding of Yorkshire specialised in many kinds of cloth, and soon became the most important centre of the industry. Eventually wool, which had once been exported to the continent in large quantities, was all required at home, and after 1660 its export was forbidden.

The Clothiers : As a result of the improved quality of English cloth the demand for it abroad increased, and enterprising merchants did everything possible to increase the output. There grew up a class of men called *clothiers,* who rode around the country buying up wool in bulk, which they then put out to be worked through the different processes—spinning, weaving, dyeing, fulling, finishing—until the cloth was ready for sale. The various tradesmen that the clothier employed still worked in their own homes and usually owned the machines and tools they used. They were paid for the work they did and controlled their own working conditions. Very many of them were farmers who undertook the manufacture of woollen cloth as a spare time occupation, to which they turned in winter or in other slack periods on the land. But there was an increasing number of men who devoted all their time to the textile trade. Some of these were employed by clothiers and worked under their supervision in large workshops, but the majority lived in their own homes and decided their own hours of work. It is because of this fact that the term *domestic system* (Latin domus : a house) has been used by historians to describe the way in which the industry was organised.

Defects of the System : The domestic system enabled the workers to live in their own homes and to own their own spinning-wheels and looms ; but it would be a mistake to assume that their lives were easier or more pleasant than those of the modern factory worker. The ' piece-rates ' paid by the clothier were, as a rule, very low, and in order to make a living men and women were obliged to toil long hours in their dreary and badly ventilated cottages. Even small children were expected to take part in the work, and Daniel Defoe in his *Tour of Great Britain* (1724-1727) remarks of Colchester that " there

The Domestic System. This picture shows the women of a family all busily engaged in the spinning and reeling of yarn. The yarn was then woven into cloth by one of the male members of the family or by a local weaver.

was not a child in the town or in the villages round it of about five years old but, if it was not neglected by its parents and untaught, could earn its bread ".

From the point of view of the clothier the system had a number of defects also. Much time was wasted in travelling around the country to collect the wool and in transferring it from craftsman to craftsman. Workers were not under his supervision, and thus, if a man were busy with farming operations or decided to take a holiday, the material the clothier was expecting might not be ready when he called. There was a great deal of the wool wasted by inefficient or dishonest workers, and the clothier had no means of determining whether the cloth, which was returned, represented the whole of the raw material that he had distributed.

Cotton: A second textile industry was the manufacture of cotton cloth, but for a long time it was of little importance compared with that of wool. The raw materials of the industry were first imported from Asia Minor by merchants of the Levant Company, who carried on trade with the Eastern Mediterranean, and later by the East India Company. The manufacture could not be as widely dispersed as that of woollens, for the brittle cotton threads snapped if spun in a dry atmosphere. Hence the industry was located in Lancashire, where the moist westerly winds provided the atmospheric conditions required. Up to the middle of the eighteenth century a number of factors hampered the development of the industry. The raw material was comparatively scarce, as it was not until after the American colonies had gained their independence that the large-scale cultivation of cotton began in the southern states. Secondly, English manufacturers had not yet succeeded in producing a cotton yarn that was strong enough for the *warp* (as the long thread in a piece of material was called), and so the cloth they produced was not fine cotton but was mixed with linen and wool. Finally the method of spinning was so slow that it usually took seven or eight spinners working hard to provide enough yarn to keep one weaver employed. Unless some faster way of producing yarn could be found, the manufacture of cotton cloth could not be increased.

The Spinning Jenny (1764): In the eighteenth century a great deal of attention was given to this problem, and several unsuccessful attempts were made to speed up the production of yarn, before James Hargreaves invented the 'spinning jenny' in 1764. Hargreaves was a Blackburn weaver and carpenter, who loved tinkering about with machines. One day when his wife's spinning wheel had been knocked over, he noticed that the wheel continued to turn, and he got the idea of a machine on which a single wheel could turn six or eight spindles, so that one person could produce six or eight times as much yarn as previously. This was a simple and inexpensive piece of machinery which could be used by the worker in his cottage, and

This picture gives some idea of how large and crude the machines were in factories and bleachworks in the early stages of the Industrial Revolution.

thus, though it greatly increased the output of yarn, it did not destroy the domestic system. The new machine was taken up rapidly in Lancashire, and it is estimated that twenty thousand were in use by 1788. But the jenny had one serious defect : the yarn which it produced was not strong enough to be used for the *warp* or long thread.

The Water-Frame (1769) : A few years later another Lancashire man, Richard Arkwright, invented a machine which turned out a stronger thread. Arkwright had begun life as a barber and wig-maker, but the wearing of wigs went out of fashion and he was forced to take up a new occupation. He turned to cotton and before very long devised a new spinning machine which was called the water-frame. Unlike Hargreaves' jenny this did not resemble the spinning wheel at all. It consisted of a number of pairs of rollers, each pair turning faster than the one in front of it and thus stretching the cotton wool into a thread that was strong enough to be used for both *warp* and *weft*. It was now possible to make a material composed entirely of cotton.

The new machine was worked by water and was too expensive to be used in the cottages. Large buildings were erected on the banks of fast-flowing rivers to house a number of machines, and workers were employed to operate them. This was the beginning of the *factory system*. In 1771 Arkwright established a spinning mill at Cromford, on the banks of the river Derwent in Derbyshire, and began to produce cotton yarn in large quantities. The spinners, who worked at home, found that they could not compete with the new machines and attempted to burn down the factory. Arkwright was not deterred by these threats but went on to build more factories in Lancashire and Scotland. He was a man of great business ability rather than an inventor (his ' frame ' was an improvement of the earlier machines of Wyatt and Paul), who devoted his whole life to the development of the cotton industry. When he died in 1792, he left a fortune of £500,000.

The Mule (1779): The only drawback with Arkwright's water-frame was that the yarn it produced was somewhat coarse. What was needed was a machine which could turn out both fine and strong thread, and enable cotton cloth of the highest quality to be produced. This was invented by Samuel Crompton of Bolton, when he combined the best features of of Hargreaves' jenny and Arkwright's water-frame to make a new machine which he called a mule. At first he used the machine only to supply his own needs as a weaver, but the finely woven materials which he produced eventually aroused the curiosity of his neighbours. He was persuaded to make the machine public, on the understanding that a subscription would be taken up for his benefit. But once they had learned how to construct and work the 'mule', the local manufacturers treated Crompton badly, and the public subscription raised only £67 6s. 6d. This angered and embittered him, and, when later he invented a carding machine, he smashed it to bits, crying "They shall not have this too." In the end the nation realised its debt to Crompton (fine muslins which had hitherto been imported from India were now manufactured in England), and Parliament made him a grant of £5,000. But this did little more than pay his debts, and he died penniless in 1827.

Result of Inventions : The jenny, the water-frame and the mule among them had revolutionised the cotton industry. Great quantities of raw material were now being imported from America, and towns were springing up in Lancashire around the new mills. In the beginning these mills were placed where the rivers came rushing down from the Pennines, in order to take advantage of the water-power, but in 1785 steam was first used to drive the cotton-spinning machinery, and factories moved down to the coalfields. More yarn was now being produced than the weavers could use, and there was a great demand for their services. The 'piece-rates' which they were paid rose accordingly, and weavers could be met strolling about the streets of northern towns, carrying £5 notes in their hat-bands to impress their less fortunate neighbours.

The Power Loom (1785): The prosperity of the hand-weavers did not last long, however, for efforts were already being made to devise a machine for manufacturing cloth. As early as 1733 John Kay had invented the 'flying shuttle' to speed up the process of hand-weaving, but yarn was scarce at that time and his machine was not generally adopted. What was required now was a power-driven loom to take advantage of the vast quantities of yarn that the spinning mills were capable of producing. Most men in the business thought that this was impossible, but a clergyman, Edmund Cartwright, who knew nothing about machines and had never seen a weaver at work, decided to try. His first attempts were very clumsy, but, in 1785,

Cartwright at last made a weaving machine and used one of James Watt's engines to drive it. Cartwright naturally encountered a good deal of opposition from the hand-weavers, who feared that their independence and prosperity were threatened ; but manufacturers adopted and improved on the loom, and by 1832 there were 100,000 power-looms in use in England and Scotland. The effect on the output of material was startling. Where previously an experienced weaver, working full-time, took a week to make 48 yards, now a boy of fifteen and a girl of twelve operating the power-loom could produce 432 yards, i.e. nine times as much.

Changes in the Woollen Industry : Mechanisation was much slower in the woollen than in the cotton industry. There were several reasons for this. The supply of wool was limited to what England could produce, and there were enough workers to deal with it. Not until the great sheep-runs were established in Australia and New Zealand, early in the nineteenth century, were abundant supplies of raw material available. Then factories grew up in Leeds, Bradford, Halifax, Huddersfield and other towns, and the West Riding of Yorkshire became the centre of the woollen industry. Other areas like Gloucestershire, Wiltshire, Devonshire and East Anglia declined in importance, and the making of worsteds, which took its name from the village of Worstead in Suffolk, left that district completely and was concentrated in Bradford. But change was slow, for woollens was an old-established industry with conservative habits, and hand-loom weavers continued at work into the second half of the nineteenth century. They are still to be found in rural areas of Ireland and Scotland and have no difficulty in selling their tweeds.

Factories and Towns : The inventions which we have read about in this section brought about a revolution in the textile industries and had a startling effect on the lives of the people engaged in them. Under the domestic system, as we saw, the worker usually lived in his own home, owned the tools he used and decided when he would begin and finish his job. With the introduction of costly machinery this was no longer possible, and the manufacturer employed the workers on his own premises, and under his own supervision. Most of these factories were quite small at the beginning, but they grew larger as the demand for English textile goods increased abroad. The early machines were driven by water-power and were concentrated in the upland valleys, but eventually they moved down into the coal-fields to be near the source of power. Towns grew up around them, and little care was taken in choosing the sites or in planning the lay-outs. They were not yet as big as they were later to become, but most of them were already ugly places. Tall chimneys blackened the sky with their smoke, and the workers lived in mean little back-to-back houses without sanitation or running water. The country people who came to settle there were not accustomed to the congestion of urban life and piled up their refuse in passages and streets thus providing a breeding ground for germs. The factories themselves were dirty and unhealthy, and hours of work were long. Twelve to fourteen hours a day were common, even for the little children, since the manufacturers wanted to get as much work as possible out of their expensive machines. " Whilst the engine runs the people must work," wrote a contemporary. " The animal machine . . . is chained fast to the iron machine, which knows no suffering and no weariness." The wealth of England was increasing by leaps and bounds, but at a great cost in human health and happiness.

2. The Iron and Coal Industries

Charcoal and Coke : The early machines used in the cotton industry were not made of iron but of wood. Iron was very scarce in Britain, not because there was a lack of ore but because there was a lack of fuel to smelt it. For centuries the fuel used for smelting was charcoal, and the principal iron-producing areas were the Weald in Sussex, the Forest of Dean in Gloucestershire and the Wrekin district of Shropshire. But the timber resources of these areas were almost depleted, and by 1740 Britain was producing less than 18,000 tons of iron a year. Coal was tried instead of charcoal, but it was found that the sulphur, which it contained, mixed with the iron and made it brittle. However, in 1709, Abraham Darby of Coalbrookdale in Shropshire discovered that iron could be smelted successfully with coke. His son, also called Abraham, improved on his father's process and prevented a deterioration of the metal by the use of limestone. The Darbys kept their new process secret for a long time, but in the second half of the eighteenth century it became generally known. From then on the iron industry left its old home in the forests and moved to the areas of the north, the midlands and South Wales where coal and iron were found in close proximity.

Henry Cort : Abundant supplies of cast iron were now available, but it was easily broken and not suitable for the engineering industry. A successful and quick method of producing wrought or malleable iron was discovered by Henry Cort in 1784 : it was known as ' puddling '. The pig-iron was heated by coal and stirred with long hooks, until the impurities were driven off in the form of gas. The iron was then passed between rollers, and sheets of any thickness could be produced.

Revival of the Iron Industry : Britain had large deposits of coal and iron, and so these new processes gave a great fillip to the iron industry. Just as the cotton inventions produced great mill-owners like Arkwright, so the new methods brought forward a number of outstanding ' iron-masters '. John Roebuck established the Carron Works near Falkirk in Scotland and made cannon for the Peninsular War. Anthony Bacon held the lease of all minerals for miles around Merthyr Tydfil, and Samuel Walker founded the great iron industry of Rotherham. But the greatest ' character ' of the age was John Wilkinson, whose works were at Broseley, near Coalbrookdale. He had such faith in the material he manufactured that he wanted to use it for every purpose. He made the first iron barge and sent it by canal to Birmingham; he built an iron bridge over the Severn; he proposed to make iron houses and iron roads—and, at his death, he left instructions that he was to be buried in an iron coffin. It is easy to understand why he was called ' Iron-mad Wilkinson '.

Coal : Small quantities of coal had been mined on nearly all the modern coalfields, but there was not the same demand for it as there is to-day, and the pits were small, employing only a few men each. One great difficulty was that of transporting the coal, for the roads were bad, and the only important coal exporting area was Tyneside, whence " sea-coal " was sent by boat to London. The coal was quarried only from deposits near the surface, as in open-cast mining today, for it was found very difficult to keep deep digging free from water or to raise the coal to the surface. Even before the increased demand for coal came in the second half of the eighteenth century, all sorts of devices had been used to draw off water but without a great deal of success. In 1698 Thomas Savery invented a steam-pump for the purpose, but it was unable to work at great depths and was superseded by the more efficient one invented by Thomas Newcomen in 1709. The new engine could pump water from the deepest mines but used a great deal of coal when doing so. As it was used mainly on coalfields this was not a serious defect, and many hundreds of Newcomen's pumps were installed in the eighteenth century.

James Watt : In 1757 a model of Newcomen's engine, used for demonstration purposes in the University of Glasgow, was given to a young laboratory technician named James Watt to repair. Watt took the opportunity to study its principles, and, after experimenting with it for a number of years, he designed a new machine that consumed only half as much coal as Newcomen's and was far more efficient. He was not able to develop his invention until he met Mathew Boulton, who owned the Soho Works in Birmingham. The two went into partnership, and Boulton and Watt, one of the most famous firms in the history of engineering, was born. Boulton supplied the capital for the enterprise, while Watt devoted all his time to experiment and research. In 1769 they patented the steam-engine. It was used only for pumping water from mines at first, but eventually it was applied to all sorts of machinery, and, in 1785, the first steam-powered cotton mill was opened at Papplewick in Nottinghamshire.

Ventilation : Now that the main obstacle to mining had been overcome, workings were going deeper than ever. But the problem of ventilation remained. Some small improvements were made in the eighteenth century; boys were employed underground to open and close trap-doors and to operate fans to control the dangerous gases, but as a burning candle was the only means of illumination explosions were frequent. In such conditions loss of life was so common that inquests on victims of pit disasters were never held. Eventually a mining engineer, named John Buddle, invented a fan which sucked foul air up one shaft of the mine and caused fresh air to rush down the other. But it was only with the introduction of Sir Humphrey Davy's safety lamp in 1815 that the mines could have illumination without danger.

Working Conditions in the Mines : The output of coal increased enormously to meet the demand. The five million tons produced in 1770 had doubled by 1800, and doubled again by 1820. Industry everywhere was demanding coal—textiles, hardwear, engineering, pottery, glass-making etc.—and existing mines were worked more extensively and new ones were opened. Working conditions underground were terrible. Women were harnessed like animals to trucks and sometimes crawled on all fours dragging heavy loads behind them. Children of eight or nine sat in dark corridors for long periods, opening and closing the trap-doors that controlled the ventilation, or worked beside the miners filling the trucks with coal. Brutality was common, and miners wore leather belts which they used to beat the children when they were too weary to work any more. The excessive labour from an early age, the long hours of darkness, the dust-laden atmosphere—all these combined to give the miner a distorted and stunted body, and usually brought him to an early grave. But they persisted well into the nineteenth century, for it was not until 1842 that the employment of women and children in mines was forbidden.

3. A Revolution in Transport

English Roads Before the Eighteenth Century : Nowadays roads are built and kept in repair by the Government or by the county and district councils, and skilled surveyors and engineers are employed for the purpose. But in the eighteenth century the Government did not do work of this sort, and local councils, as we know them, did not exist. The result was that English roads were in a very bad condition. In 1555 Parliament had passed a law making each parish responsible for its own roads : the big landowners were to provide the horses and carts, and the poor people were to give six days' unpaid labour. But the country people had little interest in their roads and avoided their responsibilities when they could. Even when the work was done, it was not done very carefully. Some gravel or broken stones were thrown into the larger holes and ruts, and, in a short time, the roads were as bad as ever. The best way of getting from place to place was on horse-back, women riding pillion behind the men. Goods had to be carried in this way also, and long lines of mules or ponies with great packs strapped on their backs plodded along the roads of England. In winter movement was almost impossible, and people living in remote areas spent months in isolation.

Turnpike Roads : After the Restoration efforts were made to improve this situation, and, in 1663, Parliament passed a *Turnpike Act*, permitting the justices of the peace to put the main roads of a district into good order and to collect a toll or fee from all who used them. There was a fixed charge for every farm animal, horse and vehicle that moved along the road, and the money collected was to be used for its improvement and repair. But the system was not a success and was later modified. In 1706 a number of influential men in Buckinghamshire came together and agreed to improve a certain road at their own expense. They sought the approval of Parliament, and an act was passed, permitting them to erect a gate at each end of the road and to collect tolls from all who used it, on condition that the money was to be expended in keeping the road in good repair. This was the first *turnpike trust,* and it was so successful that there was a steady increase in their number all through the eighteenth century, especially in districts where coal, iron and manufactured goods were being moved to factory and town.

Some of the turnpike trusts did their work well, charging reasonable tolls and keeping their roads in excellent condition. Others were mainly concerned with making a profit and enriching themselves. Arthur Young, whom we read about in the last chapter, encountered some dreadful turnpike roads on his journeys about England in the 1770's. Describing the road from Preston to Wigan in Lancashire, he says : " This turnpike is very bad. I know not terms sufficiently impressive to describe this infernal road. Let me most seriously caution all travellers to avoid it as they would the devil ; for a thousand to one they may break their necks or their limbs by overthrows or breakings down. They will here meet with ruts which I actually measured four feet deep and floating with mud—only after a wet summer; what therefore must it be after a winter? The only remedy that it receives is the tumbling in of some loose stones, which serve no other purpose but jolting a carriage in the most horrible manner. These are not merely opinions but facts, for I actually passed three carts broken down in these eighteen miles!"

The Road Builders : The bad condition of turnpike roads was not always due to the carelessness or dishonesty of those who controlled them. Often they just did not know how to make good roads, for since Roman times little thought had been given to the subject. In time, however, some of the trusts began to engage skilled men to make and repair roads for them, and so the new profession of surveyor or road-builder came into being at the end of the eighteenth century. Famous amongst these road-builders were John Metcalfe, Thomas Telford and John Macadam.

John Metcalfe (1717-1810) : A Yorkshireman, John Metcalfe contracted the dreadful eighteenth century disease of small-pox when only six years old and lost the sight of both his eyes—hence he is often called 'Blind Jack of Knaresborough', and he wandered from town to town, playing the fiddle and dealing in horses. During the second Jacobite rebellion he recruited men for the government forces and was present at the battle of Culloden. On his return to Yorkshire, he continued to peddle his goods from town to town, and, in 1754, he started a stage-coach service between York and Knaresborough. His fame, however, rests on his skill as a builder of roads and bridges. In 1765 a turnpike trust engaged him to improve the road between Harrowgate and Boroughbridge. He did the work so speedily and so efficiently that his services were in great demand. His greatest achievement was a road through the Pennines from Huddersfield to Manchester, which connected the industrial areas of Lancashire, Yorkshire and Derbyshire. Metcalfe laid his road on a firm foundation of stone blocks, cambered it so that rain water would run off into a ditch on either side, and surfaced it with broken stones.

Thomas Telford (1757-1834) : Telford was probably the greatest of these eighteenth century surveyors and ended his career as first President of the Institute of Civil Engineers. The son of a Scottish shepherd, he began life as a stone-mason and worked for some time in Edinburgh. But he was ambitious, and, in 1782, he set off for London taking only his hammers and chisels in a pack. He worked in the capital for a number of years and showed such skill at his trade that he was appointed surveyor of public works for Shropshire, and supervised the building of the Ellesmere Canal. In 1802 the Government made him chief engineer of a large scheme for improving communications in the Scottish Highlands, and during the following ten years he built nine hundred miles of roads and over a hundred bridges. He built the Caledonian Canal in Scotland and the Gotha Canal in Sweden. His last great achievement was to improve the road from London to Holyhead and to build the famous Menai Suspension Bridge joining the mainland to Anglesea. Travel between England and Ireland was increasing, and this made the journey less dangerous and more convenient.

John Loudon Macadam (1756-1836) : John Macadam was also a Scot but spent part of his early life in America, where he acquired a fortune before he was thirty years of age. He then returned home and settled in the west of England. He had always been interested in roads, and, now that he had the leisure and means at his disposal, he began to travel about the country to study the different methods of construction that were being used. Before long he was recognised as an expert, and in 1815 he was appointed surveyor for the Bristol turnpike trust. This gave him an opportunity to put his theories into practice. Unlike Telford, he did not lay a strong foundation, which he maintained was expensive and quite unnecessary. He dug down to the subsoil which was drained and levelled and then covered over with a layer of small stones. The wheeled traffic ground a fine powder from the stones, which, when mixed with rain, formed a smooth and waterproof surface. Roads made in this way were less expensive than those of Telford, and Macadam's method was widely copied. The nation recognised its debt to him, and in 1823 Parliament made him a grant of £10,000.

Coaches : The improvement of the roads was reflected in the vehicles. The stage-coach had first appeared in England about the middle of the seventeenth century, but it was heavily built

Travelling by Stage-coach in the Eighteenth Century

and uncomfortable, and, owing to the condition of the roads, was used only in the summer months. But, after the improvements we have described, lighter and faster coaches were built, and services were begun between most of the big towns. The fastest and most punctual coaches were those which carried the mails. They followed time-tables strictly and had fresh relays of horses at stopping places along the route. The result was that travelling time between towns was greatly reduced, and it was possible to get from London to Exeter or to Manchester within a day. Ordinary stage-coaches had to improve their services to compete with them, and travelling conditions improved immensely. The period 1790 to 1830 was the golden age of the stage-coach, and as many as six hundred coaches left London every day for all parts of the country.

The Problem of Heavy Goods: No improvement in road

transport was adequate to meet the demands now being made by industry and trade. What was needed was a cheap and reliable method of moving fuel, raw materials and manufactured goods in increasing quantities over long distances. The roads were unable to cope with this amount of traffic, and so, wherever possible, bulky goods were sent by river or by sea along the coast. There was a limit to what could be done in this respect, however, as many of the new industrial centres were not on navigable rivers. The only solution to their problem was to bring water to them by building canals.

The Bridgewater Canal : The most famous of these canals was that built between 1759 and 1761 to connect Worsley and Manchester. The Duke of Bridgewater had opened up a large colliery on his estate in order to supply the needs of Manchester. At first he used pack horses to carry the coal, but they did not carry enough at a time and took too long to cover the seven miles between his estate at Worsley and Manchester. Coal accumulated in great heaps at the colliery, while manufacturers in Manchester went short. These circumstances convinced the Duke that, if he could cut a canal from his colliery to the city, he would render a public service by providing a cheap and reliable coal supply for the inhabitants, and at the same time he would probably make a fortune. He engaged James Brindley to plan and build the canal. Brindley was an uneducated genius, who had already helped Josiah Wedgwood in modernising the pottery industry of Staffordshire. He began his work at Worsley and cut a channel south-westwards towards the river Irwell. There he met his first great test—the carrying of the canal across a river—but he built a great aqueduct on three arches across the Irwell and continued the journey to Manchester. Even then his difficulties were not over, for the canal had to be carried over Trafford Moss on a raised embankment, and it did not reach Manchester until 1761. The scheme was a great success. Coal was moved more quickly now and cost only half its former price. The Duke was so pleased that he began another canal, leaving the first at Trafford Moss and running to the Mersey estuary at Runcorn. This large canal became known as the Bridgewater Canal, and, when it was completed in 1776, it brought the Duke an income of £100,000 a year.

By the end of the eighteenth century England possessed a network of canals, connected with one another and with the navigable rivers. Birmingham was the centre of the system and was joined to London, the Bristol Channel, the Mersey and the Humber. One of the most interesting of the canals was that connecting Liverpool with Leeds, begun in 1769 and not completed until 1810. It had to be lifted, by means of locks, through a height of five hundred feet, and for a mile of its course ran in a tunnel bored through the Pennines.

Benefit of Canals : During the period 1790 to 1840 the canals provided the chief means of transporting heavy and bulky commodities about the country. Food was conveyed from the agricultural areas of the south and east to the factory towns of the north and midlands. Coal, iron ore, china clay and building materials were nearly always moved by canal, while manufactured goods were sent on barges to the merchants in the towns or to the ports for export. Any individual might use the canal, on condition that he paid a toll and provided his own horse and barge. Each canal was built by a different company, and there was no uniformity of width or depth. Thus long distance traffic had to be loaded and unloaded as goods passed from one waterway to another. But despite this defect the canals were a boon to the manufacturer and merchant, and unified the country in a way no other transport system did until the coming of the railways.

Questions and Exercises.

1. Describe the system under which the manufacture of woollen cloth was carried on in the eighteenth century. What were the defects of the system ?

2. What contributions to the development of the cotton industry were made by each of the following : James Hargreaves; Richard Arkwright; Samuel Crompton ?

3. Describe the " revolution " in the iron and steel industry during the eighteenth century.

4. Explain the growth of demand for coal after 1760. What difficulties had to be overcome before the demand could be met?

5. "The need for more efficient transport became urgent in Britain during the eighteenth century." Why ? How was the need met before 1815 ?

6. Describe the career of James Brindley and indicate the importance of his work.

CHAPTER SIXTEEN

Ireland 1775-1800:
The Volunteers and the
United Irishmen

1. Henry Grattan and the Volunteers

Grattan : Henry Grattan was born in Dublin in 1746. His father was a leading member of the Irish Bar, and his mother was the daughter of a Chief Justice. It is not surprising, therefore, that young Henry aspired to the legal profession, and, after graduating from Trinity College in 1767, he went to London to study at the Middle Temple. He remained there for five years, and, when he returned in 1772, he was called to the Irish Bar. He soon discovered that the life of a barrister had no appeal for him, and he found himself more and more attracted to politics. He was a supporter of " the Patriot Party," to which we have earlier referred, and a close friend of its leader, Henry Flood. Consequently when Lord Charlemont offered him a borough seat in 1775, he immediately accepted it.

Political Aims : Grattan had three great political aims :

  (i) the removal of all those restrictions which hindered
      the development of Ireland's overseas trade;

    (ii) the repeal of Poynings' Law and the Declaratory Act of 1719;

    (iii) the repeal of the penal laws against Catholics.

The first two aims were those of the " Patriot Party," but in the third Grattan was, at this time, far in advance of the other political leaders. Lord Charlemont and Henry Flood were willing to allow Catholics to practise their religion freely and even to own landed property; but they were absolutely opposed to their being granted any political rights at all.

The New Leader : Grattan entered the Irish Parliament at an exciting time. Flood had just accepted from the Government the post of Vice-Treasurer of Ireland, with a salary of £3,500 a year, and had left the " Patriot Party " without a leader. Grattan stepped forward to take his place, and for the next twenty-five years his whole life was centred on the Irish House of Commons.

The American War: The entrance of Grattan to public life was marked by another important event : the outbreak of war between Britain and her American colonies. It was only natural that the " Patriot Party " should take a great interest in that struggle, for they believed that the colonists' grievances were substantially their own, and that, if the right of the British Parliament to impose direct internal taxation in America were admitted, then a similar fate awaited Ireland. As a Dublin newspaper said : " By the same authority as the British Parliament assumes to tax America, it may also and with equal justice presume to tax Ireland, without the consent or concurrence of the Irish Parliament."

Apart from that, large areas of America were almost wholly settled by people from the north of Ireland, and some of the most vigorous leaders of the colonists were of Ulster birth or descent. The Presbyterians were especially interested, for as the Rev. Steele Dickson of Portaferry pointed out in a sermon : " There is scarcely a Protestant family of the middle classes

Henry Grattan

among us who does not reckon kindred with the inhabitants of that vast continent." In the *Belfast Newsletter* the events of the opening stages of the war were described so fully that all other news was crushed out, and James Magee, a Belfast bookseller, published a large-scale map of the northern colonies so that the struggle could be followed in all its details.

Very little of this pro-American feeling was represented in Parliament, and, when the House of Commons met in October, 1775, the members pledged their support to the King "in the assertion of his just rights". Permission was also granted for the withdrawal of four thousand troops from Ireland for service in America. But, after France and Spain entered the war in 1778 and enemy ships began to appear on the seas around the British Isles, some people began to fear for the safety of the country, now that a large part of the army was serving abroad. Matters came to a head in April, 1778, when an American privateer, named Paul Jones, sailed into Belfast Lough and captured the *Drake*, a naval sloop that was anchored there. The merchants of Belfast at once appealed to the Government for protection, but were informed that all they could have was "a troop or two of horse and part of a company of invalids" (i.e. reservists unfitted for active service). It was clear that, if the town was to be defended, the people would have to undertake the task themselves.

The Volunteers: In 1760, when the French had landed at Kilroot and captured Carrickfergus, the people of Belfast had combined to defend the town. They decided to do the same now, and, in a short time, they had formed three Volunteer companies, all arrayed in the most colourful uniforms : the First Belfast Company with scarlet tunics turned up with black velvet, white waistcoats and breeches; the Belfast Volunteer Company, known as ' the Blues ' from the colour of their uniform ; the Belfast Union in scarlet faced with blue.

The example of Belfast was followed by the country as a whole, and soon there were forty thousand men in arms. It was essentially a Protestant movement, and for a long time Catholics were not admitted to its ranks. In the towns, it was officered by the leading merchants or the local clergy, while, in the country, landlords usually organised their tenants under their command. The Lord Lieutenant, Buckinghamshire, watched the growth of this new army without enthusiasm, the more so as the leading members of the " Patriot Party" had been active in the movement from the start. The Earl of Charlemont was a prominent spirit among the Volunteers of the north ; the Duke of Leinster commanded the Dublin Volunteer Company, and Henry Grattan the Dublin Independent Volunteers. Indeed there can have been few members of the " party " who did not wear the uniform of some company raised in their constituencies.

The Lord Lieutenant's fears were justified, for, shortly after their formation, the Volunteers began to interest themselves in the great political questions of the day, and the " Patriot Party " decided to use them to force 'free trade' from a reluctant British Government.

Free Trade for Ireland (1780) : As the American War developed, the British Government found it more and more difficult to obtain sufficient food to supply the needs of the soldiers and sailors. England, with its growing population, could not provide this alone, and so in 1776 an embargo (i.e. a prohibition) was placed on the export of Irish provisions, in order that they might be available for the army's use. In all the big centres of the provision trade—Cork, Limerick, Waterford, Belfast—government contractors bought up supplies of beef, pork, butter and flour, and shipped them to England. Through time these purchases caused a scarcity of some foods, and unscrupulous merchants began to charge very high prices. In Derry, for example, butter, which had cost 4d. a pound in 1776, rose to 8d. a pound in 1778, and the price of potatoes trebled from 2d. to 6d. a stone. The poor suffered greatly from this rise in prices, and in several southern towns hungry mobs tried to prevent the removal of food supplies by government buyers.

The " Patriot Party " decided to take advantage of this

situation, and, when the Irish Parliament met on October 12, 1779 Grattan urged the necessity of government action to relieve the country's distress. The members felt strongly on the matter, and a resolution in favour of free trade was adopted by the House of Commons. The British Government gave an ambiguous answer, and so the Volunteers decided to throw their influence behind the resolution. On November 4, William III's birthday, they paraded round his statue in College Green, with two cannon decorated with placards bearing the words, 'Free Trade—or this'. Four days later, a draper's shop was sacked and cleared of English goods, while the Attorney General's home was attacked by a mob. Grattan followed this up by moving a resolution in Parliament that it was "inexpedient to grant new taxes". Many of the Government's most faithful supporters voted for the resolution, which was carried by 170 votes to 47. The Lord Lieutenant advised the British Government to give way, and at the beginning of 1780 the restrictions on Irish trade were removed. Ireland could export woollen goods and glass, and the trade of the colonies was thrown open to her. Grattan and the Volunteers had won their first victory.

Religious Toleration : During these years there was also a growth of religious toleration, and two important relief acts were passed, one for Catholics, the other for Presbyterians. By Gardiner's Act of 1778 Catholics were given the same rights in land ownership as Protestants : they could buy land, inherit it or take it on long leases. An estate owner was no longer compelled to divide his land, at death, among all his sons, but could hand it on intact to his heir.

The Presbyterians benefited also. In 1780 the Test Act was repealed. From now on they could hold official positions and were put on an equal footing with members of the Church of Ireland. When news of this reached Belfast on March 6, 1780 the town was brilliantly illuminated, and an address of thanks was sent to the King.

The Dungannon Convention : Having achieved his first

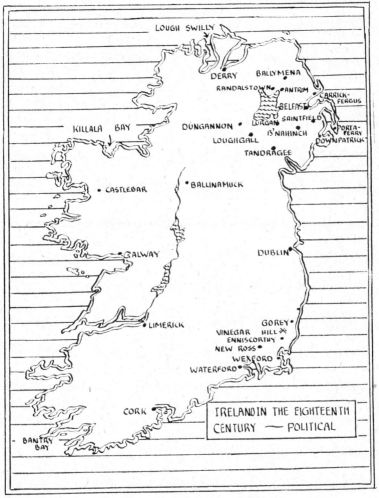

Ireland in the 18th Century—Political

political aim, Grattan now resolved to concentrate on his second : the repeal of Poynings Law and the Declaratory Act of 1719 (sometimes called *the Sixth of George I*). Once more he relied on the assistance of the Volunteers, and during the years 1780-1782 many new companies were organised throughout the country, until there were 80,000 men under arms. Efforts were also made, in some counties, to combine the separate companies into regiments. The first move in this direction took place in the north, when the officers of all the Armagh companies met at Tanderagee in January, 1780 and agreed to form a regiment under Lord Charlemont. The idea proved popular and, by the summer of 1780, most of the companies of Down and Antrim were joined in larger units and were meeting together for reviews and manoeuvres. This not only made them better soldiers; it also gave them an opportunity to discuss political questions and to decide on the best means by which the Volunteers could help the " Patriot Party " in their effort to obtain an independent Irish Parliament. Their opportunity came soon.

On April 19th, 1780 Grattan moved a resolution in the House of Commons that " no power on earth save the King, Lords and Commons of Ireland has the right to make laws for Ireland ", and supported it by one of his most famous speeches. It was obvious, however, that the Government had organised a majority against the resolution; and it was not proceeded with. This annoyed the Volunteers of Ulster, and they arranged for a convention of delegates from the different companies to be held at Dungannon on February 15, 1782. Nearly two hundred and fifty Volunteers attended and passed a number of resolutions, among which were the following two :

(a) " That a claim of any body of men, other than the King, Lords and Commons of Ireland, to make laws to bind this kingdom is unconstitutional, illegal and a grievance."

(b) " That as men and as Irishmen we rejoice in the relaxation of the Penal Laws against our Roman Catholic fellow subjects, and that we conceive the measure to be fraught with the happiest consequences to the union and prosperity of the inhabitants of Ireland."

No sooner had the Dungannon resolutions appeared in the newspapers than meetings of Volunteers were held throughout the country in order to adopt them.

Legislative Independence (1782) : Grattan and the Volunteers had chosen their time well. The war across the Atlantic was going badly for Britain : the French navy had secured control of the American coast, and Lord Cornwallis was forced to surrender Yorktown. Lord North was blamed for these reverses, and he was replaced as Prime Minister by the Whig Lord Rockingham. Many members of the new Government were friends of Grattan and Charlemont, and the hopes of the " Patriot Party " soared. A new Lord Lieutenant, Portland, was sent to Ireland, and, two days after his arrival, Grattan moved in Parliament a " Declaration of Irish Rights ", which was in effect a re-statement of the Dungannon resolutions. This time there was no opposition. The Irish Parliament repealed Poynings' Law, the English Parliament repealed the Declaratory Act of 1719, so that in 1782 legislative independence was achieved. Grattan was the hero of the hour and was given a reward of £50,000 in appreciation of his services to the nation.

2. Grattan's Parliament (1782-1800)

Government and Parliament : It is necessary to remember that, while the Irish Parliament was now nominally a sovereign body, it did not differ very much from the previous Parliaments. It was still an assembly of great landowners or their nominees, and much power remained in the hands of the Lord Lieutenant and of the Chief Secretary. They were able to control the decisions of Parliament by distributing titles, places and pensions among its members. But the greatest defect of all was that the Irish Government was not subject to parliamentary control. The Lord Lieutenant and his officials represented the British Ministry of the day, and went in and out of office with each administration at Westminster. There was no party system

in the Irish Parliament. In England, when an important measure was defeated, the Government was expected to resign, but
nothing of the kind happened here. If a measure was rejected
by the House of Commons, the Irish executive dropped it for
the moment, got busy in winning over more members to their
side and introduced it again. But government defeats were rare,
for there were always enough members ready to do as they
were told in return for places and pensions.

Industrial Development : In spite of its defects, Grattan's
Parliament did a great deal of good for Ireland. The granting
of free trade in 1780 had not brought much immediate benefit,
for the war made it impossible for Irish merchants to trade
with the American colonies or with France. But from 1783
onwards industries expanded rapidly. The manufacture of
woollen cloth, which had been almost crushed at the end of
the seventeenth century, revived, while in the northern counties
the manufacture of linen goods was flourishing and cotton was
established in Belfast. Practically every large town had its
brewery or distillery, its tannery or sugar refinery, and the
beautiful glass made in Waterford was world famous. Dublin
and Belfast (about which we shall have more to say in the
next chapter) were thriving places, but, apart from them, Irish
market towns generally had a new air of prosperity and revealed
in their better housing and tidy shops the rising standards of
living of their inhabitants. There were many reasons for the
improved conditions, but it was only natural that contemporaries
(and indeed some later historians) should have ascribed it all
to the independent Irish Parliament.

Foster's Corn Law (1784) : Ireland's prosperity ultimately
depends upon her agriculture, and, as many of the members
were landowners, it was only natural that Parliament should
devote a good deal of attention to it. In 1784 Foster's Corn Law
was passed, whereby a bounty of 3s. 4d. was granted on every
barrel of wheat exported when the price in the home market
did not exceed 27 shillings. A duty of ten shillings a barrel
was placed on imported wheat when the home price was under

Belfast in the 18th Century

30 shillings. This stimulated the growth of wheat, and large
areas of grassland were put under the plough. The new industrial
towns of England provided a ready market for Irish cereals,
and in the twelve years from 1785 to 1797 more corn, meal
and flour was exported than in the previous eighty-four years.
Mills sprang up everywhere, and the gaunt remains of many
of these can be seen scattered about our countryside to-day.

The Peasantry : The peasantry had little share in this prosperity but still lived in their tumble-down hovels and scraped a bare existence from their rack-rented land. There was indeed more employment for labourers, and, during the harvest, crowds of men, called " spalpeens ", might be met in the fertile counties, carrying their scythes or sickles and selling their labour for a shilling a day. But this was only occasional work, and there were long periods when none was available at all. The population of the country was increasing rapidly, and competition for land put up the rents. Farms grew smaller, and the cottier was forced to depend entirely on potatoes. When these failed, there was hunger and death.

3. Wolfe Tone and the United Irishmen

The French Revolution : There were many in Ireland, as in England, who regarded the French Revolution as the dawn of a better era. Foremost among these were the Presbyterians of Ulster, and in Belfast, on July 14, 1791, the Volunteers paraded to celebrate the second anniversary of the capture of the Bastille. Portraits of Mirabeau and other French leaders were carried, and a place of honour in the procession was reserved for a tableau representing ' Releasement of the Prisoners from the Bastille '. In the evening there was a dinner in the Linen Hall at which numerous toasts were drunk, and a message of good wishes was sent on behalf of the townspeople to the National Assembly of France.

The United Irishmen : The celebrations in Belfast attracted the attention of a young Dublin lawyer named Wolfe Tone. For some time he had been convinced that Grattan's Parliament would continue to be controlled by Britain unless it was reformed and made representative of the whole nation, Catholic and Protestant alike. He believed that there were some men in Belfast who would support his views. So in October,

1791, he came north to found a new society which he called the United Irishmen. The aims of the society were, *firstly*, to promote " a brotherhood of affection, a communion of rights and a union of power among Irishmen of every religious persuasion ", and *secondly*, to have the Irish Parliament reformed and made representative of the people. Many leading Belfast businessmen—Samuel Neilson, Samuel McTier, William Sinclair, Henry Haslett—supported him and believed that they could achieve their aims by peaceful means.

Branches of the United Irishmen were founded in Dublin and later in other places, but the real strength of the society was among the Presbyterians of Antrim and Down.

Attitude of the Catholics : The position of Catholics had improved greatly over the past twenty years : the last of their religious disabilities had been removed and they were able to own land like everyone else. But these grants only made the remaining restrictions more irksome, and they began to agitate for the right to enter any profession and to vote at parliamentary elections. The British Government was anxious to help them, the more so as they had shown no sympathy for the French Revolution and no inclination to join the United Irishmen. But the Irish Government was slow to act, and only with the greatest reluctance did they make concessions. In 1792 they agreed to allow Catholics to practise law, to educate their children as they pleased, and to intermarry with Protestants. But they would not grant them the franchise, for that was regarded as endangering the Protestant ascendancy. However, when war broke out between England and France in 1793, Pitt compelled the Irish Government to pass a Relief Act, enabling Catholics to vote as forty-shilling freeholders in the counties and in the open boroughs, to serve as grand jurors and magistrates, to take university degrees and to hold commissions in the army below the rank of general. Two years later, in 1795, to gain the support of the bishops the Government founded Maynooth College for the education of Irish priests and endowed it with a grant of £8,000 a year.

The Fitzwilliam Episode : Pitt's policy appeared to be justified. The Catholic bishops and clergy were totally opposed to the doctrines of the French revolutionaries, and the peasantry showed no inclination as yet to join the United Irishmen. While the Catholics remained loyal, there could be no large-scale rebellion in the country and little support for a French invasion. But this state of affairs was drastically altered by what is usually called 'the Fitzwilliam Affair'.

In 1794 a group of English Whigs had joined Pitt's Government in order to carry on the war against France. This had caused some changes in the cabinet, and it was decided to send the Earl Fitzwilliam to Ireland as Lord Lieutenant. His appointment raised hopes there, for he was a friend of Henry Grattan and known to favour the granting of full political rights to Catholics. But, before he left for Ireland, Pitt advised him to postpone, if possible, any discussions on the matter until the war with France was over. His arrival in Dublin aroused such enthusiasm, however, that Fitzwilliam was convinced that the question would have to be dealt with at once, if the loyalty of the Catholics was to be retained. He informed the British Government of his decision, but had not received a reply when Parliament opened on January 22, 1795.

Fitzwilliam had no tact and soon ran into serious difficulty. A few days after his arrival in the country he dismissed a number of his ministers who were strong opponents of Catholic Emancipation. Among them was John Beresford, the Commissioner of Revenue, a man of great influence and large family connections, who had been nicknamed the 'King of Ireland'. Beresford immediately went over to England to lay his complaints before the Government. Pitt was naturally annoyed with Fitzwilliam for causing dissension in the ranks of the Irish executive.

It was under these circumstances that the Irish parliamentary session opened on January 22, 1795. The Catholic Question was raised at once, and a stream of petitions poured in from all quarters. Fitzwilliam decided to grant the Catholics' demands and wrote to Pitt accordingly. " The time I believe propitious to the purpose," he said, "not a single petition against it to the House of Commons from any Protestant body, though the subject has already been six weeks in agitation." Leave was given to Grattan to introduce an Emancipation Bill —when, suddenly, and to the consternation of all, Fitzwilliam was recalled! March 25th, the day of his departure from Ireland was marked by special mourning. Shops were closed, all business was suspended, and, when he left his residence, his coach was drawn through the streets of Dublin by crowds of sympathisers.

Historians are still not agreed as to why Pitt acted as he did; but the most probable explanation is that, on reflection, he thought it unwise to make drastic changes in the government of Ireland while the war was going on, especially if these were going to antagonise Britain's most reliable supporters in the country. But whatever about causes, there can be no doubt at all about the consequences of Fitzwilliam's recall. The Catholics, whose hopes had been raised, were bitterly disappointed. For the first time they began to flock into the United Irishmen, and the numbers of the society increased by leaps and bounds.

Suppression of the United Irishmen: Meanwhile Wolfe Tone had got into trouble with the authorities. In the spring of 1794 the French Committee of Public Safety had decided to send William Jackson to Ireland as an emissary to establish contact with the United Irishmen. He met a number of leading members of the society, and discussions took place on the possibility of a French landing. Tone drew up a memorandum to help the French in their preparations, and, when Jackson was eventually arrested, this document was found among his papers. Tone fled to America, and the Society of the United Irishmen was suppressed. In 1795 it was revived as a secret revolutionary body, and its aim now was to separate Ireland from England. It was this new body that the Catholics joined after Fitzwilliam's recall.

Peep-of-Day Boys and Defenders: In the north two other secret societies were active at this time among the poorer classes of Protestants and Catholics. The " Peep of Day Boys" were Protestants who came early in the morning to wreck Catholic homes; their Catholic opponents were known as "Defenders". Both groups were strong in Armagh, South Down, Louth, Monaghan and Tyrone. It is difficult to say what the origin of the societies was, but it may have been due to the fact that, in some areas, Catholics were now competing with Protestants for land and thus forcing up the rent. Bad feeling was created between the two groups—they fought, maimed and killed each other and did immense damage to property. Wolfe Tone was concerned about these incidents and had spent some time in 1792 trying to reconcile the Protestants and Catholics of South Down. But religious animosity was too strong for him to have much success, and " the brotherhood of affection . . . among Irishmen of every religious persuasion" was never really attained outside Belfast and the surrounding areas. Matters came to a head on September 21, 1795, when the " Peep-of-Day Boys " and " Defenders " clashed in the " The Battle of the Diamond ", near Loughgall, Co. Armagh. The Protestants, though fewer in number than the Catholics, were better armed, and the Defenders were defeated with the loss of thirty lives. That evening the Protestants who had taken part in the battle formed the Orange Society and vowed to do all in their power " to maintain the laws and peace of the country, and the Protestant Constitution ". From then on the position in Ulster changed significantly. Many Protestants, who had half-heartedly supported the new radicalism, renewed their allegiance to the King and to the constitution, and supplied most of the recruits for the " yeomanry " raised by the Government to preserve law and order. The Catholic " Defenders ", on the other hand, were recruited into the ranks of the United Irishmen, who were preparing for rebellion and awaiting the arrival of help from France.

Bantry Bay : On December 15, 1796 a French fleet of forty-three ships, with 15,000 men aboard, sailed from Brest, under the command of General Hoche. On one of the ships was

Wolfe Tone, who had been in Paris for some time and was now an adjutant-general in the French army. The French hoped to make a landing in the south-west of Ireland, and they carried with them a large supply of arms and ammunition. Misfortune dogged the expedition from the start : the ships were separated in a fog, and more than half of them, including the vessel which had Hoche aboard, never came within sight of Ireland at all. Finally, when fifteen or sixteen ships reached Bantry Bay on December 22, a strong easterly wind was blowing accompanied by snow. For four days they remained there waiting for a chance to land, but the storm did not die down, and eventually they were forced to sail back to France.

The Disarming of Ulster : Though the French expedition had failed, the Government was seriously alarmed and decided that the conspiracy must be suppressed. The Habeas Corpus Act was suspended; the tendering of unlawful oaths was made a capital offence, the yeomanry were recruited to help in the disarming of Ulster. On March 13, 1797 General Lake issued a proclamation at Belfast, ordering all persons who were not peace officers or soldiers to hand in their arms. Houses in the area were searched and weapons of all kinds were confiscated. The methods used were brutal, and men were sometimes tortured until they gave the information that was required of them. Lake believed that conditions in Ulster justified the severity : " You may think me violent," he wrote to the authorities in Dublin Castle, " but I am convinced it will be a mercy in the end. . . . I have patrols going night and day, and will do everything I can to rid the country of these rebellious scoundrels." Some feared that the methods being used were more likely to provoke rebellion than to prevent it, and the British Government intervened to ask whether, even at this late hour, something could not be done for the Catholics to break their alliance with the dangerous United Irishmen. In the House of Commons Henry Grattan made a last attempt to persuade the Irish Government to accept his plan of parliamentary reform, but his plea was rejected by an overwhelming majority, and he withdrew sadly from the House to await the insurrection that now appeared inevitable.

Rebellion : In 1797, the ' Black Year ', when British ships mutinied at Spithead and the Nore, a Dutch fleet was assembled in the Texel to carry fifteen thousand French soldiers to Ireland. Wolfe Tone was there also, and contact had already been made with the United Irishmen who were awaiting the expedition. But the Dutch ships were kept in port by adverse winds until the mutinies were over, and, when they did finally come out, they were defeated by Admiral Duncan at Camperdown. The United Irishmen then decided to rebel without waiting any longer for foreign aid. The rising was planned for the spring of 1798, and Lord Edward Fitzgerald, a brother of the Duke of Leinster, was chosen as commander-in-chief. But the Government was kept fully informed of their plans by the many spies which the organisation had in its ranks, and in March, 1798 it arrested almost all the leaders in one swoop. Lord Edward Fitzgerald evaded capture for some time, but eventually he was discovered at a house in Thomas Street, Dublin, and arrested. He died later of wounds he received when he tried to resist arrest. Nevertheless, the insurrection did break out in Wicklow and Wexford, and in Antrim and Down, but the rebels had little hope of success and were easily suppressed.

Wexford : The rebellion began first in Wexford, a county where the United Irishmen were not numerous. It appears to have been provoked by the harsh behaviour of the militia and yeomanry who, among other things, burned the little chapel of Boulavogue, near Enniscorthy. The curate of the parish, Father John Murphy, put himself at the head of his outraged people and called on others to join them. Though they had no weapons except pikes and pitchforks, they quickly captured the towns of Wexford, Enniscorthy and Gorey, and made their headquarters on Vinegar Hill near Enniscorthy. The Protestant gentleman, Bagenal Harvey, allied with them and tried to take New Ross but failed. While the battle was in progress a horrible massacre took place at Scullabogue, about eight miles

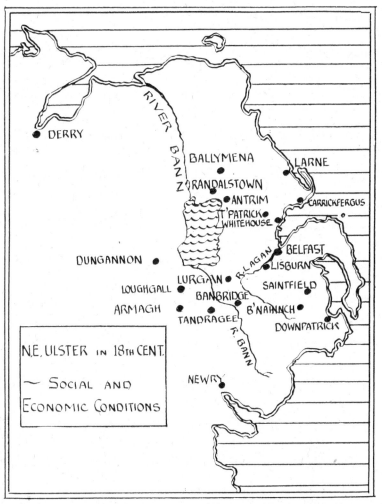

N.E. Ulster in the 18th Century—Social and Economic Conditions

from the town. The rebels held a large number of Protestants as prisoners there, most of them in a large barn. On the evening of the defeat at New Ross, some of these were slain and the remainder (about two hundred in all) were crowded into the barn and burned to death. Bagenal Harvey was horrified by the massacre, and it was with relief that he laid down his command.

By this time reinforcements had arrived from England, and General Lake had surrounded the main rebel camp at Vinegar Hill. On June 21, 1798 he began his attack with 15,000 men. The rebels fought bravely, but they had neither the arms nor the skill of the soldiers and were soon overcome. This ended the rebellion. Father John Murphy, Bagenal Harvey and some of the other leaders were executed, but Michael Dwyer and Joseph Holt escaped into Wicklow with a small band of insurgents and kept up a guerilla warfare.

Rebellion in the North: The rising in the north was confined to Antrim and Down. On June 7th, 1798 the town of Antrim was attacked by a force of about three thousand men under Henry Joy McCracken, a Belfast cotton manufacturer, but the rebels were repulsed by the forces stationed there and retreated leaving two hundred dead in the streets. On the same morning Randalstown and Ballymena had been occupied by the United Irishmen, and a detachment under Colonel Clavering was sent against them. When his order to the insurgents to surrender was ignored, he set fire to Randalstown. Ballymena at once gave in, and the remnants of the rebel force withdrew to Donegore Hill. Clavering offered a pardon to those who would lay down their arms, and most obeyed with eagerness. McCracken with a few friends tried to escape, but he was arrested and executed in Belfast.

The rebellion in Down was just as brief. It had been planned for June 6th but did not take place until three days later, by which time the rebels in Antrim had been defeated. The only big engagement was fought at Ballynahinch. Seven thousand rebels encamped in a strong position outside the town and

chose Henry Munro, a Lisburn linen draper, as their leader.
General Nugent marched against them and defeated them with
a loss of five hundred men. Nugent then issued a proclamation
threatening " to destroy the towns of Killinchy, Killyleagh,
Ballynahinch, Saintfield and every cottage in the vicinity" if
the rebels did not lay down their arms. As in Antrim, they
complied at once, and dejectedly returned to their homes.
Munro tried to escape but was caught and hanged in Lisburn.

Death of Tone: A month after the rebellion ended, a small
French force, under General Humbert, landed at Killala, in
Co. Mayo. From there they marched inland, winning a battle
on the way at Castlebar, but they were surrounded at
Ballinamuck (Co. Longford) and forced to surrender. A few
days later, another French expedition arrived in Lough Swilly
carrying Wolfe Tone on one of the ships. A British squadron
attacked them, and among the prisoners taken was the founder
of the United Irishmen. He was brought to Dublin for trial and
condemned to death. He asked to be shot as a soldier, and,
when this request was refused, he committed suicide rather
than allow the authorities to hang him.

The Union: On a number of occasions in the previous five
years the French had attempted to invade Ireland, and General
Humbert had actually succeeded in landing at Killala. Napoleon
was master of France now, and was determined to conquer
Britain. It was essential that he should not be allowed to use
Ireland as a base for the large-scale invasion of England. Therefore in Pitt's eyes a parliamentary union of the two countries was
a military necessity. Apart from that, he believed that, sooner
or later, Catholics must be admitted to the Irish Parliament,
and would inevitably form a majority there. In such circumstances he saw that there was a possibility that they might wish
to sever their connection with England and establish an Irish
republic. But if there was only one Parliament for the whole
of the British Isles, the Catholics would be outnumbered by
the Protestant members. To gain Catholic support for his plan

Pitt promised that the parliamentary union would be followed by Catholic Emancipation.

But the opposition was formidable.. First of all there were those like the Duke of Leinster, the Earl of Charlemont and Henry Grattan who cherished their " Independent " Parliament and would fight hard to retain it. Then there were the owners of " rotten " and " pocket " boroughs who feared the loss of their property. In addition there were those who held sinecure posts and places; the lawyers who regarded the Parliament in College Green as a good means of advertising their abilities; the Dublin traders and property owners who realised that, if there was no parliamentary season, their shops and houses would lose their value. Added to this was a feeling that in giving up her legislature Ireland was losing some of her dignity : instead of having an independent existence the country would henceforth exist only as part of England.

Passing of the Act of Union : Pitt was determined to effect a union and instructed the Lord Lieutenant, Cornwallis, and the Chief Secretary, Castlereagh, that they were to use every means to overcome the opposition to it. Bribery was no new thing in the Irish Parliament, but on this occasion it was practised on a scale never used before. Prominent individuals who opposed the Union were severely punished whenever the Government could possibly do so. Sir John Parnell, the Chancellor of the Exchequer and Prime-Sergeant Fitzgerald were dismissed from office and replaced by men who would support the measure. Large sums of money were spent in buying up seats, and borough owners were promised £15,000 for each borough that was abolished. Twenty-eight men were made peers, and twenty-six peers were promoted to a higher rank. These methods shock us to-day, but in the eighteenth century political bribery was an every-day affair and was the usual means whereby a British Government had got its way in the Irish Parliament.

After a majority had been created in this way, the Bill of Union was introduced into the House of Commons on May 21, 1800. Grattan opposed it, dressed in his old Volunteer uniform, but the result was a foregone conclusion, and the measure was carried through all its stages in a few weeks. On August 1, it received the royal signature, and the long drama was over. The following day the election of the twenty-eight peers to represent Ireland in the House of Lords took place, and immediately afterwards the Irish Parliament dispersed for the last time. The Union came into effect on January 1, 1801.

Terms of the Act of Union :

1. The two kingdoms were to be joined, and to be known as the United Kingdom of Great Britain and Ireland.

2. Ireland was to be represented in the Parliament at Westminster by (a) four spiritual peers (i.e. Protestant bishops) and twenty-eight temporal peers in the House of Lords, and (b) one hundred members in the House of Commons.

3. The Church of England and the Church of Ireland were to be united " into one Protestant Episcopal Church ", and this arrangement was " to be an essential and fundamental part of the Union ".

4. There was to be complete free trade between Great Britain and Ireland.

Catholic Emancipation : The Catholics were disappointed that there was no mention of Emancipation among the terms of the Act of Union. It was not entirely Pitt's fault, for when he proposed to introduce a Catholic Relief Bill, he met with such opposition from the Irish Government that he had to drop it. After the Union had taken place, Pitt tried again, and proposed to bring in a measure allowing Catholics to sit in Parliament. But now George III opposed the measure, and said he would not sign such a bill. Pitt resigned, and the matter was dropped. Many Catholics believed they had been deceived, and the Union got off to a bad start.

Questions and Exercises

1. Describe the part played by Henry Grattan in Irish affairs from 1775 to 1800.

2. What was the origin of the Volunteers? Describe the part played by them in securing (a) free trade, and (b) parliamentary independence.

3. Give an account of the work of Grattan's Parliament (1782-1800) in the sphere of industrial and agricultural development.

4. By whom and for what purpose was the Society of United Irishmen founded? Give an account of the activities of the society up to 1794. Why was it suppressed in that year?

5. Write an account of *two* of the following: —
   (a) The Fitzwilliam episode; (b) the Bantry Bay expedition (1796); (c) the rebellion of 1798 in Wexford.

6. Why did Pitt consider a union between Britain and Ireland necessary? What were the terms of the Act of Union?

CHAPTER SEVENTEEN

Ireland in the Eighteenth Century: Social and Economic Conditions

1. The Linen Industry

Early History of the Industry: Linen was manufactured in Ireland from early times, but it was a coarse and hard material like canvas, and was only made by the farmers for their own use. In the seventeenth century Thomas Wentworth (later Earl of Strafford), who had been sent as Lord Deputy to Ireland by Charles I, made great efforts to improve the quality of Irish linen. He imported flax-seed from Holland and brought over experts to instruct the farmers in the best means of growing the crop. He introduced the Dutch spinning wheel and had better looms built, so that pieces of linen twenty inches wide could now be produced. All these were useful reforms and led to an increase in the quality and in the quantity of the material manufactured. But Wentworth's methods were harsh, and those who persisted in the old ways were fined and imprisoned. Thus despite the assistance which he gave to the industry (and he spent a good deal of his own money on it) Wentworth was hated bitterly in Ireland and was known as 'Black Tom Tyrant'. Any benefits which the linen industry had derived from his changes were lost in the decade of war which followed the rebellion of 1641.

After the Restoration the encouragement of the linen trade was continued, the more so as it did not compete with any English manufacture. The Lord Lieutenant, the Duke of Ormond, introduced skilled Protestant linen workers from Holland and France, most of whom settled among their co-religionists in East Ulster. A typical settlement was the Flemish colony established by Samuel Waring at Waringstown, Co. Down, where cloth of a quality hitherto unknown in Ireland was produced. Thus there was already the nucleus of a linen industry in the north before the end of the seventeenth century.

Louis Crommelin : After the Revolution a number of influential English cloth manufacturers petitioned William III to crush the Irish woollen industry, which had begun to compete with them on the home market. The King agreed to do so, but at the same time promised to do all in his power to assist in developing the linen industry. He kept his promise, and it was he who persuaded Louis Crommelin to make a Huguenot settlement at Lisburn.

Crommelin was a member of a well known Huguenot family, which had moved from France to Holland and set up as merchants and bankers in Amsterdam. William, Prince of Orange, was acquainted with him there, and so, in 1699, he invited him to come to Ireland. He gave him the title of Overseer of the Royal Linen Manufacture and promised him a salary of £300 a year and an interest of 8% on any capital he might invest in the industry. Crommelin brought over twenty-five Huguenot families from the Low Countries, imported looms and spinning wheels, and built a bleach green at Hilden to serve the needs of the area. The colony prospered and grew until there were five hundred Huguenot families in the vicinity of Lisburn.

The Linen Board : During the eighteenth century the industry made rapid progress, so that at the time of Crommelin's death in 1727 linen formed one-third of Ireland's exports. The

Irish Parliament gave what assistance it could and imposed heavy duties in order to protect the home manufacturer from foreign competition. In 1711 a Linen Board was established to regulate methods of production and to administer the various grants and bounties voted by Parliament. This Board gave prizes for high quality material, set up schools for instructing the young in spinning and weaving, and helped in developing new markets. It lasted until 1827, and for over a century spent, on the average, about £20,000 a year in helping the industry.

The Domestic System : From the beginning there was a very close connection between agriculture and the manufacture of linen. After he had grown and harvested his flax, the farmer ' drowned ' it in a ' lint hole ' or ' flax hole ' until it was ready for scutching, a process which separated the outer covering of the plant from the fibres. The women of the household next spun the fibres into yarn, and the farmer or his sons wove the yarn into cloth. All the processes were thus carried on in the home, hence the term *domestic system* used to describe this kind of industry. The cloth was then known as ' brown linen ' and it was usually taken in that condition by a farmer to the market of a nearby town. The ' drapers ' who purchased it there had it bleached and finished before sending it to Dublin for sale. The Linen Board had set up a White Linen Hall in the capital in 1721, and English buyers came there to buy the finished cloth.

The Weavers : Through time a number of men came to give their whole time to weaving, either because they preferred it to farming or because they found it more profitable. The draper then toured the cottages in his district, giving out yarn to the weavers and paying them for the work they had done. But this was not a very satisfactory method, for the workers were not reliable and the draper could not be sure that the cloth would be ready when he called. Thus the draper sometimes built a large shed onto his house, and became a manufacturer. He installed a number of looms there and paid his workers a weekly wage. The system did not become widespread, however, for the weavers preferred to work in their own homes.

The weavers took their webs of linen to markets in one of the large towns of the area—Lisburn, Lurgan, Banbridge or Newry. Arthur Young has left us this description of a linen market which he saw in progress:

"This being market day at Lurgan, Mr. Brownlow walked to it with me, that I might see the way in which the linens were sold . . . . When the clock strikes eleven, the drapers jump upon stone standings, and the weavers instantly flock about them with their pieces; the bargains are not struck at a word, but there is a little altercation whether the price shall be one half-penny or a penny a yard more or less."

When the draper and weaver agreed on a price, this was clearly marked on the web, and the money was paid out afterwards at the purchaser's inn or hotel.

The Bleachers : From about 1750 onwards a change took place in this system. By that time a number of wealthy bleachers had begun to dominate the industry and to buy up linen for bleaching and finishing. The bleaching of linen was a slow process and entailed the steeping of the material in buttermilk before spreading it out on the grass to be acted on by the air and sun. The whole process took seven or eight months, and, as the small farmer or weaver could not lie out of his money for this length of time, he sold his linen to one of the rich bleachers. They had imported machines to speed up the bleaching process—beetling machines, wash mills and rub boards—and these were driven by large water wheels. The bleach works were built where the fast-flowing tributaries of the Lagan tumbled down from the hills on the northern edge of the valley—at Hilden, Dunmurry, Ballysillan and Ligoniel. To get their linen the bleachers employed buyers and cut out the middleman or draper altogether. These buyers travelled on horseback from market to market and dealt directly with the weavers. They were paid a salary for their work, usually £110 a year, with an allowance for their horses. As they

The Lagan Valley showing places important in the early years of the Linen Industry

always carried money, they travelled in groups for safety and were a familiar sight as they rode about the countryside in their enormous overcoats and glazed hats. They had to be men of great strength and endurance, for they usually rode about four thousand miles a year. They would be in Banbridge on Monday, in Armagh on Tuesday, in Tanderagee on Wednesday, in Newry on Thursday, in Lurgan on Friday, and in Downpatrick or Ballymena on Saturday.

Belfast Becomes the Centre : Small linen halls had been built in Belfast for the convenience of merchants in the first half of the eighteenth century, but they dealt only in unbleached material, and the town was not as important a market centre as Lisburn, Lurgan or Armagh. White linen continued to be sold only in Dublin. This was not a very satisfactory arrangement. Dublin was a hundred miles away, and the heavy wagons carrying linen southwards might take a week, or even a fortnight, on the journey. Some of the bleachers, therefore, decided to make Belfast the centre of the trade. In 1784 they built a White Linen Hall on the site of the present City Hall, and from then on less and less linen was sent to Dublin. English and continental buyers began to attend the Belfast linen markets, and banks grew up to facilitate the trade.

Though Belfast had become the principal market centre for linen before the end of the eighteenth century, little of the material was yet manufactured in the town. It was still chiefly centred in the valleys of the Lagan and the Upper Bann, and most of the weavers continued to work in their own homes. It was in the cotton industry rather than the linen industry that the factory system made its first appearance in Ireland.

2. The Cotton Industry

In 1778 Nicholas Grimshaw, a Lancashire man, suggested to the Belfast Charitable Society that it should introduce the manufacture of cotton into the poorhouse of the town. The society accepted his proposal, and two of its members, Robert

Joy and Thomas McCabe, were permitted to install machinery and to employ pauper children in the manufacture of yarn. The industry developed with amazing rapidity, and in a short time factories were built in Belfast and the surrounding districts. Some idea of the growth of the industry can be gained from the numbers that were employed in and around town:

1709—8,000
1800—13,000
1811—50,000

The first cotton spinning mill was built at Whitehouse in 1784, and its machinery was driven by water power. Six years later, one of Watt's steam engines was imported by James Wallace and installed in a cotton mill at Lisburn. Its arrival caused tremendous excitement in the district and great crowds came out to see it at work. Others followed Wallace's example, and by 1811 there were fifteen steam-driven mills in Belfast, and large quantities of coal were imported to supply them. The fact that the industry depended upon imported raw material and fuel meant that most of the cotton mills grew up around Belfast Lough, at Whitehouse, Carrickfergus, Larne and Bangor.

Weaving was done at home on the handloom, and, as it was easier and more profitable to weave cotton than linen, many workers abandoned the older textile for the new. Hand-weaving was not confined to Belfast but spread up the Lagan Valley as far as Moira.

Grattan's Parliament did everything possible to help the new industry. Bounties were paid on home and foreign sales, while a high duty on imported cotton ensured that the Irish manufacturers had the market to themselves. Even when the Union came into effect in 1801, cotton was given preferential treatment; duties on imports were not to be changed until 1808, after which date they were to be gradually reduced. But Irish businesses were too small to compete with the great Lancashire manufacturers, and one by one they were forced to close. A sign of the times was the fact that, when Thomas and Andrew Mulholland's large cotton mill in York Street, Belfast, was burnt down in 1828, they rebuilt it as a flax spinning mill, thus inaugurating the mechanical production of linen. But short though its life was, it would be difficult to exaggerate the importance of the cotton industry in the development of Belfast. It was cotton spinning which first brought industrial workers into the town in large numbers, and they were there to meet the needs of the linen industry when it was eventually mechanised, while the repair and maintenance of the new machines was the origin of what was to become a world-famous textile engineering industry.

3. Belfast in the Eighteenth Century

Early History : One of the most significant developments during our period was the great increase that took place in the size and importance of Belfast. At the beginning of the seventeenth century it was only a village, a cluster of houses built by Sir Arthur Chichester where the little river Farset emptied itself into the Lagan. Hence its name Beal Farset : the mouth of the Farset. The town developed slowly, and a map of 1660, which has survived, shows a small settlement of five streets, some lanes and two hundred houses, all centred on the Farset, which still ran open down the middle of the town. The main street, or High Street as it was called, which had grown up on both sides of the river, was naturally the first market place. There the merchants gathered and the country people exposed their produce for sale, a market house being erected for their use at the corner of Cornmarket about 1665. A number of bridges were built over the Farset, but it was not until the eighteenth century that the river was covered over, thus giving High Street the attractive curve that it has today.

Parallel to High Street, on the north, were Waring Street and its continuation, Rosemary Street. At the foot of Waring Street a second quay was built later, and in the eighteenth century this became the merchants' quarter of the town. There, too, was ' the Four Corners ' at the junction of Bridge Street, North

Street, Waring Street and Rosemary Street, where the merchants met daily to transact their business. To facilitate them Lord Donegall built an Exchange there in 1769.

Parallel to High Street, on the south, was Ann Street, where the shops specialised in flesh-meat and provisions, for Belfast was already exporting large quantities of salted beef, pork, hides, tallow and butter. William Sacheverell, who visited the town in 1698, commented on the importance of the trade: "The quantities of beef and butter which it sends into foreign parts are almost incredible. I have seen the barrels piled up in every street." A large part of this trade was with America and the West Indies, from which sugar and tobacco were brought as return cargoes.

We can thus picture Belfast at the end of the seventeenth century as a busy town and seaport. The majority of its inhabitants were merchants or found employment as butchers, tanners, coopers and salters or packers of beef. What the population was we have no means of knowing, but an estimate made in 1685 said there were two thousand people living in the town.

Growth in the Eighteenth Century : During the next hundred years considerable changes took place in the size and shape of Belfast, and in the nature and extent of its trade. The Farset was covered over, thus adding to the width of its main street, but a map drawn in 1757 shows that the actual area occupied by the town had not greatly increased. What had happened was that the vacant spaces between the houses had been built upon, so that Belfast had now a more compact shape. Such extensions as had been made were to the west and to the north-west. To the west, Mill Street, Barrack Street and the Falls were attracting workers for the bleach greens that had been built in the area. To the north-west a new wide thoroughfare, six hundred yards long and sixty feet wide, had been built—the present Donegall Street. Expansion southwards was checked by the castle grounds of Lord Donegall and by the woods of Cromac, Ormeau, Stranmillis and Malone. But towards the end of the century Donegall Place and the adjoining streets were built on the castle gardens. There also, as we have seen, the White Linen Hall was erected in 1784, and soon it was the centre of a lovely square, surrounded by terraces of dignified Georgian houses in which the richer merchants and professional people lived.

Commercial Development : For much of the eighteenth century the export of provisions continued to be the principal business of Belfast. But from about 1750 onwards, as we have seen, a number of large linen bleachers began to develop their industries on the outskirts of the town and to employ the poorer classes to work on their bleach greens. They also began to use the port for the export of their goods, and, after the founding of the Linen Hall, dealt directly with their English customers instead of through Dublin. The extent of their success is shown by the statistics for the port. In 1710 the value of linen exported from Belfast was £14,000 ; by 1801 it had risen to £2,500,000.

Towards the end of the century the linen industry was for a time in decline, and its place as the maker of Belfast's prosperity was taken by cotton. But the town did not depend entirely on its textile and provision trades, for at the time of the Union (when its population must have been over 20,000) it had a great variety of industries: tanneries, ropeworks, papermills, glass works, sugar refineries, breweries, iron works.

Social Life : It would be a mistake to regard Belfast merely as a busy commercial centre and port. A newspaper, the *Belfast Newsletter,* had been established in the town in 1737, and there were later publications such as the *Belfast Courant* and the *Northern Star*. From a study of their columns we can today get some indication of the vigorous intellectual life of the town. The number of societies was remarkable. One of the best known of them was the Belfast Reading Society founded in 1788 to form a library and for the collection of " such productions of Nature and Arts as tend to improve the mind and excite a spirit of general enquiry ". Its first librarian was Thomas Russell, a friend of Wolfe Tone and one of the founders of the United Irishmen. There was also a Musical Society and several convivial clubs, which met in taverns such as the 'Donegall Arms' in High Street. Over the Exchange a magnificent Assembly Room had been built, where dances and card parties were frequently held. There, too, was held the Harpers' Festival in 1792, after which Edward Bunting, the organist of St. Anne's, travelled through Munster and Connacht noting down the traditional music of Ireland. There were two theatres in the town, and among the great artistes who played there were Mrs. Siddons, Kean, Macready and the Kembles.

The Congregations : The population was overwhelmingly Presbyterian, and there were three meeting houses, situated beside one another in Rosemary Street. Their ministers were leading citizens of the town and took a prominent part in every good cause, whether it was in caring for the sick and the poor or in providing schools such as the Belfast Academy.

The Episcopalian congregation worshipped at the old Chapel of the Ford in High Street; but because the structure became unsafe, this church was pulled down in 1774 and the new St. Anne's in Donegall Street became the parish church of the town. Though its congregation must have been small, the Episcopalian Church had an influence out of proportion to its numbers, for it was the religion of the aristocracy and of the ruling class. Thus Episcopalians monopolised the official positions of the town. The vicar, Rev. William Bristow, was sovereign (i.e. mayor) for ten years, and, after the Test Act, Presbyterians were excluded from any share in local government.

Catholics had begun to settle in Belfast during the eighteenth century, and the census of 1757 estimated that there were 556 of them out of a population of 8,549. Socially they were of little consequence, and they took no part in the life of the town. They met to worship in an old sand-pit opposite the gate of Friars' Bush graveyard until 1768, when they opened a little chapel behind the houses in Mill Street. There they worshipped quietly until 1784, when they built St. Mary's Church. On the day it opened, the Volunteers paraded to Mass in full dress and the leading men of the town attended to show that they were pleased.

4. Georgian Dublin

A Gay Time : No account of social conditions in Ireland during the eighteenth century would be complete without a section on Dublin, for during that period were erected many of its fine public buildings and some of the best examples of Georgian domestic architecture to be found in these islands. Moreover, the last two decades of the century were a time of great political excitement, when orators made brilliant speeches in the Irish House of Commons and Volunteers paraded in their colourful uniforms in College Green. The aristocracy flocked into the capital and built for themselves town houses, where they lived when Parliament was in session. The city expanded north and south of the Liffey, and great new squares were built in the fields of the Gardiner and Fitzwilliam estates: Mountjoy and Rutland Squares in the north, Merrion and Fitzwilliam Squares in the south. During the parliamentary session three hundred Commoners and about eighty Peers resided in Dublin, and there was a continuous round of balls and parties, of visits to the theatre or to the music hall. Sometimes there were reviews of the Volunteers in the Phoenix Park, with bands playing and flags flying ; sometimes there were the more formal receptions of the Lord Lieutenant in Dublin Castle or in the Viceregal Lodge.

Public Buildings : The most important of the public buildings were the Parliament House, the Four Courts and the Custom House. The Parliament House was built first. After the ' Wood's Halfpence ' affair, the Lords and Commons were feeling so elated by their victory that they decided to erect a splendid new building in College Green. The foundation stone was laid in 1728, but the work of enlarging and embellishing

The Custom House, Dublin

the Parliament House went on all through the century. When completed, it was a beautiful building, the receding front with its grouped Ionic columns giving an effect of rare dignity and splendour. John Wesley, who visited it in 1787, was very impressed by the chambers in which the members met : he considered the House of Lords to " exceed " that of Westminster, and described the Commons as "a noble room indeed".

The Four Courts and the Custom House were the work of James Gandon, an English architect who came to Dublin in 1781 and spent the rest of his life in Ireland. After the repeal of Poynings' Law and ' the Sixth of George I ', the Irish Government decided to erect a number of public buildings in Dublin which would be in keeping with its new position as the capital of an independent nation. Gandon was engaged for the work : he designed the Custom House and the Four Courts and placed them most effectively on the banks of the Liffey. They are beautiful edifices in the classical tradition—indeed the Custom House has been described as " one of the noblest buildings in Europe ".

A great many improvements were also carried out during these years by the Wide Street Commissioners. They replaced the narrow and crooked streets of the city centre with great wide thoroughfares, and built a new bridge, Carlisle Bridge, over the Liffey, thus giving access from the Parliament House to Sackville Street (the modern O'Connell Street).

Town Houses : The great nobles vied with one another in the luxury and splendour of their town houses. Stately and dignified mansions, they were decorated and furnished with exquisite taste. This was the golden age of Irish craftsmanship ; silver, glass, metalwork and furniture were produced in great quantity and high quality. The walls and ceilings were decorated with elaborate plasterwork, the staircases had delicately-wrought iron balustrades, and the heavy mahogany doors were fitted with silver handles. Many Irish gentlemen went on the ' Grand Tour ' of Europe and decorated their rooms with the treasures they brought home : pictures and statues, vases and urns, marbles and medallions.

The most magnificent of the town houses was that of the Earl of Kildare and was called Leinster House ; but the Co. Down nobleman, the Earl of Moira, had one scarcely less imposing on the southern quays. In 1775 Wesley paid a visit there. " I waited on Lady Moira," he says, " and was surprised to observe . . . a far more elegant room than any I ever saw in England. It was an octagon, about twenty feet square and fifteen or sixteen high, having one window, the sides of it inlaid throughout with mother-of-pearl reaching from the top of the room to the bottom ; the ceiling, sides and furniture of the room were equally elegant."

Many of the town houses were on the south side, in Kildare

Street or Fitzwilliam Square or around St. Stephen's Green, where Henry Grattan lived. But the most fashionable quarter was north of the Liffey, where the slightly rising ground faced the midday sun and gave a view of the distant hills to the south. There in Rutland Square, for example, the Earl of Charlemont built a beautiful little residence and library, while in nearby Henrietta Street lived the Protestant Primate, the Earl of Kingston, the Earl of Thomond and Lord Mountjoy. Today this area retains little of its former elegance, and the houses are often let out in squalid and depressing tenements.

Life of the Rich : The life followed by the nobles and gentry was in keeping with their splendid surroundings. Everyone lived above his means. There was a passion for show, and houses swarmed with servants, ten or twelve being not unusual. Even a gentleman of moderate income kept a coach and four horses, with a coachman, a footman and at least one postilion. In the morning St. Stephen's Green would be crowded with lords and ladies, taking the air and discussing the latest news from London or the continent. Parliament met in the afternoon (rarely before 4 p.m.) and nearly always adjourned for dinner. Then began the interminable round of concerts, plays and masked balls. Those with ' an itch for gambling ' went to Daly's Club in Dame Street, where, it is said, the room was darkened in daytime and candles brought out to add to the excitement. High stakes created tension among the players, and duels were frequent. Indeed extravagance in dress, food, drink and gambling brought many of the gentry to the verge of bankruptcy, and estates were burdened with a mountain of debt.

More commendable was the interest of the upper class in drama and music. Many of the gentry had their own private play-houses, and there were professional theatres in Crow Street, Smock Alley and Fishamble Street where the great stars from London played—Garrick and Mrs. Siddons, Samuel Foote and Tate Wilkinson, Mrs. Abingdon and the Kembles. The greatest event in the cultural history of the city was probably the visit of Handel in 1741. A few weeks before his visit he had composed the *Messiah*, and thus the first public production of the sacred oratorio was given at the Music Hall in Fishamble Street by the combined choirs of St. Patrick's and Christ Church Cathedrals.

The Royal Dublin Society : Not all the aristocracy were taken up with drinking, gambling and duelling. Some, as we have seen, were interested in politics ; others threw themselves into the development of agriculture and trade. In 1731 the Dublin Society was founded for " the improvement of husbandry, manufactures and useful arts ". It did good work in all these spheres. Books on farming by English and Dutch writers were circulated; new implements were introduced, and new methods of tillage were recommended. Prizes were offered to those who produced the best crops or the highest quality of seeds. Industries were assisted and encouraged, especially the silk and linen industries, and prizes were given for the making of beer, glass, hemp, paper and hats.

At first the Society depended upon the subscriptions of its members, but eventually the Irish Parliament voted it a sum of money each year. The Society then extended its activities. In 1792 it began a natural history museum and, two years later, opened the Botanical Gardens. Just before the Union it appointed professors of Botany and Chemistry, and arranged lectures in these subjects. In its early days it met in Trinity College, but, after the Union, it moved to Leinster House, and from then on it became known as the Royal Dublin Society, because it had the patronage of George IV. It is still in existence, carrying on the aims of its founders, but is perhaps best known for the great shows it holds at Ballsbridge (its present headquarters) in the spring and summer of each year.

Life of the Poor : Behind all the big houses and the gracious living were the slums of Dublin, where the poor lived in terrible squalor. They were herded together, sometimes two or three families to a hovel, without sanitation or drinking water, while all around them, in the lanes and alleys, refuse and filth of every kind decayed, providing a fertile breeding ground for germs and disease. Excessive drinking added to the poor's miseries, and when fever moved through the slums they died by the thousand. Some of them moved into the better parts of the city to beg, but there was little sympathy for them there, and they were frequently collected by ' the Black Cart ' and carried off to the Workhouse. During periods of political excitement or of economic depression, they flocked down to College Green to demonstrate in front of the Parliament House or even, on occasion, to invade the chambers and make noisy scenes. This was particularly true of the weavers, who lived in ' the Liberties ', as the older parts of the city near Christ Church and St. Patrick's Cathedrals were called. In times of unemployment they attacked those who imported or sold English goods, which they believed were the cause of all their misery. The following extract from the *Dublin Evening Post* of May 14, 1737 will give some idea of the terror they caused :

" *A mob of weavers of the Liberty rose in order to rifle the several shops in this city for English manufactures, and stopped at the houses of Messrs. Eustace and Lindsay, woollen drapers in High Street; who, having notice of their coming, shut up their shops—as did all the other woollen drapers—at their approach. They forced off the hinges of Mr. Eustace's shop windows with hammers and chisels, but were prevented doing further mischief by the timely assistance of the sheriff and his bailiffs, whom the mob attacked. They then attacked several other shops of woollen drapers, but without committing any acts of depredation, except carrying off one small piece of English goods. Several were made prisoners in one house they broke into, and were sent to Newgate. They retired in a body to the Liberty, and threatened to pull down several houses if their associates who had been captured were not released. At length the army had to be brought against them, and a fight ensued in which one of the weavers was killed. Large bodies of military are still parading the streets. From Tuesday to Thursday several engage-*

ments took place between the troops and the rioters, in one engagement seven were reported to have been killed and nine wounded."

This is an aspect of Georgian Dublin that must not be overlooked. It was not overlooked at the time. There was no end to pamphlets explaining how the poor might be reformed, and a host of charitable and philanthropic societies were formed. But there was little real understanding of the causes of their misery—bad housing, unemployment, low wages. It was so much easier to blame it all on laziness, dishonesty and addiction to gin. In Ireland, as in Britain, it was not until the nineteenth century that the problems of poverty were seriously tackled.

Questions and Exercises

1. Give an account of the development of the Irish linen industry up to the middle of the eighteenth century.

2. Describe the changes which took place in the organisation of the linen industry from 1750 onwards, paying particular attention to (a) the influence of 'the bleachers', and (b) the development of Belfast as a marketing centre.

3. Outline the history of the cotton industry in Ulster.

4. Write an essay on *either* Belfast in the eighteenth century *or* Georgian Dublin.

CHAPTER EIGHTEEN

William Pitt and the French Revolution

1. Pitt's Political and Financial Reforms (1783-1793)

"A Kingdom Trusted to a Schoolboy's Care": A few months after the American War of Independence ended, George III invited a young man of twenty-four to become Prime Minister of Britain. He was William Pitt, son of the Earl of Chatham, who had led the country to victory during the Seven Years' War. The new Prime Minister had not a majority in the House of Commons and had practically no political exper- ience. A wit expressed the feeling of most politicians when he wrote :

> *A sight to make surrounding nations stare :*
> *A kingdom trusted to a schoolboy's care.*

Pitt formed his Government in December, 1783, and his opponents referred to it as " a mince-pie administration " meaning that it would last only for the Christmas season. But they were wrong. Pitt was a cold, aloof man of great deter- mination, and, though he was defeated again and again in the House of Commons, he refused to resign until he thought the time right for a general election. In March, 1784 he dissolved

Parliament and was returned with a substantial majority. To the consternation of his enemies " Young Mr. Pitt " remained in office for the next seventeen years !

Pitt as Prime Minister : The tasks before the new Prime Minister were enormous. The American War had cost a great deal of money, and the National Debt amounted to almost £250,000,000. Trade had decreased, taxation was high and smuggling was prevalent round the coasts. Unless some drastic financial reforms were undertaken, the nation seemed headed for bankruptcy. Pitt became Chancellor of the Exchequer as well as Prime Minister, and devoted the opening years of his rule to tackling this problem. He followed the earlier policy of Sir Robert Walpole in his strict supervision of government expenditure, and abolished many useless posts. He re-established the ' Sinking Fund ', which had been allowed to lapse. Every year £1,000,000 was to be paid into it, to accumulate at compound interest, and Pitt calculated that, if the fund were properly managed, the National Debt could be paid off in twenty-eight years. He issued invitations to financiers to lend money to the Government and selected those who charged the lowest rate of interest. When war broke out in 1793, he had reduced the National Debt by almost £10,000,000.

Pitt and Free Trade : Pitt was a supporter of the ' free trade ' doctrines of Adam Smith, a professor of Glasgow University, whose book *The Wealth of Nations* was published in 1776. Smith said that the more each country concentrated upon what it could best produce and the more all countries traded with one another, the more prosperous the world would become. In accordance with this idea Pitt negotiated a commercial treaty between Britain and France in 1786, whereby the two countries lowered their duties against each other's goods. He reduced the import duties, set up bonded warehouses for tobacco and spirits, and put an end to smuggling on a large scale. To make up for the money lost to the Exchequer by these changes, Pitt devised a number of new taxes. Some of these we would think strange— a tax on racehorses, on servants, on windows : but he did intro-

William Pitt addressing the House of Common

[National Portrait Gallery, London]

duce one that most adults pay today—income tax. Pitt first
imposed income tax in 1797 as a means of paying for the war
against France.

Other Reforms : Apart from tax and trade reforms, Pitt supported a number of movements which were not finally successful until after his death. In 1785 he introduced a Parliamentary
Reform Bill, in which he proposed that thirty-six small
boroughs returning members to the House of Commons should
be abolished, and their seventy-two seats allocated to the new
industrial towns of the north and midlands which were not
represented at all. The bill was defeated, and Pitt did not try
again. On the contrary, after the outbreak of the French
Revolution, he did his utmost to stamp out the movement for
Parliamentary Reform and dealt harshly with those who supported it.

Another movement which Pitt supported was that for the
abolition of slavery, which had been started by William
Wilberforce, Thomas Clarkson and others in 1787. They
revealed the horrible conditions under which Africans were
carried across the Atlantic, herded together between decks that
were often only four feet apart, chained to their seats and
brutally beaten. Pitt approved of Wilberforce's efforts to have
a bill passed through Parliament to end the slave trade, but
the influence of the Bristol and Liverpool merchants secured
the defeat of this measure, and it did not become law until 1807,
a year after Pitt's death.

Finally Pitt did something to make life easier for Catholics
in England and Ireland. A measure of Catholic relief had been
granted in 1778, but when, two years later, Lord North proposed to allow Catholics to exercise their religion freely, a
fanatical nobleman, Lord George Gordon, roused the London
mob with the cry of " No Popery ", and led an armed attack
on the House of Commons. The mob eventually got out of hand,
and for five days looted and burned houses all over London. But
this was the last great outburst of intolerance in British history,
and in 1791 Pitt passed a bill allowing Catholics to build

churches and schools. At the same time, and, largely as a result of pressure which he used, Irish Catholics were given similar rights and in 1793 were actually given the vote at parliamentary elections.

Pitt and the Empire : Pitt's period of office was marked by a number of important imperial reforms. In 1784 he passed an *India Act* under which that country was governed for the next seventy years. A Board of Control was established in London to supervise the political activities of the East India Company, and the consent of this Board was necessary before higher offices, such as those of Governor-General or Commander-in-Chief of the Company's forces, could be filled. The act also prohibited the Company from making alliances with native rulers or taking part in Indian wars. In 1788 Pitt sent out an expedition to Australia under Captain Arthur Phillip consisting of seven hundred convicts and a strong guard of soldiers, and from the settlement they made there developed a new colony in the South Seas. Three years later Pitt passed a *Canada Act* which created two provinces—*Upper Canada* (or Ontario where the population was predominantly British, and *Lower Canada* (or Quebec) where the French were in a majority. Each province elected its own Assembly and had its own Governor and Council nominated by the British Government.

Pitt and the War : Pitt hoped for a long period of peace to enable Britain to recover from the strain of the many wars in which she had engaged during the eighteenth century. This would give an opportunity for the financial reforms he had introduced to show their good effects. But in 1793, as we shall see, France declared war on Britain, and for the rest of his life Pitt was engaged in a life and death struggle with the traditional enemy. The Prime Minister was often criticised for his mistakes in conducting the war, but he did show great determination and never lost hope, even in the darkest days. That is why he is sometimes referred to as " the pilot who weathered the storm ". Pitt was modest about his achievements. A few months before his death in 1806, the Lord Mayor of London referred to him as " the saviour of Europe ". Pitt's reply to the Mayor has become famous. " I return you many thanks for the honour you have done me ; " he said, " but Europe is not saved by any single man. England has saved herself by her exertions, and will, I trust, save Europe by her example."

2. The French Revolution

France in the Eighteenth Century : During the seventeenth and eighteenth centuries France had fought many wars, first in Europe under Louis XIV, and then in India and North America in an effort to establish empires there. Wars cost money, and the French people were burdened with heavy taxes to pay for campaigns that brought little gain to the country. Money was spent in other ways as well. Louis XIV had built a beautiful palace at Versailles on the outskirts of Paris and had spent a fortune in furnishing it and laying out its gardens. His successors, Louis XV and Louis XVI, had continued his extravagance ; great crowds of nobles congregated at Versailles and idled away their time in amusement and frivolity.

In order to pay for this the people of France were taxed heavily. The principal source of revenue was the *taille,* a land tax, but many of the nobles who owned large estates obtained exemptions from its payment, and thus the ordinary people had to pay more than their share. A notorious tax, the *gabelle,* was levied on salt, and every person over seven years of age had to buy seven pounds of salt a year whether he needed it or not. The Government did not gather these taxes itself but sold the right of collection to men called " tax-farmers ", who squeezed as much as they could from the people and paid as little as they could to the Government. There was so much injustice, corruption and inefficiency in the levying and collection of taxes that the Government was always short of money.

The Privileges of Nobles and Clergy : Though they did nothing to deserve it, the nobles and higher clergy were exempt from many of the taxes that had to be paid by the rest of the population. They had a number of other valuable privileges as well. The peasant had to have his corn ground at the lord's mill and his bread baked in the lord's oven. He had to bring his animals to the lord's abattoir and his grapes to the lord's wine-press. For all these services the lord charged a heavy fee, and the peasant had no option but to pay. In addition, by a system known as the *corvée* the peasant could be taken out of his fields where he was busy and put to work on the public roads.

The archbishops, bishops and higher clergy had all the privi-leges of the nobles, and, many of them led useless and disedify-ing lives. Many of the bishops were absentees and frequently took political posts under the Crown. But the parish priests were very poor, recruited from the common people and sharing in all their hardships. When the Revolution came, they supported the rebels against the King.

It must also be remembered that the Church owned large estates, probably as much as one-fifth of the land of France. Consequently writers like Voltaire had little difficulty in find-ing support when they attacked the Church, for many hoped to gain from a distribution of its lands.

The Government of France : There was no way in which the people's resentment against these abuses could be made known. The States General, as the French Parliament was called, had not met since 1614, and thus there was no place where the grievances of the country could be attended to. All power was centered in the king. If he wanted a new law or required a new tax, he simply issued an edict, and for advice he turned to his favourite nobles. The middle-class professional men—the ' bourgeoisie '—resented this state of affairs, especially as they were convinced that they had the ability to help the King rule the country more efficiently. But things might have remained as they were for a long time had not a number of events occurred at the end of the eighteenth century which gave the bourgeoisie an opportunity of leading a revolt.

The War in America : One of these events was the American Revolution. In 1776 the English colonists in North America had rebelled against the mother country and had declared their independence. Louis XVI and his ministers regarded the war which followed as an opportunity of avenging themselves on Britain for the loss of Canada and India in the Seven Years' War. French troops were sent across the Atlantic to help the rebels and made a contribution to their ultimate victory. But the intervention had unforeseen consequences for France. The soldiers returned with democratic ideas and were even more dissatisfied with conditions at home. The Americans had rebelled because a Parliament, in which they were not represented, had attempted to tax them ; but the French had no Parliament at all, and their system of taxation was far more inequitable and unjust than that against which they had just fought. The American victory must have encouraged many a Frenchman to hope for a like success. Nor was this all: in helping to defeat Britain, France had bankrupted herself. A new system of taxation would have to be devised, and so, in desperation, Louis XVI decided to call the States General after a lapse of one hundred and seventy-five years.

The French Revolution : The States General met at Versailles in May, 1789, and the bourgeoisie determined to make the most of the King's difficulties. They had no wish to harm Louis XVI but only to reform his Government, and a cleverer man than the King might have been able to handle them. But Louis XVI had no policy at all and shifted from side to side until no one would trust him. Crowds of hungry people gathered in Paris, and there on July 14th they attacked the Bastille, the city prison. This was the beginning of rioting, which got worse and worse as the months passed. In October the King and his family were taken by the mob from Versailles to Paris, and spent the next three years there in terror of their lives. In June, 1791 Louis XVI escaped from the capital in a coach with his family, but they were captured at Varennes, near the German border, and brought back to Paris. The King's popularity was now gone, and the crowds jeered him as his carriage passed.

Death of the King and Queen : War broke out in 1792 with Prussia and Austria, but the undisciplined French soldiers were routed in the Netherlands and driven into retreat. Immediately there was panic in Paris. The King was deposed, and France was declared to be a republic. Nobles who were suspected of sympathy with the invading armies were taken into custody, and hundreds were sent to the guillotine. A 'Reign of Terror' ensued, and finally, in January, 1793 the King himself was executed. The Queen, Marie Antoinette, was held a prisoner for some months longer, but eventually she too was put to death. Their executions were not the end of trouble, however, but its beginning.

3. Britain and the French Revolution

A Difference of Opinion : At first many people in England had welcomed the Revolution. The poet Wordsworth, then only nineteen years of age, hailed it as the beginning of a new age of happiness for France. He wrote :

> " Bliss was it in that dawn to be alive,
> But to be young was very heaven."

The Radical, Charles James Fox, on hearing of the capture of the Bastille exclaimed, " How much the greatest event that has happened in the world, and how much the best." Those who favoured parliamentary reform were also jubilant and believed that, if the revolutionaries established a democratic form of government in France, England would be forced to follow her example. But when events beyond the Channel began to take a violent course, and first the nobles and then the King were sent to the scaffold, Englishmen became less enthusiastic in their support of the Revolution. Edmund Burke, the great Whig politician, had opposed the Revolution from the beginning, and in 1790 he warned Englishmen against it in his book *Reflections on the French Revolution.* "No monarchy," he wrote, " . . . can possibly be safe as long as this strange, nameless, wild, enthusiastic thing is established in the centre of Europe. Revolution can only lead to bloodshed and disorder. They in turn will give place to a military tyrant." The disturbances of the succeeding months convinced many of the accuracy of Burke's prophecies, and they became bitter opponents of the Revolution. An indication of the change in public opinion was the riot which took place in Birmingham in July, 1791. The supporters of the Revolution met to celebrate the capture of the Bastille, but the mob rose in fury against them and almost wrecked the city. From then on relations between England and France got worse and worse.

Outbreak of War : But Pitt was anxious to avoid war : he believed that a period of peace was necessary to allow his financial reforms to have their full effects. In 1792 he cut down the strength of the army and navy, and said that he was looking forward to fifteen years of peace. But the English people were so incensed by the happenings in France during the following year that war between the two countries became inevitable. In 1792 the revolutionaries took up arms against Austria and Prussia and issued this threat : " Come all the Kings of Europe in arms against us, and we will hurl at their feet, in defiance, the head of a King." On January 21, 1793 they carried out their threat and executed Louis XVI in the Place de la Concorde in Paris. Earlier they had driven back the invading armies and declared that they would make war " against all Kings and on behalf of all peoples ". The revolutionary forces then overran the Austrian Netherlands and obtained control of the Channel coast. They captured Antwerp and opened up for trade the river Scheldt in violation of the Treaty of Utrecht (1713). Pitt made a spirited protest : the French reply was a declaration of war (February 1, 1793).

Repressive Measures: Even before the war began, the Government had taken steps to prevent the spread of dangerous political ideas in Britain. In 1791 Tom Paine, an English Quaker who had fought for the Americans during the War of Independence, had published an answer to Burke which he called *The*

Rights of Man. In the next year he added a second part to the book in which he advocated the abolition of the monarchy and the establishment of a British Republic. Pitt's Government banned the book and decided to prosecute the author for a " scandalous, malicious and seditious libel ". Paine fled to France, but the Government determined to stamp out in England all sympathy for the French Revolution. In 1793 an Aliens Act was passed to deal with French spies, and in 1794 the Habeas Corpus Act was suspended so that people could be imprisoned without trial. Seditious writings were made punishable, and it was made treason to utter words against the King or to communicate in any way with the French. One can understand Pitt's determination, now that Britain was at war, to ensure that supporters of the enemy should not be allowed to hamper the national effort, but in his anxiety he went too far. Societies advocating parliamentary reform were harassed and could hold no meetings without official approval. Even trade unions were suspect, and in 1799 and 1800 Anti-Combination Acts were passed, forbidding workers to form associations for improving their working conditions. Pitt was determined that England should not imitate France.

Questions and Exercises

1. Give an account of William Pitt's domestic and imperial reforms (1783-1793).

2. What were the causes of the French Revolution ? Summarise the course of the Revolution (1789-1793).

3. What was the attitude of the British people towards the French Revolution ? Why did this attitude change ? How was the change reflected in government legislation (1793-1800) ?

4. Why did Britain and France go to war in 1793 ?

CHAPTER NINETEEN

The Wars with France (1793-1815)

1. The War at Sea: Nelson and Napoleon

The First Coalition : In 1793 the new French Republic was surrounded by a ring of enemies—Britain, Austria, Prussia, Spain and Holland—and they formed what is called *the First Coalition*. At the start the French were overwhelmed and driven out of the Netherlands, but then the revolutionaries reorganised their forces and hurled back the invading armies across their frontiers. Pitt's contribution to the war was a force of ten thousand men, which he sent to Dunkirk under the command of the Duke of York. The nursery rhyme indicates how little the British army achieved :

> *The grand old Duke of York,*
> *He had ten thousand men,*
> *He marched them up to the top of a hill*
> *And marched them down again.*

The Duke of Wellington, who served with the expedition as a junior officer, said afterwards that he had learned one good lesson there : how not to do it. The allies did not have any

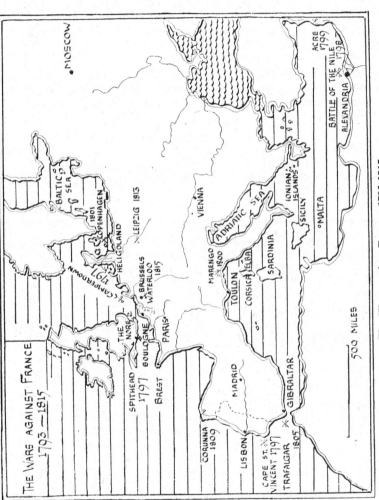

The Wars against France, 1793-1815

plans, and one by one they dropped out of the coalition until only Britain and Austria were left. Pitt then tried to make peace, but the French, intoxicated by their success, laid down unreasonable terms and so the war continued.

The Naval Mutinies : 1797 was a black year for Britain. The coalition had broken up, and some of its former members, notably Spain and Holland, had gone over to the side of France. The navies of these three countries began to prepare for an invasion of England, and the British Government feared the consequences. To add to their worries they had a financial crisis on their hands at home and the threat of a revolution in Ireland. Everything depended on the strength of the Royal Navy. But to the horror of the Government, this was the moment chosen by the British fleets at Spithead and the Nore to mutiny. They had good reasons for doing so : many of the sailors had been press-ganged into the navy against their wills, and were flogged to make them work. Their food was bad, consisting of salted meat and ships' biscuits, and hundreds died every year from scurvy. Pay was small and often years in arrears ; they were rarely allowed shore-leave and went for long periods without seeing their families. The Spithead mutiny was settled first, and the crews returned to their posts, once they were promised better conditions and a royal pardon. But the mutineers at the Nore refused to yield until certain harsh and unpopular officers were removed. They were led by Richard Parker, a former midshipman who had been reduced in the ranks for insubordination, and they decided to blockade the Thames and starve out London, as a means of forcing the authorities to concede their demands. But the Government held firm, and, one by one, the ships of the Nore fleet were forced to surrender. The ring-leaders were punished severely: thirty-nine were executed, and the remainder were flogged with a ' cat-o'-nine-tails '. Parker was hanged from the yardarm of his ship, in order to impress upon the crews the Government's determination to stamp out such behaviour in the future. This severity was due, in large measure, to Pitt's belief that the mutineers were in sympathy with the French, a charge which the sailors stoutly denied. By their action, however, they had left England open to invasion at a critical time, and it was only the sea-victories of Cape St. Vincent over the Spaniards (which actually took place before the mutiny) and of Camperdown over the Dutch that restored Britain's confidence in her fleets. Cape St. Vincent was important for another reason: it first brought into prominence Horatio Nelson, one of the great heroes of British history.

Horatio Nelson (1758-1805): Nelson, the son of a Norfolk clergyman, was born in the village of Burnham Thorpe on September 29, 1758. Frail and delicate as a child, he never enjoyed the robust health one associates with a sailor, and he frequently suffered from sea-sickness. An uncle on his mother's side was a captain in the Royal Navy and, when only twelve years old, young Horatio joined his vessel as a midshipman. During the next eight years Nelson gained great experience, serving in merchant vessels as well as ships of war and even participating in a voyage of exploration to the Arctic. Before he was twenty-one, he had been made a captain, and he served with distinction in the West Indies and off the coast of North America.

When the American War of Independence ended, Nelson, like many other seamen, was put on compulsory leave, with half-pay, because there was nothing for him to do. He remained ashore for six years. But, on the outbreak of war with France in 1793, he was recalled and given command of the battleship, *Agamemnon*. His commander-in-chief, Lord Hood, put him in charge of a naval party which was to capture the French island of Corsica in the Mediterranean, and it was during the fighting there that Nelson lost the sight of his right eye.

Battle of Cape St. Vincent (1797): In 1796, when the first coalition was breaking up, the British Government decided to abandon the Mediterranean, and Nelson was given the difficult task of organising the withdrawal. This done, he joined Sir

John Jervis on the eve of the battle of Cape St. Vincent, fought off the coast of Portugal in 1797. This was the first great naval encounter of the war, and Nelson played a decisive part in gaining a British victory. The Spaniards outnumbered the British by twenty-seven ships to fifteen, but Nelson, in a brilliant manoeuvre, broke line as the two fleets joined battle, and attracted to himself at least seven of the enemy, including the *Santissima Trinidad,* the largest warship afloat. The Spanish ships were thrown into confusion, and Nelson attacked them for over an hour, until one by one they surrendered. Nelson himself led a boarding-party and received the submission of the ships' captains and of the dying Spanish admiral. For his part in the victory (though he had broken the order of his commander by his tactics!) Nelson was made a rear-admiral.

Not long afterwards Nelson was put in charge of an expedition against the Spanish base of Santa Cruz in the Canary Islands, but failed to capture it and lost his right arm. He had already lost his right eye, and for a time he was depressed, as he feared his naval career might be ended. " I am become a burden to my friends and useless to my country," he said. But his spirits soon revived, and, after a short leave, he joined Admiral Jervis's fleet aboard the *Vanguard.*

The Battle of the Nile (1798) : Meanwhile in France a young general, about whom we shall hear a great deal, had come to the fore. He was Napoleon Bonaparte who, by his brilliant victories in 1796 and 1797, had forced Austria to sue for peace and so had brought about the end of the first coalition. Only Britain was now left at war with France, and Napoleon believed she could be most seriously injured in her overseas possessions. He decided to overrun Egypt and Syria, and to create a French eastern empire of which India would be part. He gathered a large army and fleet at Toulon in the spring of 1798, and Nelson was sent into the Mediterranean to watch him. At this stage no one knew what the French proposed to do but many thought they would sail for Ireland, where the United Irishmen were preparing to revolt. But whatever Napoleon's destination,

Nelson was patiently waiting outside Toulon ready to give battle.

Napoleon escaped from the harbour unnoticed when the British fleet had been driven off-shore by a storm. Nelson did not know where Napoleon had gone, but guessed that he might have sailed for Egypt and hotly pursued him. Napoleon delayed on the way at Malta, and so, when Nelson reached Alexandria, the French had not yet arrived. Fearing that his guess had not been correct, Nelson now began a frantic search for the enemy, and sailed to and fro in the Mediterranean for nearly a month. At last, almost in despair, he paid another visit to Alexandria and saw the French fleet anchored in Aboukir Bay at the mouth of the Nile. Though it was late in the afternoon, Nelson decided to attack at once, and the battle lasted all night. The French ships were anchored close to the shore, and all the guns were lined along the starboard (or seaward) side, as the commander expected the attack to come from there. But once more Nelson showed his courage and foolhardiness. Without pilots or charts, he sailed between the French ships and the coast and took them from the rear. Never was there a more complete naval victory than the *Battle of the Nile* (August 1, 1798). Of the thirteen French ships nine were captured, two were burnt and two escaped. With the fleet destroyed, Napoleon was a prisoner in Egypt. He decided to march northwards through Syria and Turkey and to return overland to France. But at Acre he was held up by a Turkish garrison, reinforced by a British force under Sir Sidney Smith. Thwarted now on every side, Napoleon deserted his troops, returned by sea to France and made himself virtually the dictator of the country with the title of First Consul (1799).

Battle of Copenhagen (1801): While he had been out of Egypt, a second coalition had been formed, consisting of Britain, Austria and Russia. Napoleon decided to break it up. With his usual speed he crossed the Alps, defeated the Austrians at the battle of Marengo (1800) and compelled them to make peace by the Treaty of Luneville. Russia withdrew from the coalition.

and for the second time Britain was left to face France alone.

As in previous wars, Britain had insisted on searching the vessels of neutral nations to ensure that they were not carrying war materials to France. This interference with their trade was resented by many countries, and so Napoleon decided to organise the Baltic powers of Denmark, Sweden, Prussia and Russia into the *Armed Neutrality,* to protest against this practice and to defy it. Britain's reply was to send a fleet into the Baltic, under Sir Hyde Parker, with Nelson as second-in-command, either to negotiate a settlement with the dissatisfied fleets or to destroy them. When the British ships reached Copenhagen where the Danish fleet was anchored, Parker hesitated, but eventually he gave Nelson permission to attack. Copenhagen was strongly fortified, and Nelson took great risks in coming close to the shore in an effort to destroy its guns. Three of his ships ran aground and the others suffered heavy casualties. Fearing a disaster, Parker ordered the ships to withdraw, but, when the admiral's signal was pointed out to Nelson, he raised his telescope to his blind eye, and said, " I really do not see the signal." After four hours bombardment the Danes surrendered. The British losses were heavy, but Nelson had made Britain mistress of the Baltic as well as of the Mediterranean.

Peace of Amiens (1802) : Both sides were now tired of war and wanted peace. William Pitt had disagreed with George III on the question of Catholic Emancipation, and was replaced as Prime Minister by Addington. Addington negotiated with Napoleon the Peace of Amiens, whereby Britain gave up all her conquests, except Ceylon and Trinidad, and promised to restore Malta to the Knights of St. John. The British understood that Napolean would withdraw his armies from Holland, Switzerland and Italy. The peace was very popular. The British Prime Minister called it " a genuine reconciliation between the two first nations of the world ", and, when the new French ambassador arrived in London, his carriage was pulled through the streets by delighted crowds.

The Invasion of Britain : The Peace of Amiens was only a breathing space. Napoleon needed time in order to consolidate his position in France, to come to terms with the Church and to prepare the Code Napoleon. In 1803 he began his conquests again ; he sent an army to reconquer San Domingo in the West Indies and began to stir up trouble in India. The British, therefore, did not trust him, and refused to surrender Malta as they had promised to do by the Treaty of Amiens. In addition the English newspapers bitterly attacked Napoleon and carried caricatures of " the Corsican ogre ". Angrily Napoleon ordered the imprisonment of ten thousand British tourists who had taken advantage of the peace to visit France. In these circumstances war could not be long delayed, and in May hostilities began again.

Napoleon decided to invade Britain. He gathered an army of one hundred thousand men at Boulogne and began the building of sufficient boats to ferry them over the Channel. There was a great deal of panic in England, for the people were by now aware of Napoleon's military ability. Half a million men joined the volunteer corps, and Martello towers were built to protect the coasts. But as usual Britain really depended upon her navy for, if the seasoned French troops had succeeded in making a landing, they would have been difficult to defeat. The Royal Navy was determined that Napoleon should not cross the Channel, and Admiral Jervis quipped, " I won't say the French can't come ; I only know they can't come by water!"

In 1805 Napoleon prepared a plan. As many of his fleets as possible were to put to sea and sail across the Atlantic to the West Indies. There they were to unite to form a large force, and then return to seize control of the English Channel so that Napoleon could move his huge army over to England. In the beginning the plan looked like succeeding, Villeneuve, who was being blockaded by Nelson in Toulon, escaped with his fleet and, having been joined by some Spanish ships from Cadiz, sailed for the West Indies. Nelson followed him, but Villeneuve was awaiting the arrival of the Brest fleet in Martinique and kept out of the British admiral's way.

Brest was so closely blockaded, however, that the French fleet there could not put to sea, and so Villeneuve decided to return to Europe on his own. Nelson followed close behind him and sent a fast ship to warn the Admiralty of Villeneuve's return. Sir Robert Calder was sent out to intercept him, but Calder was not Nelson and, after a brief encounter, the French fleet was allowed to take refuge in Cadiz. This was the end of Napoleon's invasion scheme. In August, 1805 he broke up his camp at Boulogne and marched his army eastwards against the Austrians and Russians. Once more Britain had been saved by her fleet.

The Battle of Trafalgar (1805) : Nelson was disappointed that Villeneuve had been allowed to escape, and, once he had taken some leave (he had been two years continuously at sea), prepared to destroy him. The French admiral had been accused by Napoleon of cowardice and was anxious to prove his worth in an engagement with Nelson. On October 21, 1805 the two fleets joined, off Cape Trafalgar, in the most famous naval battle in history. Nelson split his fleet into two parts—one led by himself in the *Victory,* the other by Collingwood in the *Royal Sovereign.* The battle began just before noon, and by three in the afternoon the enemy was defeated. But Nelson was dead : about a quarter past one a ball hit him on the left shoulder and shattered his spine. As he lay dying, he knew from the cheers of the crew that victory was already won. " Thank God, I have done my duty " were his last words.

The death of Nelson was a tragic loss to Britain, but he had completed the task to which he had dedicated his life. Napoleon's armies might be invincible on land, but his mastery ended at the shore. At sea the British warships had no rivals. That is why the war from now on is sometimes called " the struggle between the elephant and the whale ". Were there any means by which either could overcome the other ? Napoleon thought there were, and it was in attempting to carry them out that he brought about his own downfall.

The Death of Nelson on H.M.S. Victory, 1805

2. The War on Land: Wellington and Napoleon

Napoleon Bonaparte (1769-1821): Napoleon Bonaparte was born at Ajaccio on the island of Corsica in 1769. His parents were of noble birth but were then quite poor and had a large family. From his earliest years he was determined to be a soldier, and when he was ten his parents sent him to a military academy in France. From then on, the army was his career, but an opportunity to show his qualities as a leader did not come until the outbreak of the Revolutionary War in 1793. Put in charge of the army in Italy, he provided the French with some of their most spectacular victories, and forced the Austrians to sign the Treaty of Campo Formio (1797). His words to the soldiers at the opening of the campaign have become famous: " You are badly fed and nearly naked. I am going to lead you to the most fertile plains in the world. You will find there great cities and rich provinces. You will find there honour, glory and wealth."

Napoleon's second great expedition was to Egypt in 1798, but Nelson cut short his stay there by the Battle of the Nile. He returned to France, overthrew the Government and made himself First Consul. From then on he ruled the country, and in 1804 became the Emperor Napoleon. In that year, also, he began to gather troops at Boulogne for the invasion of England, but Nelson's final victory at Trafalgar put an end to his hopes. He had to find some other way of subduing his most obstinate enemy.

The Continental System : Napoleon's new plan of campaign against Britain was the *Continental System*. He believed that, if he could prevent her from importing food and raw materials and from exporting manufactured goods to pay for them, Britain could be starved into surrender. His navy was destroyed at Trafalgar and thus Napoleon could not blockade Britain, but, if he could prevent the nations under his domination from importing British goods, then he believed he could bring his enemy to her knees. In 1806 and 1807 by the Berlin and Milan Decrees he ordered the countries of Europe to boycott British goods and not to allow British ships into their harbours. To this Britain replied by an Order in Council, refusing to allow any ships to enter ports from which British ships were excluded.

Napoleon made strenuous efforts to make his decrees effective, and one country after another was forced to submit. The weak links in the system were Spain and Portugal, and through their ports British goods were being smuggled into the continent. In 1808 Napoleon decided to close the gap. A French army was sent into the Peninsula under Marshal Junot; it forced the King of Portugal to flee to Brazil and overthrew the Spanish royal family. Napoleon then made his brother Joseph King of Spain and sent him to Madrid with a large army. But this time Napoleon had bitten off more than he could chew. The national pride of the Spaniards and the Portuguese was aroused, and for the first time he found himself in conflict with a nation, and not merely with its ruler. Britain controlled the seas and compelled the French to bring all their supplies across the Pyrenees. On this journey bands of Spanish guerillas ambushed and harassed them every mile of the way. In an effort to stop this Napoleon sent more and more men into Spain, until the great part of his army was engaged permanently there. The British Government was quick to see the possibilities of this situation, and an army was sent to the Peninsula under Sir Arthur Wellesley.

Wellesley : Sir Arthur Wellesley, later Duke of Wellington, was the son of Lord Mornington and was born in Ireland in 1769. For a time he represented Trim (Co. Meath) in the Irish Parliament, then entered the army and served in India. But it was in Europe that he won fame, and it was for his victories over the French that he was made Duke of Wellington.

His first engagement in the Peninsula was not very promising. He defeated Marshal Junot at Vimiero (1808) and was planning the capture of Lisbon, when a senior officer who had just arrived in Spain intervened and allowed the French to escape. For a time Wellesley was blamed for this blunder, and returned to England while the matter was being investigated. He was replaced by Sir John Moore, who is chiefly remembered for his retreat to Corunna. He fell in the final battle outside the town, and Wellesley returned to the Peninsula once more as commander of the British forces.

The Peninsular War : The war in the Peninsula continued for another three years, but it is unnecessary to trace Wellesley's part in it in any detail. In 1809 he won a great victory at Talavera, for which he was made Viscount Wellington. He was often short of arms, clothing and food, but he courageously fought on, harassing Napoleon and thwarting his plans. In 1812 he captured Madrid and the next year drove the French out of Spain. Napoleon had made his task somewhat easier by withdrawing many of his more experienced troops for the Russian campaign. Before the end of 1813 Wellington had crossed the Pyrenees into France—the first foreign general to invade France since the early days of the Revolution.

The Invasion of Russia : In 1811 the Czar of Russia broke away from the Continental System and began to trade with Britain. Napoleon feared that other rulers might follow his example, and so he decided to teach him a lesson. With an army of over half a million he invaded Russia in the summer of 1812. The Russians retreated before him, destroying their crops as they went, and drawing the French forces through a country that was little more than a barren waste. Napoleon expected that when he reached Moscow he would be able to replenish his supplies there, but in September the Russians burned their capital to the ground and the French were forced to retreat across the devastated land. The snow came and the cold east wind, but Napoleon's troops were clad only for a summer's campaign. The story of the retreat is one of the best known in history. His men were unprepared for the hardships they had to endure : some deserted and were eaten by the wolves, thousands died from hunger and disease. The Cossacks attacked them continuously, and only the skill and courage of Marshal Ney, who commanded the rearguard, prevented the army from being annihilated. But it was a terrible blow to Napoleon's prestige : of his fine army of six hundred thousand, only twenty thousand returned alive, and few of them would ever fight again.

The War of Liberation : From now on, everything seemed to go wrong for Napoleon. He hastened back to France and raised a new army, even young boys being pressed into the ranks. Russia, Prussia and Austria formed an alliance against him, and England supplied them with the money they needed. In October, 1813 they attacked Napoleon at Leipzig, and, after a great battle lasting for three days, they defeated him. He retreated towards France with his enemies in full cry after him, while Wellington crossed the Pyrenees and advanced on Paris from the south. Napoleon wanted to fight on, but his generals forced him to abdicate. The allies placed Louis XVIII, brother of Louis XVI,* on the throne of France, and banished Napoleon to the island of Elba in the Mediterranean.

The Battle of Waterloo (1815) : Representatives of Russia, Prussia, Austria and Britain then met in congress at Vienna in order to decide the future of France, to draw up a new map of Europe and to take steps to ensure that a war of this kind would never occur again. But while the congress was in session, Napoleon suddenly escaped from Elba and returned to France with eight hundred men. He was received with enthusiasm : his veterans joined him in crowds, and a regiment, sent to arrest him, marched behind him to Paris. He declared that he intended to rule as a constitutional sovereign and to live at peace with the rulers of all countries. But they were not prepared to trust him, and they began to mobilise their forces once more. By June, 1815 two of their armies were ready : a mixed force of

---

*Louis XVI's son, whom royalists regarded as Louis XVII, died in 1795.

British, Dutch and German troops under the Duke of Wellington, and a Prussian army under Field Marshal Blücher. Wellington's force was at Brussels, with an advance guard some distance to the south of it at Quatre Bras ; Blücher, with his Prussian army, was at Ligny. Their plan was to combine for an attack on Napoleon, but he tried to forestall them by invading Belgium and engaging each separately. On June 16, Napoleon attacked the Prussian position at Ligny and dispatched Marshal Ney against Wellington at Quatre Bras. Blücher was defeated and began to retreat, so Wellington fell back along with him, the two armies keeping in close contact. The allied commanders decided to make a stand at Waterloo and turned to face Napoleon. Throughout the whole of June 18, the French charged against the rising ground where Wellington's forces were, but failed to make any impression on his lines. Finally in the evening, Napoleon called on ' the Old Guard ' to make one last effort, only to see his veterans repulsed. Wellington then began a counter-offensive, and, aided by Blücher's troops who had now joined him, drove the French before him from the field of Waterloo. Napoleon fled and tried to escape to America, but he was captured by a British ship, *H.M.S. Bellerophon.* This time the allies decided that he must be placed at a safe distance from Europe, and sent him to the lonely island of St. Helena in the South Atlantic, where he died in 1821.

British Gains from the War : The powers of Europe whose work had been interrupted by Napoleon's return assembled once more at Vienna after his defeat. They dealt first with France. Louis XVIII was recognised as King, but an army of occupation, under Wellington, was left in the country for a few years until a large war indemnity was paid ; and the states bordering France were strengthened in an effort to prevent any further French aggression. It is not necessary to describe in detail these arrangements, except to say that, in general, the countries which had supported Napoleon were punished and those which had opposed him were rewarded. Britain's gains

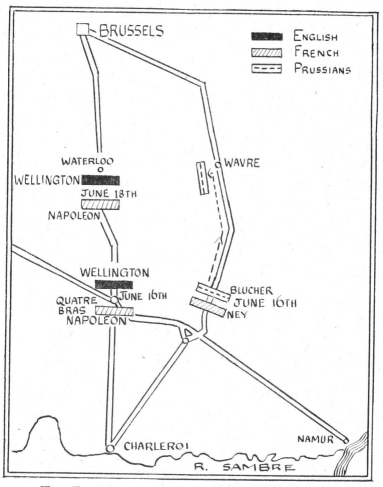

THE BATTLE OF WATERLOO ~ JUNE 18TH, 1815.

were small but important, and were mainly islands of strategic or economic value. In Europe she acquired Malta and Heligoland which she used as naval bases, and the Ionian Isles which gave her control of the entrance to the Adriatic Sea. Britain had taken Ceylon and the Cape of Good Hope from the Dutch in the early stages of the war, and was allowed to retain them by the treaty. These, along with Mauritius and the Seychelles, which she took from France, were regarded as important acquisitions, because they strengthened British control of the sea route to India. In the West Indies she obtained the sugar-growing islands of Tobago and St. Lucia from France, and Trinidad from Spain.

Thus only a generation after the loss of the American colonies a new British Empire had been created with territory in every continent—Canada, India, Australia, South Africa and the West Indies—and a large number of islands and trading ports scattered all over the seas of the world.

Questions and Exercises

1. Trace a large map of Europe and the Mediterranean Basin, and on it mark and name the following :—

    (a) The river which the French opened for trade, against British wishes, in 1793.

    (b) The two places where naval mutinies occurred in 1797

    (c) Nelson's three victories of 1798, 1801 and 1805.

    (d) The island where Napoleon was born, and the island to which he was exiled in 1814.

    (e) The great victories of Wellington over the French : 1809 and 1815.

    (f) The harbour where Napoleon gathered his forces for the invasion of Britain.

    (g) The place where Sir John Moore was killed (1809).

(h) The battle in which Napoleon was defeated after his retreat from Moscow (1813).

(i) The city where the victorious powers met in conference after the war (1815).

(j) The islands acquired by Britain in Europe : Heligoland, Malta, Ionian Isles.

2. Why did Britain and France go to war in 1793? What part did Britain play in the war, between 1793 and 1802?

3. Describe the career of Lord Nelson, and discuss the importance of his naval victories.

4. Explain the different plans which Napoleon had for conquering Britain. Why did each of them fail?

5. What were the causes of the Peninsular War ? Describe the part played by the British forces in defeating Napoleon there?

6. Describe, with the aid of a sketch map, Napoleon's campaigns and defeats from 1812 to 1815.

7. On a map of the world indicate the extent of Britain's over-seas possessions in 1815.

The Wars against France (1702–1815)

Britain's Gains and Losses

War	Date	Treaty	Terms
War of the Spanish Succession	1702–1713	Utrecht	Louis XIV's grandson, Philip V on throne of Spain. Emperor Charles got Netherlands, Milan, Naples and Sardinia. *Britain gained* Gibraltar, Minorca from Spain, Newfoundland, Nova Scotia and lands round Hudson Bay from France. The Old Pretender was expelled from France.
War of the Austrian Succession	1740–1748	Aix-la-Chapelle	Frederick II of Prussia kept Silesia. Britain restored Louisburg to France in exchange for Madras. *Britain gained little from the War.*
The Seven Years' War	1756–1763	Paris	*Britain gained* Canada and Cape Breton Island from France, while the French finally recognised British possession of Nova Scotia, Newfoundland and lands round Hudson Bay. Britain also gained Dominica, Grenada, Tobago and St. Vincent in the West Indies, as well as receiving Florida from Spain. France recognised British predominance in India and surrendered Senegal in West Africa. British Empire now greatest in world.
The War of American Independence	1775–1783	Versailles	*Britain lost* her thirteen colonies, which became the United States of America. Restored Senegal to France, Minorca and Florida to Spain.
The Revolutionary War	1793–1802	Amiens	*Britain retained* Ceylon (taken from Holland) and Trinidad (taken from Spain), but promised to restore other conquests including Malta to the Knights of St. John. Understood *France retained* Belgium and Rhine frontier. Understood she would leave Holland, Switzerland and Italy.
The Napoleonic Wars	1803–1815	Vienna	British gains: *From France* St. Lucia and Tobago in the West Indies, Mauritius and Seychelles in Indian Ocean. *From Spain* Trinidad. *From Holland* Cape of Good Hope, Ceylon and part of Guiana in South America. *Also* Heligoland, Malta and a protectorate over the Ionian Isles. Britain's gains were of strategic and commercial importance.

CHAPTER TWENTY

Georgian England

The eighteenth century was a period of warfare. It opened with Britain and France engaged in a conflict about the succession to the Spanish throne : when it closed Napoleon Bonaparte had not yet been defeated. We have studied the course of each of these wars, in turn, because of their tremendous importance for Britain. As a result of them she not only established her naval supremacy over France and increased her overseas trade; she also added greatly to her territory. Though the thirteen colonies of North America were lost, a new empire was already taking shape in India, Canada, the West Indies, Australia and South Africa. It would be a mistake to assume, however, that these wars affected the lives of the ordinary Englishman in the way that a war would affect our lives today. Most of the campaigns were fought in far-away places with strange names, and only the professional soldiers and sailors were involved. No doubt, the war against Napoleon was carried on nearer home, and there was always the danger that ' Boney ' might invade the country and bring it under his control. But, even then—apart from an occasional invasion scare—most people went about their business as usual and were far more concerned about the great changes that were taking place in agriculture and industry than about anything else. The new wealth, which these changes were creating, was responsible for the higher standards of living of the upper and middle classes. They now had better designed and more comfortable homes, decorated and furnished by superb craftsmen and often surrounded by beautifully laid out parks and gardens. They were, too, patrons of artists and musicians, and filled their houses with furniture by Chippendale or Hepplewhite, with Wedgewood china and beautifully wrought silver, with portraits by Reynolds and Gainsborough or landscapes by Turner and Constable. Few periods in British history have left a more impressive record of cultural achievement than the eighteenth century.

But there was another side to the picture. The beautiful country houses were often surrounded by the hovels of the workers, and behind the imposing terraces of town houses were horrible slums where coarse and ill-clad men and women drank their lives away in gin. In these homes there was no culture, only sordid crime, disease, brutality and death. But before the century ended, there were signs of improvement here also, for the eighteenth century had a number of great humanitarians; Thomas Coram who established the Foundling Hospital, John Howard who devoted his life to the reform of the prisons, and Edward Jenner who helped to control smallpox, which was the dreaded disease of all countries at that time.

1. The Rich and their Pleasures

Homes and Gardens : When dealing with the architecture of Georgian England, text-books sometimes concentrate on the vast palaces and mansions, designed by architects like Sir John Vanbrugh and Sir William Chambers for wealthy nobles and great landowners. No doubt Blenheim Palace near Oxford and Holkham Hall in Norfolk are impressive buildings and reflect the taste of the wealthier members of the aristocracy—but they are not typical of English architecture of the time. More characteristic of the period are the moderate sized private houses, examples of which still exist in many an English town. These are generally built of brick—red or yellow or grey—and delight the eye by their simple exteriors and graceful proportions. Their doorways are often beautiful and have elaborate fanlights, while the railings and lantern holders are fashioned in wrought iron.

Another characteristic of the period was the care which architects took in the lay-outs of their buildings. Whole areas were planned and mapped out, before any work began, to give harmony in the grouping of houses and to contrast formal terraces and crescents with villas set among trees. John Nash (1752-1835) planned large areas of London in this way and arranged Regent's Park and St. James's Park as landscape gardens surrounded by dignified terraces. John Wood laid out Bath on similar lines and planned the famous Crescent with plenty of open spaces and with tastefully arranged ponds, and trees and flower-beds. As most of the town's inhabitants were wealthy people, there was no difficulty in getting sufficient money to meet the cost of his work.

Inside the houses, the rooms were large and comfortable, and there was usually a beautifully carved staircase rising from the main hall. The most important room in the house was the drawing room, and it was decorated and furnished on a lavish scale. This was the place where the family entertained its guests, and so it looked out upon the gardens. The best efforts of the plasterer and stucco worker were lavished upon the walls and ceiling of the room, and the richest damask or satin was used for curtains. Between the windows were hung tall mirrors, richly carved and gilt, while on the walls were the most valuable pictures that the family possessed. Settees, armchairs and stools were upholstered with damask, and tables were placed about the room. Glass chandeliers suspended from the ceiling added to the brilliance of the scene.

Out-of-doors, great attention was paid to gardens, and enormous sums were often spent on trying to reproduce the wildness of uncontrolled nature. Lakes and fountains were made, and hermitages and " ruins " were scattered about the parkland. Sometimes an attempt was even made to find a suitable inhabitant for one of these odd buildings. In George II's reign the Hon. Charles Hamilton of Pain's Hill, Surrey, offered seven hundred guineas to anyone who would live for seven years in his hermitage, without cutting his hair or nails, and with only a mat to sleep on but with food supplied regularly from the house. The only applicant left after three weeks however, and the Hon. Charles had to make-do with a stuffed figure!

Dress : The portraits of men and women by Reynolds, Gainsborough and the other artists of the period provide us with excellent examples of the magnificent dress worn by the upper classes. Gentlemen had coats of silk, satin or velvet, richly embroidered and laced, with cravats, gorgeous waistcoats, knee-breeches, silk stockings and buckled shoes. Sometimes they wore their own hair, but more often they had their heads shaved and wore wigs. For dress occasions or social gatherings they had magnificent white wigs, that were perfumed, powdered and curled; but for everyday use they wore low wigs tied at the back with a black ribbon. Their hats were three-cornered and made of felt, and they usually carried long and slender canes.

The dresses worn by the ladies were naturally even more colourful. They were made from silks and brocades of pink, lavender, yellow and grey shades, and covered with elaborate patterns and designs. They had a tight bodice, but the skirts were wide and were stretched out on hoops round the hips. Usually they were ornamented with frills and ribbons, and had panniers of the material draped to the back and falling in a tail to the hem of the dress. The most striking feminine feature was the elaborate hair style. Ladies wore great wigs of false hair, which was piled high over cushions, then curled and powdered, and finally decorated with imitation fruit and sprays of flowers. Hair styles were sometimes carried to ridiculous lengths, and it is said that women, on their way to a ball or to the theatre, had to travel in their sedan chairs with the roofs open because their wigs were so high.

Towards the end of the Georgian period the clothes worn by both sexes became more plain and simple. Gentlemen had coats of dark material, tightly fitting and short at the front, but with " tails " at the back. They still wore light-coloured breeches, hose and shoes, but no longer wore wigs. Their hair was now fairly long again, and surmounted by what looks like the beginning of a " top-hat." The dresses worn by ladies had changed even more radically. They were now very long and full in the skirt, with a high waistline but without frills, flounces or hoops. Women now wore their own hair loosely curled, and had hats such as those worn by the ladies in Sir Joshua Reynolds' later portraits.

Style of Living : The upper classes, who lived in such splendour and dressed with such taste, divided up their day with visiting, eating and merry-making. Dinner was the chief meal and was taken late in the evening—sometimes as late as nine o'clock. Breakfast was only a snack, as on the continent, consisting of tea and a roll of toast, and did not begin until mid-morning. The lateness of the hour made it possible to surround the meal with some of the ceremony which the aristocracy loved, and breakfast parties were common. The morning was considered to last until dinner time, and a lady relates that it was usual " to walk out in a sort of négligé or morning dress, your hair not dressed but merely rolled up in rollers, and in a frock and boots."

Dinner was a formal affair for which everyone dressed elegantly. Huge quantities of food were eaten, and Parson Woodforde in his *Diary* gives us an example of a typical meal. A roast leg of mutton and a baked pudding for the first course were followed by a roast duck, a meat pie, eggs and tarts; while for supper there were a brace of partridges, some cold tongue, " potatoes in shells " and more tarts. When the company had done eating, the table was cleared, the ladies withdrew, and the bottles and glasses were produced. Everybody drank too much, and many a gentleman ended the evening in a drunken stupor. Horace Walpole, writing in 1741, described how after a ball " Lincoln, Lord Holderness, Lord Robert Sutton, young Churchill and a dozen more grew jolly, stayed till seven in the morning and drank thirty-two bottles."

The Spa : Considering the amount they ate and drank it is not surprising that the upper classes suffered frequently from gout and felt it necessary to go to spas to take the waters. There were many of these places in England—Tunbridge Wells, Cheltenham, Harrowgate, above all Bath—and, though they were at first visited only by invalids, eventually they became centres of fashion and pleasure.

Bath was the first spa to become popular. This was largely due to Richard Nash, a penniless adventurer who settled there in 1705 and turned it into one of the most beautiful towns in England. A new ballroom and a theatre were built, and a pump room where people could sit to drink the waters. Aristocrats flocked to the town, and private villas were laid out in terraces and squares. It is interesting to see how the ladies and gentlemen spent their time. Every morning they went to the baths, where they walked about in the water dressed in voluminous bathing costumes. After this they adjourned to the pump room to drink from the springs and to discuss the scandal of the town. It was only then that they took breakfast after which all repaired to Bath Abbey for morning service. In the afternoon they drove in their carriages or shopped, and dined in style at three o'clock. After dinner all strolled in the gardens or on the streets in their best clothes, before ending the day with a dance, a visit to the theatre or a game of whist. We would find a life like this dull and pointless, but it exactly suited the polite and leisured society of the eighteenth century.

In the latter half of the period Cheltenham became popular. In 1788 the royal physicians recommended it to George III, and in a short time the aristocracy followed him there, and Bath began to decline. George III also went to the seaside at Weymouth, and resorts grew up on the south coast. However, it was not until the nineteenth century that Blackpool and the other northern holiday centres that we know today grew up as playgrounds for the factory workers.

Amusements : Horse-racing, hunting, shooting and fishing were the natural sports of a country-dwelling people. Horse-racing was not the strictly regulated affair that it is today. Rules were vague and not very strictly enforced; horses were not trained, and jockeys had little skill. But they were noisy and enjoyable events, and the whole countryside turned up to watch the fun. Races were run in heats, and courses might be anything up to four miles long. To win a race a horse might have to complete three or four heats and cover up to twenty miles. Thus what was required of the winner was not so much speed as stamina. During the course of a race there was a good deal of jostling among the jockeys, and attempts were sometimes made to knock over a rival who seemed likely to win. Towards the end of the eighteenth century the famous English classics were established—the St. Leger in 1776, the Oaks in 1779 and the Derby in 1780.

Often on the evening of a race meeting cock-fighting would take place, for this cruel " sport " was still popular with all classes. A French visitor to England in 1728 has left us a description of a contest that he saw : " The stage on which they fight is round and small. One of the cocks is released and struts about proudly for a few seconds. He is then caught up and his enemy appears. When the bets are made, one of the cocks is placed on either end of the stage; they are armed with silver spurs and immediately rush at each other and fight furiously. It is surprising to see the ardour, the strength and courage of these little animals, for they rarely give up until one of them is dead . . . . the noise is terrible, and it is impossible to hear yourself speak unless you shout . . . . Cocks will sometimes fight an hour before one or the other is victorious."

Boxing was almost as cruel. The pugilists were usually backed by noble lords, who arranged the fights and put up the " purse " or prize-money. A great deal of money was involved, and men fought until they had battered each other into insensibility.

In an earlier chapter something was said about the football which had been played in England for centuries. It bore no resemblance to any of our present varieties of ball game, but

was a disorderly and boisterous contest played across country
or through the streets of a town. Towards the end of the
eighteenth century it began to decline, and in the country
districts it was replaced by cricket, then becoming organised
as it is today. Thus we read of a match staged at Kennington
Common in 1735, where great crowds saw the Prince of Wales
lead a team from London and Surrey " from a pavilion specially
erected " to do battle against a Kent team captained by Lord
George Sackville. The Sackvilles were great patrons of cricket,
and one of them, who captained the Old Etonians against all
England, staked 1,500 guineas and had side bets of £25,000 on
the match. Little wonder that noble lords were known to
promise large farms and favourable leases to brilliant
cricketers who were prepared to play for their teams.

The recreations of the ladies were quieter and more genteel.
Their favourite pastime was dancing, in which they danced
the stately minuet to the music of the violin, the viola and the
French horn. Sometimes they spent the evenings at cards,
usually whist which became the fashion from 1740 onwards,
or employed their time in the fine needlework in which they
excelled. But most popular of all was visiting friends or entertaining guests, when, over a cup of tea, they talked about the
things women have discussed from the beginning of history.

2. The Poor and their Problems

Slums : So far in this chapter we have dealt only with the
rich and their pleasures, but the majority of the population had
little share in this good life. The housing of the poor was
appalling. In London and the older towns decrepit mansions,
that had seen better days, were turned into tenements, one
family to a room, without sanitation or amenities of any kind.
In the new industrial districts conditions were no better, and
workers were herded in dismal ' back to back ' houses, with no
regard for comfort or decency. The more unfortunate families,
whose bread-winners had suffered from accident or illness,

might be forced to live in cellars and garrets, infested with rats and other vermin. All household refuse was thrown into the streets, where it gave off foul smells and became a fertile breeding ground for disease. Pure drinking water was almost impossible to obtain, for much of the water came from polluted rivers or from wells contaminated by sewage. The lack of personal hygiene aggravated the situation. The poor rarely washed and wore heavy and filthy woollen clothing that was in keeping with their sordid surroundings.

Gin : It is not to be wondered that people who lived in conditions such as these led degraded and depraved lives, or tried to forget their miseries by excessive drinking. Ale and beer were bad enough, but in the eighteenth century the Government encouraged the manufacture of gin to provide the farmers with a market for their surplus grain. No duty was placed upon it, and it could be sold anywhere without a licence. Gin shops sprang up all over the place : the drink was sold from street stalls and barrows and from alleys and back-rooms of city slums. Temptation beset the poor on every side, and they succumbed to it. Outside a shop there was sometimes a notice ' Drunk for 1d., dead drunk for 2d., clean straw for nothing '; inside poorly clad and undernourished paupers drank themselves to death. Families were neglected when both mother and father led lives like these (indeed infants were frequently abandoned by their callous parents), and a child's chance of growing to maturity was remote indeed. Crimes of every kind were common, and the gaols were full; yet it was not until 1751 that the Government could be persuaded to tax spirits and limit their sale.

The Philanthropists : There can have been few periods in British history when the gulf between rich and poor was as wide as during these years. The upper classes had very little understanding of the causes of poverty and no sympathy for its victims. There were some, however, who were deeply shocked by the terrible evils they saw around them and who tried to do something to remedy them. We have already seen how John Wesley went out to preach to those whom the ministers of the Church of England never reached, and how he not only brought them the consolations of religion but also started a dispensary in London where they could get free medicine, and organised Sunday Schools to give them some education. But there were other generous and philanthropic gentlemen who devoted their lives and spent their fortunes in helping the poor and the unfortunate, and it would be a pity to leave the eighteenth century without knowing something about their work. We can consider only a few : Thomas Coram and Jonas Hanway who worked for foundlings or for abandoned babies; James Oglethorpe and John Howard who concentrated on reforming the prisons.

The Foundling Hospital : Every year thousands of children were abandoned in the streets to perish of hunger and cold, while respectable citizens passed by with a shrug of the shoulders. Thomas Coram was not one of these. He was a kind and generous sea-captain who, on his journeys through East London to join his ship, was horrified to find infants deserted in this way. He conceived the idea of a Foundling Hospital to care for these children, and persuaded a number of aristocratic ladies to sign a document in which they undertook to raise money to support such an institution. He then approached the King, who granted a charter in 1739 and gave a subscription of £2,000 towards the cost of the building. Other charitable people followed his example, and subscriptions flowed in. Handel gave an organ and a score of the Messiah, besides directing a number of musical performances which raised £10,000. By 1745 the hospital was opened, and deserted infants were received into its care. Coram did everything to make their lives happy and comfortable and to provide them with an education so that they should have a good start in life. Later in the century John Hanway, who was a governor of the hospital, began the system whereby some of the children were boarded out with people who were prepared to receive them. This got them out of an institution and into a home, so that they could see what happy family life was like.

Prison Reform : While Coram and Hanway were interested in foundlings, James Oglethorpe and John Howard were concerned with conditions in gaols. Prisoners were herded in terrible dungeons, often chained to the ground or to the walls, and with nothing but straw to sleep on. They had little fresh air or exercise, and their food was poor both in quality and quantity. Because of the unhealthy conditions, typhus, small-pox and ' putrid fever ' were common and large numbers of prisoners died. In 1750, when a hundred prisoners from New-gate were brought for trial to the Old Bailey, they carried their fevers to the outside world. Four of the six judges who presided on the bench died, and some forty jurymen. After this it was ordered that the prisoners to be put on trial should be washed in vinegar before being taken out of gaol, in order to protect those with whom they might come in contact.

It was not only wrongdoers who were sent to prison. A man who had encountered misfortune and could not pay his debts might find himself detained there for the rest of his life. It was the death of a friend in these circumstances which first attracted James Oglethorpe's attention to the problem. He got a parlia-mentary committee set up to investigate prison conditions in 1729, but it achieved little, apart from revealing to many people for the first time how brutally treated many convicts were. Next Oglethorpe approached the Government for permission to found a new colony in North America, and this was the origin of Georgia. The early settlers were released prisoners, who had a chance to start life afresh in a new country. Oglethorpe's trust in them was justified, for many of them became useful citizens and industrious settlers. A quarter of a century later, John Howard took up the work of prison reform again. A young man of independent means, he had been captured by a privateer when on his way to Portugal and lodged in a French gaol. The sordid conditions he found there and the harsh treatment he received made him resolve to devote the remainder of his life to the improvement of prison conditions. Although a delicate man, he travelled up and down the country for many years collecting information, and in 1777 published his famous book, *The State of the Prisons in England and Wales.* Howard was not a sentimental man who wanted prisons to be made into pleasant rest centres. He believed that wrongdoers should be punished, but he did not see any justification for the depravity, brutality and corruption that were permitted in many English gaols. Conditions like these only confirmed the prisoner in his evil ways and made it almost certain that the first offender would be back in gaol again. The recommendations which he made in his book about the treatment of prisoners and with regard to food, exercise, medical inspection and sanitary arrangements all seem reasonable to us, but he had great trouble in persuading the authorities to accept them. Indeed it was only with the legal reforms of Sir Robert Peel in the early part of the nineteenth century that an intelligent attitude was adopted towards crime, when it was realised that an efficient police force was more likely to keep evildoers in check than severe penalties or long terms of imprisonment.

3. Edward Jenner and Smallpox

Smallpox : One of the most dreaded diseases of the eighteenth century was smallpox. Young and old, rich and poor were attacked and died by the thousand, while those fortunate enough to survive might be left blind or have their faces disfigured by ugly scars and holes. It was an extremely infectious disease and was carried rapidly from place to place. When this danger was realised, those who contracted smallpox were removed to 'pest-houses', where they remained until they either recovered or died. Those who recovered were lucky, for it was noticed that they never had the disease again.

Lady Mary Montagu : In the lands bordering the Eastern Mediterranean where smallpox was very prevalent the same thing was noticed, and, when Lady Mary Montagu, wife of the British ambassador to Turkey, went to live in Constantinople, she found that it was the custom there to inoculate children against the disease. Small scratches were made with a needle on the arms and legs of a child, and matter from a smallpox sore was put into the wounds. The child then suffered a mild attack of the disease, but, when he recovered, he never contracted it again. Lady Mary had the operation performed on her own little boy and was so pleased with the result that she decided to make the practice known in England. On her return home she persuaded George I to offer a free pardon to three men and three women in Newgate prison, who were under sentence of death, on condition that they would allow themselves to be inoculated. In the presence of a number of doctors the operation took place, and all six prisoners recovered from a mild attack of the disease. Eventually the Princess of Wales had her two children successfully inoculated, and from then on the method was widely practised throughout the country.

Unfortunately inoculation did not always turn out as expected. Sometimes children developed a serious form of the disease and not a mild attack as expected. Even when the dose was mild, the patients could infect people with the more dangerous kind. Thus it soon became clear that, while inoculation might prevent smallpox, it was at the same time keeping it alive. Some safer way of ending the disease would have to be found.

Edward Jenner (1749-1823) : Jenner was the son of a Gloucestershire parson and had served his time with a Bristol doctor before completing his medical studies at St. George's Hospital, London. He then returned to his native village of Berkeley and went into practice as a country doctor. The area in which he lived was rich farmland on which there were many dairy herds. From time to time the cows developed sores on their udders, which spread to the hands of the milkmaids. This was known as "cowpox", and in the country it was commonly believed that those who contracted it were immune from smallpox. Jenner decided on a great experiment to prove or disprove this belief : he would give a person cowpox and then deliberately expose him to smallpox in the hope that he would not take it.

On May 14, 1769 a milkmaid called Sarah Neames visited him at his surgery with a number of cowpox blisters on her hands. Jenner punctured one of these with a lancet and collected the matter which flowed from it in a goose quill. Next he injected the matter into the arm of a healthy young boy, named James Phipps, and waited on the results. As he expected, the boy developed on his arm the kind of pimples which the dairymaid had got from the cow. In a short time they disappeared, and Jenner decided that Phipps had passed through his attack of cowpox. But was he immune from smallpox? Taking his courage in his hands, Jenner decided to find out. He inoculated him with the terrible disease and nervously awaited the result. But, to his delight, the disease did not ' take ', and Phipps was safe.

Vaccination : Jenner withheld his judgement until he had carried out a number of other successful experiments. Then in 1798 he announced his discovery in a pamphlet entitled " An Enquiry into the Cause and Effects of Variolae Vaccinae ". At first many doctors scoffed at Jenner's idea, and an eminent physician declared that vaccination (as the new method was called from Latin vacca : a cow) might cause people to grow cows' heads ! But by degrees doctors began to use it as they saw how successful it was.

Soon the news of Jenner's discovery spread abroad. Spain sent an expedition to South America to bring the benefits of vaccination to her colonies there, and in Havana, Cuba, no cases of smallpox occurred for two years after the expedition, although the disease had been rampant in the West Indies. In Russia the Czar ordered that every man, woman and child should be vaccinated within three years. Many public honours were showered on Jenner, and Parliament granted him two gifts from the nation, one of £10,000 and the other of £20,000.

But fame did not spoil the country doctor. After a brief stay in London, he returned to his practice in Berkeley and remained there until his death in 1823.

A Public Benefactor : Today, in most countries, children are vaccinated, and smallpox, which once caused thousands of deaths, is now a rare disease. We know now that the operation gives immunity only for a limited time, and so, whenever there is a danger of an epidemic spreading here from one of the under-developed countries, the treatment is given again. Other diseases are prevented in a similar way—diphtheria, typhoid, cholera, infantile paralysis, etc.—and inoculations are now being sought for the common cold. There are some who would take away from Jenner's fame on the plea that the method he used was not original and had been practised before. But without doubt he was a public benefactor and one of the great men of the eighteenth century.

Questions and Exercises.

1. Give an account of the life of the rich people in England during the eighteenth century, paying particular attention to (a) dwellings and gardens ; (b) dress ; (c) food and drink ; (d) amusements.

2. Tell what you know of the following and of the reforms for which they worked : Thomas Coram ; James Oglethorpe ; John Howard.

3. Outline the career of Edward Jenner. For what reasons do you consider him to have been a great man ?